Praise for previous editions of

Nevada
Off the Beaten Path®

"A top-notch regional travel book."
—*Salt Lake City Tribune*

"[The author] has the strange knack of making even the most seemingly
uninspiring travel destinations fascinating."
—*Denver Post*

Help Us Keep This Guide Up to Date

Every effort has been made by the author and editors to make this guide as accurate and useful as possible. However, many things can change after a guide is published—establishments close, phone numbers change, and facilities come under new management, etc.

We would love to hear from you concerning your experiences with this guide and how you feel it could be improved and be kept up to date. While we may not be able to respond to all comments and suggestions, we'll take them to heart and we'll also make certain to share them with the author. Please send your comments and suggestions to the following address:

The Globe Pequot Press
Reader Response/Editorial Department
P.O. Box 480
Guilford, CT 06437

Or you may e-mail us at:
editorial@globe-pequot.com

Thanks for your input, and happy travels!

OFF THE BEATEN PATH® SERIES

Nevada

THIRD EDITION

by Donna Peck

The Globe Pequot Press

Guilford, Connecticut

The prices and rates listed in this guidebook were confirmed at press time. We recommend, however, that you call establishments before traveling to obtain current information. Meal price ranges used in this book are as follows: up to $10 inexpensive, up to $20 moderate, up to $30 expensive; rooms: $40 low, $60 moderate, $80 and above high; attraction prices: $5 low; $8 moderate, $10 and above high. The area code for Clark County is 702; the rest of Nevada is 775.

Cover and text design by Laura Augustine
Cover photo by Jim Vitali/Index Stock
Maps created by Equator Graphics © The Globe Pequot Press
Illustrations by Carole Drong
Cowboy Poetry, page 18, and *Cowboy's Prayer,* page 19, courtesy the Cowboy Poetry Gathering. *The Humboldt River, the Meanest Strea*m courtesy Emigrant Trail Museum, Donner Memorial State Park.

ISSN 1537-3304
ISBN 0-7627-0886-7

Manufactured in the United States of America
Third Edition/First Printing

Acknowledgments

Special thanks to V. Rulgwan, Eugene Dillard, H.W. (Wally) Trapwell, Andrea Lynn, Bette Cole, Bonnie Stark, Marge Taylor, Myram Borders, Chris Chrystal, Kaye Medlin, Barbara Rohde, and Angela Froelich.

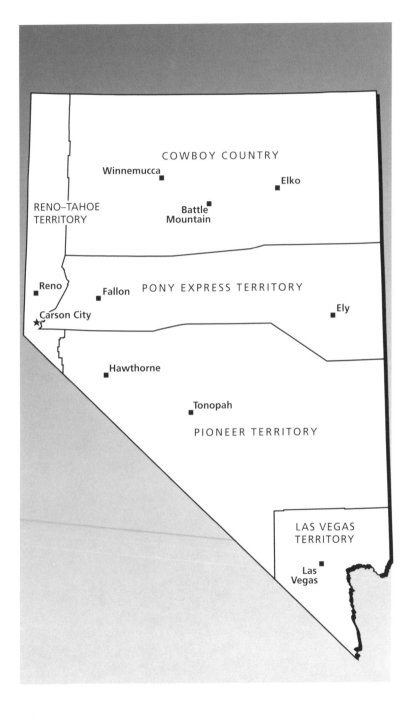

COWBOY COUNTRY

Winnemucca

Elko

RENO–TAHOE
TERRITORY

Battle
Mountain

Reno

Fallon

PONY EXPRESS TERRITORY

Carson City

Ely

Hawthorne

Tonopah

PIONEER TERRITORY

LAS VEGAS
TERRITORY

Las
Vegas

Contents

Introduction

Like many travelers, I had journeyed *through* Nevada but not to Nevada. So I jumped at the chance to load up my vehicle for an opportunity to explore the "real" Nevada. The mineral wealth of Nevada is legendary, as evidenced by the prominence in American history of the Comstock Lode. Just as prospectors had to dig beneath the surface to discover treasure, today's travelers need to veer off the interstate and dig beneath the surface. Nevada's richness in natural beauty, historic sites, and intriguing people is legendary.

Nevada derives its name from the Spanish meaning "snowcapped." Within its boundaries lie more mountain ranges than in any other state. Likewise, Nevada boasts fifty-one peaks above 9,000 feet, with Boundary Peak on the Nevada-California border southeast of Hawthorne capturing highest honors, at 13,145 feet. Pristine mountain rivers also dot the landscape, providing refreshing pause. The Humboldt River flows 500 miles from the Humboldt Mountains in north central Nevada before disappearing forever in the Humboldt Sink south of Lovelock. The Truckee River feeds Pyramid Lake, the largest remnant of ancient Lake Lahontan, located northeast of Reno.

Nevada's 110,543 square miles (it's the nation's seventh largest state) contain topography as diverse and stunning as the Jarbidge Wilderness in the east to Lake Tahoe in the west and from the inspiring Valley of Fire and Cathedral Gorge in the southeast to the treacherous Black Rock Desert in the northwest. Man-made achievements and engineering feats such as Hoover Dam and Lake Mead continue to enthrall and amaze visitors, as do the efforts of Virginia City–area underground miners who toiled in temperatures exceeding 150 degrees Fahrenheit for $4.00 per day (top wages in Comstock Lode days).

A wealth of ghost towns, rodeos, Indian powwows, state parks, hiking trails, and fishing and hunting opportunities beckon the Nevada traveler. Historic Pony Express and emigrant trails traverse the state, as does "The Loneliest Road in America." Twenty-four state parks offer refuge from the highway, while numerous historic sites impart a sense of what the West was really like during the gold and silver rushes and pioneering days. Today a new mining boom adds another chapter to this state's rich mineral history.

A word of caution is in order. On many Nevada roads you may not encounter a single soul. In addition, the heat can be fierce. Make sure your vehicle is in top operating condition. Carry spare parts and plenty of food and water in case of a breakdown. Some roads may not be passable at certain times of the year and in certain weather conditions. Inquire locally about road conditions and whether a four-wheel-drive vehicle is recommended.

In addition to a sport utility vehicle, you'll need a cellular phone. It could save you a lot of trouble and bring help in a hurry. Mining areas can be dangerous.

By no means let yourself be scared off by these comments. Off-the-beaten-path travel is not just for the fearless. Nevada has one of the best tourism networks in the nation, staffed by well-informed locals who can suggest guides so you don't have to go solo. Also don't miss the splendor of Las Vegas. Nevada's showcase to the world is an astonishing nighttime treat.

Nevada is truly a state where traveling off the beaten path will expand your horizons. Get ready to have your image of Nevada changed forever. It's likely you will be returning again and again.

Happy trails.

Facts at a Glance

Nevada Commission on Tourism

Capitol Complex, Carson City, (775) 687–3636 or (800) NEVADA–8.

Chambers of commerce, staffed by locals, are a great resource for planning your trip. They can not only recommend lodging, dining, and sightseeing but also provide directions. Folks in the rural backcountry often close up shop from the end of June through the September tourist season. Call or write to the local chambers listed at the end of each chapter.

Airports

Reno International Airport, (775) 328–6400 or (800) 766–4685, and McCarran International Airport, Las Vegas, (702) 261–5211, are serviced by the following major airlines: Southwest, Northwest, USAirways, United, Alaska Airlines, America West, American, Continental, Delta, Frontier, Air Canada, American Trans Air, Canadian Airlines, Hawaiian Airlines, KIWI International, National.

Regional Airports in Elko and Laughlin are also served by Delta Connection–Sky West, America West Express, United Express.

Motor Home Rental Companies

Bates Motor Home Rental Network, 3690 South Eastern Avenue, Suite 220, Las Vegas, 89106; (702) 737–9050

Cruise America Motorhome, 6070 Boulder Highway, Las Vegas, 89106; (702) 456–6666

Sahara RV Center, 1518 Scotland Lane, Las Vegas, 89106; (702) 384–8818.

Four-wheel drive rental companies

Priceless Car Rental, (702) 986–7500, (800) 886–7283.

Payless Car Rental, (702) 736–6147, (800) PAYLESS; www.800-payless.com.

X-Press Rent-a-Car, (702) 795–4008, (800) 795–CARS; www.xpressrac.com.

Resort Rent-a-Car, (702) 798–9856, (800) 289–5343; www.resortcar.com.

Rail Service

Amtrak, (800) USA–RAIL or www.amtrak.com.

Four-wheel-drive rental companies.

Climate

Temperatures range from a low of 9 degrees Fahrenheit in Ely in January to a high of 109 degrees Fahrenheit in Laughlin in July.

Major Publications

Reno Gazette-Journal, daily

Nevada Magazine

Nevada State Parks

Expect to pay an entrance fee, which goes toward improvements and staff salaries. Summer ranger programs enhance the camping experience. At the Cathedral Gorge Visitors Center, you can learn how to track animals, read cloud formations to predict weather, and survive outdoors in winter. Campers pay both the camping fee and an entrance fee: $9.00 and $3.00 from April 1 to November 15 and $4.00 and $1.00 from November 16 to March 31. Fees at private campgrounds are often higher.

Fun Facts

Nevada was part of the area ceded by Mexico to the United States in 1848. The discovery of the Comstock Lode in 1859 caused such an influx of settlers that Nevada soon had a big enough population to become the thirty-sixth state. Outside of Reno and Las Vegas, Nevada is a vast, open country of wide ranges and towering, snow-clad mountains. It is still a land where the old west survives, with historic main streets looking much the same today as they did in the days of Wyatt Earp and Mark Twain.

State capital: Carson City

Largest city: Las Vegas (population 1,206,152)

State bird: mountain bluebird

State animal: desert bighorn sheep

State trees: piñon pine, bristlecone pine

State grass: Indian rice grass

State flower: sagebrush

State reptile: desert tortoise

State fish: Lahontan cutthroat trout

State metal: silver

State fossil: *Ichthyosaur*

State rock: sandstone

State precious gemstone: black fire opal

State colors: silver and blue

State song: *Home Means Nevada,* by Bertha Raffetto of Reno; adopted in 1933

More Fun Facts

- Before statehood Nevada was part of Zion, as the Latter Day Saints (or Mormons) called their desert homeland. Based in Salt Lake City, the Mormons established the State of Deseret, a provisional government that included most of what is now Nevada and Utah and parts of seven other states.

- Nevada ranked third in the "Top Ten Tax Havens" by *Money Magazine* because its taxes are among the lowest in the nation. Nevada lures businesses with these advantages: no personal income tax, no corporate income tax, no unitary tax, no inventory tax.

- Nevada lists as major industries divorce and gambling.

- Marriage is another major business. Nevada has few legal restrictions, requiring neither blood tests, waiting periods, nor consent for those eighteen and older.

- When Black Rock Desert (a barren, flat moonscape stretching in every direction) was designated a National Conservation Area, 87 percent of Nevada came under federal government ownership. For information about specific areas contact the Bureau of Land Management, 5665 Morgan Mill Road, Carson City 89701; (775) 882–1631.

Unique Weddings

- Some themes played out at Vegas wedding chapels include rock and roll, Camelot, Elvis/Blue Hawaii, intergalactic, Las Vegas, Victorian, 1950s/1960s/disco, beach party, gangster, traditional. Viva Las Vegas specializes in themed weddings, (702) 384–0771 or (800) 574–4450. Out of Nevada's seventeen county clerk offices, these offices issue the most marriage licenses:

  Carson City Courthouse, 885 East Musser Street, Carson City 89701, (702) 455–3156; Clark County Courthouse, 200 S. Third Street, Las Vegas 89155, (775) 455–3156; Washoe County Courthouse, South Virginia and Court Streets, P.O. Box 11130, Reno 89520, (775) 328–3275; Washoe County Clerk, Incline Village, 865 Tahoe Boulevard, Incline Village 89431, (775) 832–4166; Douglas County Administration Building, 175 Highway 50, Stateline and P.O. Box 218, Minden 89423, (775) 586–7290.

Helpful Web Sites

- www.travelnevada.com (click on territory/cowboy). Nevada Commission on Tourism provides general information, activities, events, and travel articles.

- www.virginiacity-nv.org. Virginia City Convention and Tourism lists attractions, lodging, directions, and events.

- www.nevadanet.com. This regional online guide offers entertainment and travel specials for Reno–Lake Tahoe territory.
- www.travel.com. This twenty-four-hour online center handles air, auto, and lodging reservations.
- www.koakampgrounds.com. RV owners can preview and book reservations at KOA campgrounds.
- www.bestwestern.com. This is the directory and reservations site for Best Western.
- www.holiday-inn.com. This is the directory and reservations site for Holiday Inn.
- www.marriott.com. This directory and reservations site includes eight Marriott properties in Nevada.
- www.hotelchoice.com. This directory and reservations site helps you locate and reserve lodging at Rodeway Inn; Econo Lodge; MainStay Suites; Comfort Inns & Suites; Quality Inns, Hotels, and Suites; and Clarion Hotels (also www.choicehotels.com).

Detailed Maps

Of interest to sports enthusiasts, rockhounds, hunters, and explorers is the $8^{1}/_{2}$-inch by 11-inch bound atlas. Another favorite is the *Nevada Map Atlas,* which sells for $12; it shows back roads, ranges, peaks, streams, and canyons. To obtain these atlases, as well as detailed maps of the entire state at a scale of 1 inch for every 2 miles, write to Nevada Department of Transportation, Map Section, Room 206, 1263 South Stewart Street, Carson City 89712 (775–888–7MAP).

Movies Filmed in Nevada

Misfits, Clark Gable's last movie, filmed in Dayton and Virginia City.

The Shootist, John Wayne's last movie, filmed in Carson City.

Powwows around the State

At Powwows you learn about the Native American inhabitants of the state. The Paiutes, Shoshone, and Washo once thrived in Nevada's unique environment. Before attending a powwow, view the richly detailed dioramas of tribal life at Carson City's Nevada State Museum. Powwows consist of fancy and traditional dances, referring both to dress and dance style. Each tribe adds its own variation to the dance based on its heritage and tribal lifestyle.

- Mother Earth Awakening Pow Wow, third weekend of March, Stewart Indian Cultural Center, Carson City (702–882–1808).

- Snow Mountain Pow Wow, Memorial Day weekend, Las Vegas Colony, Las Vegas (702–386–3926).

- Quinn River Indian Rodeo, third weekend of June, Fort McDermitt Reservation, McDermitt (775–532–8259).

- Indian Days Pow Wow, third weekend of July, Fallon Fairgrounds, Fallon (775–423–3968).

Cowboy Country

Elko County

There is no better place to begin *Nevada: Off the Beaten Path* than journeying into *Jarbidge.* In fact, you can't get to this part of Nevada from within the state more than six months of the year, due to snow blocking the mountain passes and roads. To arrive at Jarbidge, enter through Idaho to the north. Take Highway 93 about 24 miles south out of Twin Falls to Rogerson, then take the blacktop road heading west (be careful—there is no road designation). Continue cautiously over the top of the one-lane, 1910 Salmon Dam. Incidentally, you also enter the state over the top of Hoover Dam in southeast Nevada. As in nearly every Nevada drive, be alert for open-range cattle country. You may round a bend to find a cattle drive in progress on the roadbed. When you aren't dodging cattle, look out across the fields for a lone coyote.

Just before you enter Nevada, about 50 miles from Rogerson, the road turns to dirt and then heads down into Jarbidge Canyon. You can't miss the border. It is doubly marked, with a boulder on the left slope that has ID/NV painted on it and a used road-grader blade containing similar markings on the left shoulder. A 15-mile-per-hour winding gravel road leads you by towering rock spires rising along the banks of the gorge. Twisted evergreens cling to the rocky banks. Keep the window rolled down to experience the roar of the tumbling Jarbidge River.

Eight miles from the state border, after you enter the beautiful Humboldt National Forest, you come upon the *Jarbidge Historical Marker,* designating Jarbidge Canyon as the site of the West's last stagecoach robbery and murder. The foul deed took place on a windblowing, snowdrifting December 5, 1916. The stage, bound from Three Creek, Idaho, to Jarbidge, carried pay for the men at the mines and mills, as well as $3,200 in small bills for Crumley & Walker, owners of the Success

> ### It's Jarbidge (not Jarbridge)
>
> *How did they come up with that name? Jarbidge, a one-time mining town in the scenic far north, is one of Nevada's most mispronounced places. Jarbidge is the anglicized version of Tsaw-haw-bitts, a word from Shoshone folklore. The giant Tsaw-haw-bitts lived in Jarbidge Canyon and preyed on Indians, tossing them into a basket slung across his back. Reaching home, he tossed them into a kettle to cook up for dinner. The Shoshone avoided the canyon until it filled up with people during the mining boom. They pronounced the canyon "Ja-ha-bich," eventually spelling it Jarbidge.*

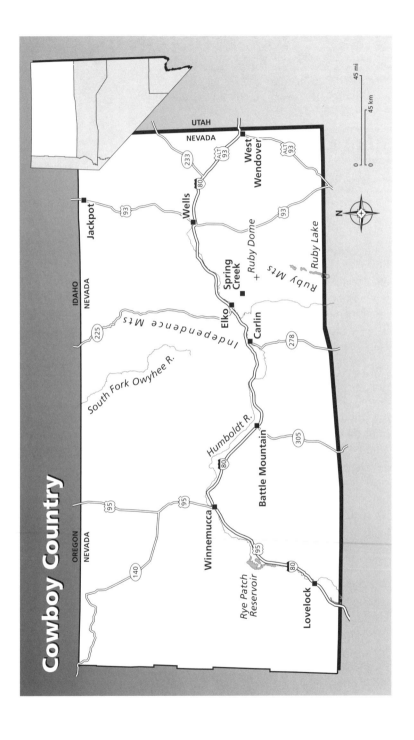

Cowboy Country

Saloon and Restaurant, and a $1,000 cashier's check for the proprietor of the candy store.

A search party, formed after the stagecoach failed to arrive on time, found the dead body of driver Fred Searcy sprawled on the seat. Mr. J. T. McCormick, owner of the general store and an excellent hunter, made casts of dog prints found at the site. After a bit of sleuthing, the search party found the stray dog that had made the prints. The dog in turn led them to a slashed mail sack with a bloody palm print later linked to gambler Ben Kuhl.

Kuhl and several associates were charged with the robbery and murder. The trial was noteworthy because it was the first time prints were introduced as evidence. On October 16, 1917, the jury delivered a guilty verdict of murder in the first degree, carrying the penalty of death by shooting or hanging, at the option of the defendant. Kuhl's sentence was commuted to life imprisonment on December 13, 1918. He served thirty-five years before being released on parole. He died of pneumonia five years later.

Accomplice Edward "Cut-Lip Swede" Beck was found guilty of conspiracy and received a life sentence, serving six years in the state prison. William McGraw, who lent the murder weapon to Beck, was never put on trial, due to lack of evidence. The loot was never recovered.

Continue another ½ mile to enter Jarbidge and go back in time to the turn of the century. Jarbidge (pronounced like *garbage* with a *J*) derives from the Native American word *Tsawhawbitts,* meaning "bad or evil spirit" and relating to a legendary cannibalistic giant who roamed the nearby mountains and valleys, capturing people, putting them into a basket, and then returning to Jarbidge Canyon to devour them. Evidence of Native American hunting parties in the area trace back more than 10,000 years.

The cry of "Gold!" by prospector David Bourne in 1909 forced Congress to carve Jarbidge out of the boundaries of the Humboldt National Forest, which had been created in 1908. More than 1,500 miners flooded into the region, helping the Jarbidge district replace Goldfield as Nevada's premier gold-producing region. The Elkoro Mining Company ranked as Nevada's number one gold producer in 1918 and 1919. Overall, Jarbidge

---

AUTHOR'S TOP PICKS

Cowboy Poetry Gathering, Elko

Tuscarora School of Pottery, Tuscarosa

Angel Lake, Wells

Emigrant Trail, Elko

Metropolis Ghost Town, Metropolis

Lamoille Glacier Overlook, Lamoille

Basque Festival or Basque dining, Elko or Winnemucca

Jaz Ranch, Ruby Mountains, Lamoille

Cottonwood Ranch, Wells

Jarbidge Wilderness Area, Jarbidge

mines produced more than $9 million in gold before the mines played out in the late 1920s, with the last mine (Elkoro) giving up the ghost in the 1930s. In the early years rooming was so scarce that hostelers rented out their bunks on a three-shift basis.

As early as the 1880s, a Basque sheepherder claimed he discovered a rich vein of gold quartz in the canyon; however, he died before he could return to the property. Some versions of the story claim that a fight broke out with a partner who was killed. In any event, the famed Lost Sheepherder's Ledge has never been relocated and awaits your discovery.

Today around twenty-eight residents keep Jarbidge alive year-round, with the population exploding to nearly fifty during the summer months. Residents know how to enjoy themselves with annual Memorial Day and July Fourth barbecue festivals, Labor Day Corn Feed, and Halloween Pig Feed. In addition, Jarbidgeites are always open to spontaneous reasons to celebrate. Weather permitting, opening of mountain passes and an influx of visitors take place around the Fourth of July.

Jarbidge is truly off the beaten path. Mail arrives on Monday, Wednesday, and Friday, and not until the 1980s, after nearly forty years of being "out of service," did the telephone return to the town. But that doesn't mean there's not plenty to see and do in the area. A walk down the center of town on the dirt street offers up both history and entertainment.

But first settle into the *Tsawhawbitts Ranch Bed & Breakfast,* located on the right as you come into the north end of town. Look for the stone walls and log arch entrance to the property. The log structure nestled in the pines was built in 1974 as a hunting retreat and purchased in 1989 by present owners Krinn and Chuck McCoy. Buildings include the main house, carriage house (originally a dairy barn in the mining days and later a machine shop), and party house. The carriage house sleeps four and contains a full kitchen and laundry facilities. The party house is used mainly for family gatherings and wedding receptions.

The spacious main house has three bedrooms on the ground floor and three upstairs, with a large common area for reading, watching television, playing games, or pursuing other forms of relaxation. Be sure to look at the historic photos on the wall in the common area, the topographic map near the river entrance, and unique area antiques. If you study the old photos of the tent-town days, you'll see the names Jahabitts and Jahabich painted on a board above the tent flaps. That gives you a clue how you can twist your tongue from Tsawhawbitts to Jarbidge.

Rooms in the main house run $65, while the carriage house goes for

TOP ANNUAL EVENTS

Cowboy Poetry Gathering,
Elko, January,
(775) 738–7508 or
(888) 880–5885.

Basque Festival,
Elko, July, (775) 738–3616
also in Ely and Winnemucca,
(800) 962–2638.

Fourth of July,
Battle Mountain,
(775) 635–5720.

Bonneville Salt Flats,
land speed races, August,
Wendover, (877) 936–6837.

Country Fair,
Lamoille, June,
(800) 428–7143.

$125. Inquire about party-house rates. A favorite is the back upstairs room, where you can listen to the movement of the Jarbidge River as it sweeps by the property at night. Another soul-soothing spot is the tree-shaded bench area (lighted at night) on the riverbank.

You can also arrange for summer wilderness adventures into the Jarbidge Wilderness area, with pack trips leaving from the B & B. The Tsawhawbitts Ranch Bed & Breakfast is open year-round. For information about rooms or the wilderness adventures, call (775) 488–2338 or write P.O. Box 260090, Jarbidge 89826.

Take a stroll through town, crossing the wooden bridge on the north end. Your first stop should be the "Best Little Store-House," **Trading Post,** for a chat with proprietors Rey and Marguerite Nystrom. On a chilly morning the old wood stove will provide comfort, as will the pleasant company. Don't worry about Fritz the dog, he's as mellow as they come. Here you can get all your necessities and browse through a selection of antiques and local crafts. The building was constructed in 1912 and moved to Jarbidge in 1923, after the mines around nearby Pavlak played out.

The **Jarbidge Jail** is right next door. As the hand-painted sign points out, FOR A TOUR, SEE THE TRADING POST, FOR A ROOM, SEE THE JUDGE. As indicated, Rey is the keeper of the jail key and he will be more than glad to give you a tour or turn over the key. Imagine living in the 6-foot, 8-inch concrete cell. The jail also holds records, such as 1920s purchase orders for the Elkoro Mine Company, headquartered at 120 Broadway in New York City. Don't miss the old mining implements hanging on the outside of the jail.

Just beyond the jail, on the right, is the red light district, with log structures featuring caved-in roofs, giving new meaning to air conditioning. There are plenty of interesting structures left over from the mining days. Check out the house with dozens of antlers on the porch roof. Local writer Helen Wilson, author of *Gold Fever,* spends part of the year in Jarbidge and is always open to jawing a bit about Jarbidge history. *Gold Fever* is a Nevadan tale about Jarbidgeites. It relates stories about her mother and father, hardships endured, and letters tied in a bundle with a blue ribbon. Helen's 1910 cabin is noted by a sign.

You will surely want to stop at the red log **Community Hall,** fully restored in 1965 and still in use for town meetings, dances, and other events. Its "floating" maple dance floor hosts the town's Harvest Ball around the end of September. Folks flock in from all around the area for this event. Helen Wilson remembered the dances of her youth and was instrumental in resurrecting the dance tradition.

The stage curtain contains many vintage advertisements for the town feed stable, freighters, and general merchandise stores. Photos in the Community Hall depict Jarbidge as a 1910 tent town, gold-mining and milling activity, and town buildings long since gone.

For food and entertainment there are a number of options, such as the **Outdoor Inn, Tired Devil Cafe,** and **Red Dog Saloon.** Meal prices are inexpensive. The Outdoor Inn features an ornate solid-mahogany bar and backbar crafted in Europe. After its trip around the Horn in 1890, it survived the 1906 San Francisco earthquake and later resided in the Golden Nugget Saloon in Las Vegas before making the journey to Jarbidge. Tall carved wood statues of Greek mythological figures Pan and Aphrodite highlight the backbar. The Outdoor Inn, like many other Jarbidge business establishments, opens the first of May and closes after hunting season. It is owned by Dot and Jack Creechley, who purchased the historic structure in 1970. For information call (775) 488–2311.

Continuing up the street, you pass over a creek race with mining equipment alongside. Stop and read the historical marker near the school. The school currently has six students, two of whom are the teacher's. Despite the small enrollment and Jarbidge's remoteness, the school is well equipped with computers to bring it into the twenty-first century.

The **Humboldt National Forest** surrounding Jarbidge provides a host of recreational opportunities. The Humboldt National Forest is broken into several distinct pieces, and we will visit other parts of it later in this and other sections of the book. Combined, the segments encompass two and a half million acres, ranging from sage-covered lowlands to canyons with sheer rock walls to towering mountain peaks. Southeast of Jarbidge, Mount Matterhorn rises to a height of 10,839 feet. For information and maps contact the Humboldt National Forest, 2035 Lost Chance Road, Elko 89801, or call (775) 738–5171.

The **Jarbidge Wilderness** remains one of the nation's least visited wilderness areas. Its varied terrain of 113,300 acres contains rugged mountains, glacial rock formations, and an opportunity to leave civilization far behind. You can travel for days without seeing another person. Many of the wilderness's most breathtaking sights, such as pristine Emerald Lake, at an elevation of 9,200 feet, are best reached on horseback. The Jarbidge Wilderness provides some of the best mountain biking and brook-trout fishing in the country. Jarbidge Wilderness information and maps can be obtained at the Ruby Mountain and Jarbidge Ranger District, P.O. Box 246, Wells 89835, or call (775) 752–3357.

The services of a professional guide are recommended. Guides and outfitters can provide the pack and transport animals, gear, food, and expertise for everything from big-game hunts to wildlife photography trips. Master guide Lowell Prunty's ***Jarbidge Wilderness Guide and Packing*** has a long tradition of guide trips in the Jarbidge Wilderness. The Prunty family homesteaded in Charleston, Nevada, only 3 miles from the wilderness. The Pruntys became well-known in rodeo circles for their bucking stock. Three generations of outfitting experience guarantee a pleasurable and safe trip. Prunty operates out of Murphy's Hot Springs, just 13 miles north of Jarbidge. You drove through Murphy's Hot Springs on the way in from Rogerson, Idaho.

Guests are limited to a maximum of six, unless you have a private group of more than six. The cost for a six-day pack trip adventure runs $1,400 per person and includes all food, tents, sleeping pads, and equipment required to make your time spent in the wilderness a real treat. Sleeping bags and your personal gear are all you need to bring with you (a list of

Jarbidge Wilderness

items you'll need will be sent with your confirmation). A money-saving tip: Make your reservations through Sierra Trading Post and receive a $200 discount. Other trips, such as a six-peak ridge hike and outfitting and packing week, are also available. All trips begin on Sunday afternoon at the Tsawhawbitts Ranch Bed & Breakfast in Jarbidge. For reservation and other information, contact Jarbidge Wilderness Guide and Packing, Murphys Hot Springs, Rogerson, ID 83302 (208–857–2270), or contact the B & B at (775) 488–2338. You can obtain a Sierra Trading Post catalog by writing Sierra Trading Post, 5025 Campstool Road, Cheyenne, WY 82007–1802, or calling (800) 713–4534.

Trivia

*The **Northeastern Nevada Museum** in Elko displays the "hoof-shoes" worn by 1930s cattle rustler Crazy Tex, who fooled experienced trackers by perfecting the stride of a cow.*

On the eastern side of the Jarbidge Wilderness, the **Cottonwood Ranch** lets you experience a real cattle ranch in transition to holistic ranching (resource management) as a team effort in conjunction with the Bureau of Land Management, a number of environmental groups, and various other interested parties.

While the holistic resource management facilitator and team members are engaged in bringing ranching into the twenty-first century, you can enjoy participating in horse drives, pack trips, cow camps, and roundups and/or a ranch retreat. The ranch is located in the historic O'Neil Basin, a notorious haven for cattle rustlers. The season begins with May horse and cattle drives and continues in June with cattle-branding activities and more drives. Pack trips through the Jarbidge Wilderness begin in July, and the season closes out in September with a cattle drive across the mountain range, with quaking aspens at their peak splendor.

"This is a real Western experience. There's plenty to do on this ranch without making up work for the guests," says Horace Smith.

Horace's grandfather purchased the ranch from the O'Neil spread, which started in the 1880s. Four generations of family members have worked the ranch over the years. Treat yourself to sumptuous beef and hearty meals. In addition to the great food, fantastic scenery, and wilderness experience, you'll make some wonderful friends with Horace's son, Agee, daughter, Kim, and all-around ranch hand Patty McCready. Five women from Detroit were so taken by their first experience at the ranch that they have standing reservations at the ranch every summer.

Cottonwood Ranch also hosts a father-and-children outing that brings out the best in family relationships. You can observe the beneficial changes in family dynamics with each passing day.

Plans for an artists' workshop are in the works, and a corral of steady, gentle horses are available for riding. Don't forget to check out the chuckwagon covered with brands. A makeshift sauna (sweat tent) and Indian teepee at the ranch provide other activities.

Six-day Jarbidge Wilderness pack trips and spring and fall horse drives cost $1,200 per person and include all lodging, camping equipment, and three hearty meals per day. Cow camp and roundups run $145 per day, while ranch retreats are $105 per day, with a two-day minimum. The highlight of the pack trip culminates with a horseback ride into Jarbidge; the whole town comes out to celebrate your arrival. For more information and reservations, write Cottonwood Ranch, O'Neil Basin, Wells 89835, or call (775) 752–3604 or (800) 341–5951.

To arrive at Cottonwood Ranch, take Highway 93 south from Jackpot, Nevada (19 miles south of the Rogerson, Idaho, cutoff to Jarbidge). You'll pass a number of rock formations of balanced rocks; continue through the town of Contact, and after 31 miles from the Nevada border, take a right at the O'Neil Basin sign, proceeding to a well-maintained dirt road. Travel another 24 miles (west) and turn right at the fork in the road. Five miles later take the left fork and drive 4 miles farther to the Cottonwood Ranch gate entrance, which features ornamental ironwork of horseback riders rounding up cattle.

The Humboldt River, the Meanest Stream

*T*he **Humboldt River** *paralleling Highway 80 was despised by emigrants traveling to California in wagon trains. Muddy and sluggish, it flows for 300 miles through broad alkaline valleys, ending in a marshy bog near the Stillwater Range, where it spreads out into the desert sand and disappears. It offered bitter, sometimes undrinkable water in the desert country between the Rockies and the Sierra Nevada. It inspired this gruesome ode:*

Meanest and muddiest, filthiest stream

most cordially I hate you;

Meaner and muddier still you seem

since the first day I met you.

What mean these graves so

fresh and new

along your banks on either side?

They've all been dug and filled by you,

thou guilty wretch, thou homicide.

—Author unknown

Returning to the main road, take Highway 93 south 36 miles to Wells. Along the way you will pass the Thousand Springs turnoff, approximately 24 miles north of Wells. Turn left (east) onto the *California Trail Back Country Byway* to follow a parallel route alongside the original California Trail or Emigrant Trail. Remnants of 150-year-old wagon ruts are still visible at many spots along the byway. You will experience the isolation of miles of sage-covered valleys broken only by sporadic juniper trees. Along part of the way, you will retrace the route of the Magic City Freight Line, a road used by mule-drawn wagons to haul freight from Toana, Nevada, to the Shoshone Basin in southern Idaho. Several streams provide ample opportunity to fish. Other popular recreations on the byway include rock hunting and photographing wildlife.

The gravel road is easily accessible by most vehicles in good conditions. Travel from November through April is not recommended, due to snow and mud conditions. Check locally for road conditions. The Thousand Springs loop to Jackpot is 76 miles, or you may want to travel a portion of the loop and then return to Highway 93 to continue your journey to Wells. Another option is to take the Jackpot-to-Thousand-Springs loop on your way to Cottonwood Ranch. For a trail map and information on the byway, write the Bureau of Land Management Office, 3900 East Idaho Street, Elko 89801, or call (775) 753–0200.

Wells (population 1,256) started out as an important resting spot and watering hole (Humboldt Wells) along the California Trail. From 1845 through 1870 thousands of emigrants traveling by covered wagon each year rested and rejuvenated themselves from their grueling trip and prepared themselves for the rest of the journey across the Humboldt Valley to California. Humboldt Wells was formally established upon completion of the Central Pacific Railroad in 1869. The town shortened its name to Wells in 1873.

The main town sprang up along the railroad track and is now in the process of restoring this historic district with hopes of establishing a museum in the *Wells Bank,* located on Seventh Street, south of the railroad tracks. The 1911 bank features a large false front with an arched window over the doorway. There's a lot of potential in other structures in the historic district, such as the Nevada Hotel and the Quilici General Merchandise Building.

The Coryell residence is the oldest standing structure in Wells, having been built in 1879. It is located on the corner of Ninth Street and Lake Avenue. Drive down a few of the alleys north of the railroad tracks and you'll discover several well-preserved railroad-tie houses, some covered with chicken wire and plaster.

Stop for tours and tasting at Ruby Mountain Brewing Company, Angel Creek Ranch. Take Highway 93 south for 8 miles to Clover Valley. Call (775) 752–2337. The mailing address is HC 60 Box 100, Wells 89835.

Wells is the gateway to *Angel Lake,* in the beautiful Ruby Mountains. From Wells, Highway 231 winds 10 miles up through pine, quaking aspen, mountain mahogany, piñon pine, and sagebrush to Angel Lake. Hike the west flank of the range on the Ruby Crest trail. Camp at Angel Creek Campground. Call (775) 738–7284 or (775) 752–3357 for winter road conditions. Humboldt National Forest maps are available at the Ruby Mountains and Jarbidge Ranger District, P.O. Box 246, 428 Humboldt, Wells 89835 (775–752–3357).

Jaz Ranch is the home of Nevada High Country Outfitters (775–777–3277), one of Nevada's finest guest ranches. Nestled at the base of the majestic Ruby Mountains, Jaz Ranch offers all-day trail rides in this unspoiled wilderness. Pack trips include fishing cutthroat trout in one of the lakes. For information call Todd Schwandt or write Nevada High Country Outfitter & Guide Service, P.O. Box 135, Wells 89835.

Wells Bank

Krenka Ranch is the home of Hidden Lake Outfitters. You can sign up for the two-day ranch-hand experience on a working cattle ranch, including cattle roundup and wild mustang viewing. For information call (775) 779–2268.

Major events in Wells are the annual chariot race, held in November, and the Wells Car Show, held in late July. For information call the Chamber of Commerce at (775) 752–3540.

Wells is also the center of an important agricultural region. Ironically, Nevada's only agricultural ghost town, *Metropolis,* lies 14 miles northwest of Wells. To reach Metropolis from the historic district of Wells, cross the railroad track at Seventh Street. A small wooden sign on the right instructs you to turn left on Eighth Street. Follow the paved road as it winds around out of town, heading west and bypassing the railroad overpass. Eleven miles later the road turns to gravel. One mile down the road, cross over a cattle guard and make an immediate left turn. Continue on another 1½ miles and you'll spot ruins on your right. There are faded wooden signs marking the way, so it's hard to get lost.

Born out of an investment dream for an innovative agricultural community, Metropolis was virtually carved out of the sagebrush with grand aspirations. East Coast financier Harry L. Pierce organized investors to form the Metropolis Land Improvement Company and related Pacific Reclamation Company (PRC) in 1910. In 1911 the PRC completed the 100-foot-high Bishop Creek Dam, partly with brick rubble left over from the 1906 San Francisco earthquake. Plans were in place to irrigate, with water diverted by the dam, 40,000 acres of land purchased by the PRC.

The PRC recruited industrious Mormon farmers with track records of improving the land under the most adverse conditions. The PRC sold land to the farmers for $75 and up per acre for irrigated land and $10 to $15 per acre for dry-farming plots. Town lots sold for between $100 and $300. More than 700 farmers, approximately two-thirds Mormons, settled into the Metropolis area. Investors envisioned a thriving town of 7,500 residents.

Streets, lots, and parks were plotted in 1911. By the fall of 1911, the Southern Pacific Railroad built an 8-mile railroad spur that carried impressed visitors into the fast-growing town. The Amusement Hall became the first Metropolis building, quickly followed by the completion of Hotel Metropolis in January 1912. The $75,000 hotel was proclaimed the largest hotel between Denver and San Francisco. Its three stories of red pressed brick boasted steam heat, electric lights, running water, a marble-tiled lobby, a billiard room, a barbershop, a newsstand, and a bank. Thirty of its fifty rooms had baths. A lavish grand opening on December 29, 1911, formally opened Hotel Metropolis. The 4-block commercial district had graded streets, concrete sidewalks, fire hydrants, and electric streetlights.

All of this was reported in the town's newspaper, the *Metropolis Chronicle,* which began publication in September 1911. All started out well; the land proved productive, with turkey red wheat growing to shoulder height, yielding thirty bushels per unirrigated acre.

Legal battles, however, initiated by local ranchers and farmers over water rights, proved disastrous for the PRC and Metropolis. The courts found in favor of the local ranchers and farmers, limiting the amount of water the PRC could draw to one-tenth the amount needed to irrigate 40,000 acres. The company went into receivership in April 1913 and finally went bankrupt in 1920. Other problems also befell Metropolis. Several years of drought, followed by an invasion of crop-eating jackrabbits, put the final nail in the coffin for Metropolis.

Hotel Metropolis closed its doors in 1913 (the building burned in 1936), the newspaper stopped its presses in late 1913, the last train departed Metropolis in 1925, the Lincoln School (opened in September 1914 at a cost of $25,000 and a student capacity of 180) discontinued high school classes in 1940 and grammar classes in 1949, and the Metropolis U.S. Post Office canceled its last stamp in 1942. Today no one lives in town, and all that remains are foundations for Hotel Metropolis and the lone-standing entrance arch of the two-story Lincoln School.

The farmers and ranchers who did remain proved successful, as the exodus of others left adequate water supplies. Likewise, the Metropolis area social life flourished, with dances, parties, hot springs outings, quiltings, and other social gatherings that are today fondly remembered by Metropolis residents. In fact, former Metropolis residents now flock to Salt Lake City yearly for a reunion.

Stop at the Metropolis memorial plaque across the road from the schoolhouse arch. It gives a brief history of the town and includes historic photographs. The arch represents a fantastic and memorable photo opportunity. For safety's sake, don't climb over the ruins. If you continue down the dirt road between the sagebrush that brought you to Metropolis, you will arrive at the newer cemetery (the old one contains only a few remaining graves and headstones, and you'll need a guide to get you there).

After a day among the ruins, treat yourself to a welcome stay at **Starr Valley Bed & Breakfast,** about 10 miles east of Wells. Starr's offers three spacious upstairs bedrooms, with handmade quilts covering the beds.

A hearty breakfast includes a variety of options, from quiche with ham to heart-shaped waffles. You won't go away hungry, guaranteed. But the best part of the stay is making friends with the proprietor, Donna McCormick.

Starr's is open year-round. Each of the three rooms in the main house costs $45–$75 per night. For information and reservations write Starr Valley B&B, P.O. Box 721, Wells 89835, or call (775) 752–3898.

Returning to Wells and heading west to Elko on Interstate 80, you come to the Halleck Interchange, approximately 30 miles from Wells. A **Nevada Historic Marker** discusses Camp Halleck (1867), later renamed Fort Halleck (1879). It was originally built to provide protection for travelers along the California Trail and for construction workers laying the tracks for the Central Pacific Railroad. Ironically, Fort Halleck troops never engaged local tribes in battle but did participate in skirmishes with the Modoc tribe of California (1873), the Nez Percé in Idaho (1877), the Bannock tribe in Oregon (1878), and the Apaches in Arizona (1883). The government disbanded the fort on December 1, 1886.

Continuing west an additional 20 miles brings you to **Elko** (population around 20,000 and counting), selected in 1994 as the Best Small Town in America. A midsize-to-large town by Nevada standards, Elko keeps growing due to a boom in gold mining in the immediate area. Elko's population more than doubled from 1985 to 1995. Four major gold-mining companies maintain offices in Elko and operate mines in the vicinity. Elko is the gold capital of North America, with the continent's largest gold mines. The nearby Carlin Trend contains 45 percent of the United States' estimated gold reserves.

Elko rose out of the Nevada landscape as a tough-and-tumble tent city alongside the track of the Central Pacific Railroad in December 1868. Legend has it that the railroad's Charles Crocker liked to name railhead towns after animals and he added an *o* to make the pronunciation easier-sounding. When the Golden Spike linked the Central Pacific and Union Pacific at Promontory Point, Utah, many of the Central Pacific's Chinese track crew were simply abandoned. A number of them made their way to Elko, where they raised vegetables. They are credited with building Elko's first water system, consisting of a reservoir and a nearly 10-mile ditch to carry water through what is now City Park.

Fur trappers visited the area in the 1820s as did famed explorers John C. Frémont and Kit Carson. The forty-niners trod the California Trail near Elko as they followed the Humboldt River westward, while the ill-fated Donner Party traveled on the Hastings Cutoff along the east side of the Ruby Mountains south of Elko.

In 1869 the state legislature created Elko County out of Lander County and made Elko the county seat, complete with new courthouse. A year later Josiah and Elizabeth Potts climbed the gallows and were hanged. The Pottses were convicted of murdering an old wealthy horse trader, Miles Faucett. Upon hearing the reading of the death warrant, Elizabeth Potts proclaimed, "I am innocent, so help me God!" She attempted to cheat the gallows the morning before the scheduled hanging by slitting her wrists with a razor, but her efforts were thwarted by the death watch of J. Stanley Taber. Elizabeth was the only woman ever legally hanged in Nevada. The gallows was constructed in Placerville, California, tested with weights, and then knocked down for shipment to Elko, where it was rebuilt in a corner of the jailyard adjacent to the courthouse.

Covering the hanging, the San Francisco *Daily Report* commented, "It is to the credit of Elko, that it hangs a woman guilty of murder. It is a dreadful thing to hang a woman, but not so dreadful as for a woman to be a murderer. . . . In San Francisco Mrs. Potts would certainly have either been acquitted or pronounced insane, and would have walked out of court a free woman."

Other Elko firsts include the first high school in Nevada and the first site for the University of Nevada, from 1874 to 1885. Continuing its firsts in education, Elko became home to Nevada's first community college, in 1967. One of the first novels, *Nellie Brown,* written by a black American was published in 1871 by Thomas Detter, proprietor of Elko's Silver Brick shaving saloon and bathing establishment. He was instrumental in forcing change in the Nevada law prohibiting black children from attending public schools. In 1875 Detter delivered a major speech in San Francisco at the anniversary celebration of the Emancipation Proclamation.

Moving its heritage a bit, Elko became the first and only town to relocate the railroad tracks that formed a barrier through the middle of town. Near the Elko Airport is the site of the nation's first successful oil shale distillation facility. Robert M. Catlin, Sr., drove the main shaft beginning in 1916. The plant operated for a few years in the 1920s, producing an average of thirty-six gallons of crude oil per ton of shale but not enough to compete with cheaper fossil fuels. The airport hosted another first. On April 6, 1926, Varney Air Lines pilot Leon Cuddeback landed his biplane at Elko, completing the first scheduled airmail run in the United States. A historical marker at the Elko Airport terminal commemorates the 460-mile flight from Pasco, Washington, to Elko with an intermediate stop at Boise, Idaho, for fuel and mail.

Your first stop in Elko should be the ***Northeastern Nevada Museum.*** It contains a wealth of Elko County and Nevada history, starting with the 1860 Ruby Valley Pony Express Station, situated outside of the museum. Originally located 60 miles south of Elko, it was moved in 1960 in celebration of the hundredth anniversary of the Pony Express. Note the vertical logs. Although the Pony Express lasted only eighteen months, it left its mark on Western history forever.

Inside you will find other interesting displays. Some favorites are the bar from Halleck Station, which was sawed off to fit the short stature of the bar's 1920s owner, Bill Rahas; an Elko-Tuscarora-Cope stage, a 1925 Seagrove fire engine, and a 1918 Dodge touring car; exceptional Native American basketry; the bighorn ram skull embedded in a tree found at 9,000 feet elevation in the Ruby Mountains; and the Basque history/customs exhibit. Other informative displays include wildlife, area flowers, bottles, mining (historic and current methods), works of area artists, and railroading. The museum is located at 1515 Idaho Street and is open Monday through Saturday from 9:00 A.M. to 5:00 P.M. and Sunday from noon to 5:00 P.M. Admission is free. For information call (775) 738–3418.

Trivia

*The **Cowboy Poetry Gathering** was voted the best special event in rural Nevada in a* Nevada Magazine *reader poll.*

The historic Pioneer Hotel houses the ***Western Folklore Center*** (WFC). It exhibits ranch-hand and ranch articles used by modern-day buckaroos but is best known for sponsoring the annual January **Cowboy Poetry Gathering,** which attracts the likes of Waddie Mitchell and other notable cowboy poets, Western artists, and musicians. The WFC also sponsors an annual Cowboy Music Gathering, WFC Roundup, and various workshops on roping, sheep camp cooking, and other Western traditions. The center is located at Fifth and Railroad Streets. For information call (775) 738–7508.

You'll see real Western horsemanship at the Spring Creek Horse Palace. Working Cowboy Rodeo performances are sponsored by the Working Ranch Cowboy Association. Follow State Route 227 outside Elko or call

(775) 753–6295. Also, ask for the Ranch Life Adventure Guide at the Elko Convention & Visitors Authority (775–738–4091).

The area is rich with Basque heritage, sheepherders who came from the Pyrenees Mountains in Spain and France. The annual three-day **Basque Festival** has drawn folks from all over for more than thirty years. Events include a parade in native clothing, traditional Basque music, Jota (Basque folk) dancing, distance-walking contests with "Basque Suitcases" (104-pound weights), and Old Country wood-chopping competitions. The festivities are typically scheduled around the July Fourth weekend. Basque or not, you can be sure you'll be greeted wholeheartedly with "Ongi Etorri" (welcome). For information, dates,

Waddie Mitchell Recites at Eagle's Nest Station

*W*hen **Waddie Mitchell,** America's favorite cowboy poet, threw a leg over his horse, a few of us inside the chuck wagon heard a seam rip. "Think I've worn out my britches," he grinned behind his waxed mustache, and followed the tiny chuck wagon down a dirt road. Crossing an old stagecoach road, the wagon pulled up to a clearing where, under a lone juniper tree, Sam the camp cook was setting out lunch meat, rolls, and potato salad. With sandwiches on our laps, Waddie began talking. He likes to do recitations, he told us, outdoors under the Nevada sky. The cowboys and Nevada: It's a natural fit. Ranchers attracted by the unfenced land brought longhorns up from Texas after the Civil War. Ranch life since then has been simple, basic, yet has spawned a lot of creativity. Cowboys find time to paint, compose songs, and to write poetry and practice reciting it around campfires. Mitchell's words spoke volumes of the loneliness of cowboy life on cattle drives. We were moved by a poem about his daughter, a true story, measured out in rhyme and meter, of how she had grown up before he knew it.

He has been busy the past fifteen years. He was out on a cattle drive when the call came from Johnny Carson to appear on the Tonight Show. Invitations blew in from everywhere. He has recited poetry at the Rainbow Room in Manhattan, for black tie events, and at Stanford University. Now he's the headliner at the Poetry Gathering. When Waddie Mitchell and Hal Cannon conceived an event in Nevada centered on cowboy poetry, Waddie was against the idea of calling it a festival. "This is what's it's like out there on a cattle drive; cowboys gathering wherever the chuck wagon bell clangs, just as we are now." A jew beetle the size of this cowboy's famous handlebar mustache whirled by as he spoke. His horse neighed; Sam the camp cook clanked the kettle; and Waddie's boyhood friend and Eagle's Nest owner, Don Farmer, just smiled. Full sun broke across the plain and sped east up the flanks of the Ruby Mountains. The Eagle's Nest, HC 30-449 Box 4, Elko 89815, (775) 744–4370.

Cowboy Poetry

"Life is like a singing river, That each of us must ford, And though our melodies may vary, We often strike a common chord." —Waddie Mitchell, Cowboy Poet

and a schedule of activities, inquire at the Elko Chamber of Commerce, 1601 Idaho Street, Elko 89801, or call (775) 738–7135.

Native Americans also celebrate a number of events in Elko each year. The annual Native American Festival, held in July, offers traditional stick games, Native American crafts, and dance competitions. In October the Elko/Te-Moak Powwow begins with a dancing competition in authentic regalia and includes a parade, a drum contest, and a free barbecue. A variety of other Elko area events await your participation: periodic National Women's Barrel Racing Association competitions, the July Silver State Stampede, the August Humboldt River Muzzleloaders Rendezvous, and September's Morroders Gambler Runs, featuring classic cars and rock-and-roll bands of the 1950s and 1960s. For information and dates on specific events or for an annual events listing, call the Chamber of Commerce at (775) 738–7135.

Make time for a ***historic walking tour*** of Court Street. Start at 421 Court Street, at the Pythian Hall Castle, built in 1927. You'll notice the Palladian-style windows, the red brick adorned with terra-cotta medallions, and the Roman numerals *CDXXI,* for 421. Now move along to Sixth and Court Streets to view the first county high school in Nevada, opened in 1895; Elko County offices now occupy the building. The John Rueben Bradley Home (1904), at 643 Court Street, is highlighted by a rounded turret and white trim. At 705 Court Street, the 1910 McBride Home is almost completely covered by vines. Wind up your tour at the 1869 Dewar Home, at 745 Court Street. Its redbrick and white porch are now surrounded by large pines.

Pick up a souvenir of the West or stock up on supplies at world-renowned ***J. M. Capriolas & Farcia Bit & Spur,*** located at Fifth and Commercial Streets. This is where the real cowboys shop for handmade saddles, bits, and spurs, all of which are crafted right in the upstairs shop. Choose some new duds from a large selection of ranchwear, other Western-style clothing, cowboy boots, and hats for the whole family. Capriola's has made saddles for President Theodore Roosevelt, Will Rogers, and Douglas Fairbanks. Sylvester Stallone is among the store's current clients. Open Monday through Friday from 8:00 A.M. to 5:00 P.M. Call (775) 738–5816.

By now you should have worked up an appetite and can enjoy some good dining, Elko-style. To be sure, you must partake of at least one Basque meal before leaving town. One of Elko's Basque restaurants, the ***Biltoki***

Basque-American Dinner House, is located at 405 Silver Street. Meals are served from 4:30 to 10:00 P.M. every day except Wednesday, when the restaurant is closed. The fireplace lounge and bar open at 4:00 P.M. Dig in for a meal of lamb or another Basque specialty. Prices are moderate. For information call (775) 738–9691.

Take Fifth Street south out of Elko 20 miles on Route 227 and you'll come to the town of **Lamoille,** at the base of the glacier-carved Ruby Mountains. Thomas Watterman, one of the first settlers in the valley, named it after an area in his beautiful native Vermont. The name stems from the French word *LaMoutte,* meaning "gull-inhabited," and was given to the Lamoille River in Vermont. The Lamoille Valley served as an important stopping point. Waterman's store, hotel, and blacksmith shop provided rest, supplies, and wagon repairs to emigrants continuing to points west.

Picturesque Lamoille Valley rivals any Swiss valley setting. Continue through the town to reach the **Presbyterian Church** for a photo opportunity that sets the tone for a relaxing and rejuvenating stay. The church's steeple is framed by the majestic backdrop of the Ruby Mountains.

Despite its smallness, there's a number of places to grab some grub in Lamoille. The **Breitenstein House** specializes in steaks and serves a fine Sunday brunch. Prices are moderate to expensive; chateaubriand for two runs $60. Coming from Elko, turn left at the Presbyterian Church where the pavement ends and go about 1 mile. Take the right fork, and the Breitenstein House parking lot is on the right. For information call (775) 753–6356.

Back on the main road into Lamoille, the **Pine Lodge Dinner House** sits south of the road, among the pines. Drawing your attention around the interior of the restaurant are numerous wildlife, such as bear, deer, sheep, and rattlesnakes, captured in striking poses. Call (775) 753–6363.

Red's Ranch represents a wonderful place to rest up before and during your adventures in the breathtaking Ruby Mountains. Located on the outskirts of Lamoille, the retreat lies in a wooded setting offering complete privacy and solitude. Built by Mimi Ellis (daughter of Red Ellis, founder of the Stockmen's in Elko) in 1987, Red's Ranch operates as an executive retreat conference center, plus has B & B accommodations.

The ranch encompasses 125 acres and includes a swimming pool, a gazebo Jacuzzi, an outdoor barbecuing and dining area, spacious rooms, a billiard table, and a pristine stream running through the property. Mimi patterned the main house after the great lodging houses of the Rockies. The expansive log structure is accented by massive beams and a large stone fireplace. A number of the decorations and Native American rugs are from the original Stockmen's. The main house has ten bedrooms, with an additional three in the guest house.

The conference center in the barn-shaped building includes a large meeting room, an office, a kitchen, a dining room, and all the requirements for a serious business meeting, such as fax and copy machines. The center is well suited for day meetings as well as extended retreats and is custom-made for those in search of a unique private retreat.

When the work is over, there's plenty to choose from in order to relax and enjoy Mimi's Western hospitality. You can shoot clays, hike, or fish, or enjoy a game of badminton, billiards, croquet, or horseshoes. Soak your body in the Jacuzzi or swimming pool while you gaze up at the majestic Ruby Mountains.

For the more adventuresome there's a variety of seasonal expeditions arranged through private operators. In the summer there's a spectacular helicopter ride over the Rubies, followed by fall hunting trips and in the winter, challenging world-class helicopter skiing. Imagine heading down the slopes on virgin powder.

In conjunction with Great Basin College, Red's Ranch sponsors a Western Women's Fly-Fishing School package with meals, accommodations, and fly-fishing instruction. Activities include a talk on "Western Women of the West," a barbecue, a trail ride, and, of course, fly-fishing.

B & B rates run $250 per day and include use of all ranch facilities. For business retreat information and B & B reservations, write Red's Ranch, P.O. Box 1406, Lamoille 89826, or call (775) 753–6281 (fax 775–753–9379).

For a bird's-eye view of Lamoille Valley and the Ruby Mountains, contact **Ruby Mountain Helicopter Skiing** for a package deal with professional guides that includes three nights' lodging at Reds Ranch. The regular helicopter-skiing season extends from February 1 through March 31; prior to February 1 and after April 2, skiing depends upon weather and snow conditions. When you return, Francy Royer, chef extraordinaire, tops off the day with an energy-packed meal to ready you for the next exhilarating day. The all-inclusive, three-day-package rate, based on double occupancy, is $2,500. Each three-day skiing experience is limited to sixteen skiers and guarantees a minimum of 39,000 feet of helicopter lift. The powder conditions in the Rubies rank among the best in the world. Make your reservations far in advance. For a complete set of terms and conditions, write Joe or Francy Royer at Ruby Mountain Helicopter Skiing, P.O. Box 281192, Lamoille 89828–1192, or call (775) 753–6867 (fax 775–753–7805).

No visit to the Elko/Lamoille area is complete without a trip up Lamoille Canyon. A two-lane, 12-mile scenic byway road winds its way to a trailhead at an elevation of 8,600 feet. Along the way you'll experience cascading waterfalls tumbling over glacier-carved rock formations as the river draws you deeper into the Ruby Mountain Wilderness Area. Stop at one of the numerous picnicking and camping facilities for wildlife viewing opportunities. On the way to the top, pull over to the *Lamoille Glacier Overlook,* where you can see the effects of two 1,000-foot-thick glaciers that carved out U-shaped Lamoille Canyon more than 250,000 years ago. Rugged glaciated peaks rise to more than 11,000 feet in elevation. Save some film for the return trip, because you will see rock formations and other sights from new perspectives and in a different light at various times of the day. Outbursts of bright wildflowers such as bluebells, iris, lupine, and larkspur mingle among the rocks. Pines and oak dot the mountainsides. Bighorn sheep, cougar, deer, grouse, hawks, and golden eagles are among the wildlife that make the Ruby Mountains their home. Ruby Dome, the highest of the peaks, towers to 11,249 feet, in excess of 5,500 feet above the valley floor.

A number of day hikes with varying degrees of difficulty can take you to pristine, jewel-like lakes nestled among the mountain peaks. One of the most spectacular trails is the Ruby Crest National Scenic Trail (trail 43), which follows the crest of the Rubies from Road's End in Lamoille Canyon to Harrison Pass, 40 miles to the south. The hike takes four to six days. The Ruby Crest National Scenic Trail is open from June 15 to September 15, depending on weather.

For those with less time, a thirty- to forty-minute, easy-to-moderate round-trip on the Nature Trail takes off from $\frac{1}{2}$ mile north of Terraces Campground. The Thomas Canyon Trail leaves from Thomas Canyon Campground for a four- to six-hour round-trip journey at moderate difficulty. The right fork of the Lamoille Canyon Trail starts at Lamoille Canyon Campground, concludes four to six hours later, and is rated moderate in difficulty. Campsites in Lamoille Canyon are typically occupied on a first-come, first-served basis. The camping fee is $5.00 per day. For information about three- and four-day guided horseback, fishing, and photography trips into the Ruby Mountains, contact Hidden Lake Outfitters at (775) 779–2268.

Permits for hiking or backpacking in the wilderness are not currently required. Humboldt National Forest maps are available for $2.00 at the Ruby Mountains Ranger District Office, P.O. Box 246, 428 Humboldt, Wells 89835 (775–752–3357). U.S. Geological Survey topographical maps can be obtained for $2.50 from the Bureau of Land Management, 3900 East Idaho Street, Elko 89801; call (775) 738–4071 for information.

For those with mountain bikes on their minds, the Elko Cyclery has published an informative booklet about a number of area trails for bikers with experience levels from beginning to very experienced. Pick up a copy at Elko Cyclery, at 382 Fifth Street. Don't forget to strap on a helmet. An estimated 75 percent of the 1,000 bicycling deaths each year result from head injuries.

Elko County contains 121 of the state's 535 streams and more than a third of Nevada's reservoirs. Most of them contain trout, but a number are managed to provide game fishing of both largemouth and smallmouth bass, crappie, and catfish. Frozen reservoirs in the winter also allow fishers to experience ice fishing.

Nevada's newest state park, *South Fork State Recreation Area,* is situated just 16 miles south of Elko. The park's 1,659-foot dam creates a reservoir for a diversity of water sports, such as boating, waterskiing, and fishing. Overnight camping is available at twenty-five campsites within 2,200 acres of scenic meadowland and rolling hills. The campsite comes complete with rest rooms, running water, and a shower.

To get to South Fork State Recreation Area, take the Jiggs Highway from the Lamoille Highway at the stoplight near Spring Creek Plaza, approximately 5 miles southwest of Elko. Entrance fees are $3.00 per vehicle; camping $8.00. For information call the park ranger at (775) 744–4346 or the district ranger at (775) 758–6493.

Now prepare yourself for a ride across (depending on weather conditions and time of year) the Rubies through Harrison Pass to the *Ruby Lake National Wildlife Refuge.* Take the Lamoille Canyon road back down to Highway 227 and head toward Elko. When you reach Highway 228, turn left (south). Twenty-five miles later you'll pass through Jiggs. You may think Jiggs is an unusual name, but the town and area post office have sported a number of monikers, starting out as Dry Creek and proceeding through Mound Valley, Skelton, and Hylton before a

U.S. postmaster with a sense of humor rechristened the town Jiggs, in 1918. Through the years Jiggs has been a social center for area ranchers who first set up shop here in the 1860s.

Continue on another 3 miles and then take the Harrison Pass Road, which forks off to the left (east). The blacktop disappears and you finish the remainder of the 15 miles across the mountain range over Harrison Pass, at 7,247 feet. When the gravel road dead-ends into Route 767, turn right (south) and follow the road to Ruby Lake National Wildlife Refuge headquarters, where you can pick up informative brochures, fishing and hunting regulations, and information on motorboat restrictions. The road is steep, winding, and rough and is closed during certain times of the year due to weather. Note that Harrison Pass is not maintained during the winter.

Before starting out, check road conditions with the U.S. Forest Service at (775) 738–5171 or the refuge manager at (775) 779–2237. The alternate route takes off from Interstate 80 about 20 miles east of Elko, at the Halleck interchange. Follow Highway 229 southeast about 35 miles, until the blacktop disappears, then stay on the gravel road until you reach the refuge headquarters, an additional 30-plus miles away. Either way, you will enjoy a spectacular drive around or through the Rubies. The nearest campground is located 1½ miles south of refuge headquarters, while a public telephone can be found a little farther south, at Shantytown. Licenses and Duck Stamps must be acquired before arrival at the refuge. Limited amounts of gasoline can be obtained on a seasonal basis at Shantytown, so begin your trip with a full tank.

Established in 1938 by President Franklin D. Roosevelt, the refuge encompasses more than 37,630 acres, consisting of marshes, open ponds, and islands bordered by wet meadows, grass, and sagebrush-covered highlands. More than 200 species of birds can be sighted. Be sure to take along your binoculars to zero in on the graceful sandhill crane, great blue heron, or red-tailed hawk. Rare birds such as the trumpeter swan and bald and golden eagles can also be sighted. In a good year the refuge can produce 5,000 canvasback and 4,000 redhead ducks.

Other wildlife also make the refuge their home. Keep a watchful eye out for antelope, badger, beaver, bobcat, coyote, mountain lion, mule deer, porcupine, weasel, and other critters. A guide to birds, mammals, fish, amphibians, and reptiles and their habitats in the refuge can be obtained at the refuge headquarters and proves an invaluable aid to wildlife viewing.

Sixty-seven miles north of Elko, off of Highway 225, you come to **Wild Horse State Recreation Area,** with 120,000 acres, on the northeast shore of Wild Horse Reservoir. The park is open year-round and offers a host of boating, camping, picnicking, fishing, and hunting activities. Facilities include a shower building, toilets, and a boat-launch ramp. Construction of the original dam took place in 1937, with a 1970 enlargement bringing the reservoir up to 3,000 acres. Wild Horse is open in winter but the lake is frozen and campground facilities are limited. There are two campgrounds on the lake, plus a private campground at the south end of the lake, where the stream enters the reservoir. Admission fees are $3.00 for day use and $10.00 overnight. For information on the recreation area, call (775) 758–6493.

Westward Bound

The world's greatest peace-time migration started in 1840. For nearly thirty years after that, over 300,000 emigrants passed through Nevada on their way west in search of a better life. They walked beside oxen-drawn wagons over dusty ruts, across dry desert basins, muddy hills, rocks, mountains, and rivers. The **Emigrant Trail,** *or California National Historic Trail, designated in 1992, has been marked across the state. Guided tours and maps are available at Elko Convention and Visitors Authority, (775) 738–4091.*

Wild horses and burros do roam the Nevada countryside. In fact, Nevada ranks first in the nation in the number of wild horses and burros, with more than 32,000 wild horses and nearly 1,800 burros. The Bureau of Land Management (BLM) maintains wild horse and burro specialists in ten locations around the state, including Elko. In 1971 Congress passed legislation to protect, manage, and control wild horses and burros on public lands, in the form of the Wild Free-Roaming Horse and Burro Act, which declared these animals to be "living symbols of the historic and pioneer spirit of the West."

By law, the BLM supervises the removal of horses or burros "in order to preserve and maintain a thriving natural ecological balance and multiple-use relationship in the area." What all this means is that you can adopt your own wild horse or burro. The BLM maintains a number of permanent centers where animals are available for adoption year-round. The adoption fees range from $75 per burro to $125 per horse. One year after signing an adoption agreement, the adopter may receive title, provided he or she has properly cared for the animal. Among the most famous horses adopted from Nevada are the mounts of the U.S. Marine Corps Mounted Color Guard, which appears in parades throughout the West, such as the Rose Parade in Pasadena, California.

Those interested in obtaining more information on the wild horse and burro adoption program can contact the BLM office serving the area in which they wish to adopt. For a list of these facilities, contact your nearest BLM office. The Nevada BLM National Wild Horse and Burro Center is located at Palamino Valley, P.O. Box 3270, Sparks 89432; for information call (775) 475–2222 or (775) 673–1150.

Backtracking a few miles south on Highway 225, take a right (west) turn at the Lone Mountain Station Corner onto Route 226, to travel a mere 24 miles (branching left onto Route 789 for the last 6 miles) but back in history more than a century to the ghost of the mining town of **Tuscarora.** During its peak mining days of 1878, Tuscarora's population rose to 5,000, exceeding that of county seat Elko. At one time more Chinese lived in Tuscarora than in any other place in America, with the exception of San Francisco. Many of the Chinese arrived at Tuscarora after they were abandoned by the railroad.

Tuscarora sprang out of the earth with the discovery of gold by John and Steve Beard in 1867. Four years later W. O. Weed discovered the rich Mount Blitzen silver lodes. The only Tuscarora gold mine, the Dexter, operated continuously until 1898. Major silver mines, such as the Argenta, Belle Isle, Commonwealth, Grand Prize, and Navajo, produced more than $7 million between 1871 and 1910. Overall, production estimates range from $10 to $40 million. Due to the lack of wood in the area, almost all of the available sagebrush was collected to fire the mills. Six mills with a combined eighty stamps processed ore from the district's most productive mines. By 1915 only a handful of people resided in town—as is true today, despite a brief flurry of gold-mining activity that threatened to devour the town in the 1990s before the mining company collapsed in a flood of lawsuits.

A single mill stack towers over the town like a lone sentinel waiting for the return of prosperity. Other remaining structures include a number of houses and the **Tuscarora School of Pottery,** run by the world-renowned Dennis Parks. Art students have come from all over the world. The facility includes a gallery with the works of both Parks and his son, Ben. Dennis won the 1990 Governor's Arts Award for Excellence in the Arts, while Ben designed the 1996 award, a very large pair of ceramic cowboy boots.

Parks's showroom is housed in the front portion of the old Zweifel Rooming House, dating to the mid-1800s, having been moved to Tuscarora from a declining mining town, Cornucopia. The building also held the post office, as evidenced by the row of mailboxes in the hallway. Out in back, Parks's handmade kiln utilizes recycled crankcase oil to fire up to temperatures as high as 2400 degrees Fahrenheit. Parks transforms local clay into unique pieces of art as diverse as garlic pots, a torso series made from large sacks, and a collection of plates of Taylor Canyon reflecting "me in different moods."

One visitor looked at an introspective image titled *Potter in Clay* and remarked, "You sure look like yourself."

Public collections that include Parks's works cover the globe, from the Nevada Museum of Art to the Musée Ariana in Switzerland and from the Museum of Ceramics in Italy to Mimar Sinan Üniversitesi in Turkey. The studio is open seven days a week from 9:00 A.M. to 5:00 P.M. You don't need to worry about your newly acquired piece of art breaking on the way home—Parks ships anywhere.

Often the gallery is open with not a soul in sight. Be patient; Ben or his wife, Elaine, will arrive soon to visit with you and take you on a tour of the kiln area and studio. To find the gallery and studio, turn left at the first street after the new post office. There's a dilapidated building on the corner with a plaque designating it the Tuscarora Mason Lodge. Parks and the Tuscarora School of Pottery can be contacted at P.O. Box 6, Tuscarora 89834 (775–756–6598).

After visiting with the Tuscarora living, stop at the well-kept cemetery at the end of town to browse among the dead and read the tombstones. Tuscarora regained a brief bit of the limelight in 1992 when director David Schickele introduced his film *Tuscarora Lives* (detailing Tuscarora citizens' battle with the open-pit mining company) at the San Francisco Film Arts Festival.

Another forgotten mining-town treat awaits you as you maneuver your vehicle over 42 miles of graveled, sometimes rutted Route 789 west to **Midas.** Riding the ruts gives you a slight taste of what the emigrants and pioneers had to endure as they traveled by wagons across these old trails and roads. Pack your fishing rod because along the way you'll pass Willow Creek Reservoir, with excellent angling. Be careful as you round the curves—many hundreds of sheep may be blocking the roadway. At the only fork in the road, turn right for the last 2 miles into Midas.

Gold was discovered here in 1907. The camp was originally called Gold Circle, because many gold mines encircled the camp. The name was changed to Midas in November 1907 with the establishment of the post office and concern from postal officials that too many Nevada towns already had the word *gold* affixed to their names. By 1908 more than 2,000 people with hopes of striking it rich filled the tent city. The first murder occurred in a duel that year. Less than a year later, fewer than 250 miners remained, as low-grade ore and high transportation costs hampered operations.

Midas rebounded in 1915 with the construction of a fifty-ton cyanide mill. Seven years later fire destroyed the mill and mining ceased. In 1926 Gold Circle Consolidated Mines built a seventy-five-ton mill and operated it until late 1929. Other mine and mill production continued until the beginning of World War II, before shutting down. Overall, Midas area mines produced more than $4 million in gold. After 1942 the town rapidly declined. The post office closed that year, followed by the school ten years later. Today both Tuscarora and Midas have populations less than the number of pounds of air in your tires.

Yet the future is a bit brighter. Mining is once again stirring in the area. A few newer homes and mobile homes are scattered among period mining shacks and abandoned machinery. Towering cottonwoods embrace the town as they stretch over the dirt lane (main street) from both sides, creating a tunnel effect.

Stop in at the **Midas Gold Circle Bar,** on the right as you drive into town. The bar ceiling is dotted with autographed dollar bills (a Nevada tradition, as you will find out). Some of the bills are from as far away as Singapore and Spain. For food you can get "anything that will fit into the microwave." Proprietor and part-time prospector Don Mellen will tell you how the prospecting is going.

"We found a rock the other day that got us quite a bit excited," says Don.

Not surprisingly, the school is still closed, but it looks in good condition. After all, you can't expect a school to be open in a town with no children. Nonetheless, as Mellen told us, "Move into town with four kids and we will open it for you."

You can write the Midas Gold Circle Bar at Star Route Midas via Golconda 89414, or call (775) 529–0439. Mellen wants to make sure people don't get lost getting to his establishment. On the back of his business card is a map showing how to find Midas from Elko and Golconda.

The **Midas Saloon and Dinner House** is just up the street on the right, past the public telephone booth. Les and Bev Matson serve the best food in town. This is no joke—besides operating the only restaurant in town, the Matsons serve first-class, multicourse meals that will make your mouth water. Choose from prime rib, live lobster, or a number of other sumptuous entrees. Prices are expensive by Nevada standards but are the least expensive fine dining in Midas. Like many ghost-town establishments, business is seasonal. For information on operating season and hours, call owners Les and Bev Matson at (775) 529–0203.

At this time you may continue on to Golconda in Humboldt County, but we recommend a loop back to Interstate 80 at Elko, to head west virtually following the route of the Donner Party in 1846. Note the red rock structures as you proceed west from Elko.

Eureka County

A little beyond Carlin you enter Eureka County. At this point emigrants had to make an important decision: They could push on along the Humboldt River with fresh water and grasses for the oxen or take a more direct route and climb over Emigrant Pass, an elevation of 6,114 feet, as Interstate 80 does today. On the Humboldt River Route through Palisade, travelers encountered steep, 800-foot basalt cliffs, leaving little room alongside the river for wagons. Most emigrants opted for the Emigrant Pass route, except when the river was low in dry years and they could use the riverbed as the road.

Take a diversion to cover the 10-mile drive to **Palisade** and see where the Donner Party traveled. Follow Route 278 south to the Palisade cut-off on the right (west). It's easy to see how Palisade (originally called Palisades) derived its name from the red cliffs. As you maneuver the narrow dirt road hugging the mountain, peer over the left shoulder (it's very close) and see where the train enters a tunnel below you. You drop off the mountain ledge into what remains of Palisade. The wooden shack, built of railroad ties, at the fork is unique and a great photo opportunity. Turn right and go over the railroad track to get a better view of the Humboldt River and canyon route. It's also a handy place to get a wonderful shot of the railroad trestle and tunnel through the mountainside.

The town was laid out by the Central Pacific Railroad in February 1870. It rivaled Elko and Carlin as a departure point for wagon, freight, and stage lines to Eureka and points south. At the peak the railroad community of Palisade reached a population of 300 people. After the Eureka mines played out and closed in 1885, Palisade went into a decline. The Western Pacific began running through the town in 1908, but a flood in 1910 damaged the rail lines and swept away Palisade's hopes for revival. The post office finally shut down in 1962.

A gravel road from Palisade joins Interstate 80 just east of Emigrant Pass but may require a four-wheel-drive vehicle and good weather.

Check locally for road conditions before venturing out. To be on the safe side, it's only a little more than 10 miles back to the interstate at Carlin. On the other side of the pass, the trail once again struck the Humboldt River at Gravelly Ford, east of Beowawe. This was the sight of several killings, and three fenced graves still remain here.

For now we will depart Eureka County, but we will resume our travels through that area in the Pony Express Territory chapter.

Lander County

The **Battle Mountain** (population 3,542) area first drew attention around the 1830s, due to plentiful beaver in nearby rivers. By 1841 the first organized party of emigrants made its way through what is now Battle Mountain. An estimated 60,000 wagons traveled along this route in 1852 alone. In 1866 prospectors discovered gold and silver in the hills southwest of town. Two years later the Central Pacific Railroad reached here and the town was born. Mining has been rejuvenated once again, with nearly twenty mines in the area operated by such firms as Barrick Goldstrike Mines, Inc., Newmont Gold Company, Pegasus Gold Corporation, Sante Fe Pacific Mining Company, and U.S. Gypsum Company.

The origin of the name Battle Mountain remains a mystery. Various versions report a skirmish between Native Americans and a wagon train (1850), a survey crew (1857), and another emigrant party (1865). Take your pick.

For a trip through a historic mining area, take Route 305 south. Just after the overpass over Interstate 80, turn left and follow the road to the foot of the Lewis Canyon, where you veer left. As you enter the canyon, look for old mill sites, wooden water pipes, and other mining relics.

Some area history provides a little color. Thirteen miles to the east stood the town of Argenta. Sixteen passengers rode the first stage from Argenta to Austin. The first passenger train arrived there on November 12, 1868, and the population shortly thereafter boomed to 500. On November 25, 1868, a drunken stage driver rolled over the Austin-bound stage (twice). The first killing took place on December 12, 1868: A desperado was shot dead, with "everyone taking credit." In February 1869 two men murdered another man in Winnemucca and fled to Argenta, where they terrorized the town before riding away. Argenta had to pack a lot of living into its short history. In March 1870 the rail began running from Battle Mountain instead of Argenta, sealing that community's fate. Argenta migrated lock, stock, and barrel to Battle Mountain.

Battle Mountain figured prominently in the women's suffrage movement as the location for the first recorded Woman Suffrage Convention, in 1870. Nevada, like a number of other Western states, approved the vote for women prior to passage of the 1920 U.S. constitutional amendment. Nevada women first went to the polls in 1915.

We will visit the rest of Lander County in the Pony Express Territory chapter.

Humboldt County

The road out of Battle Mountain follows the Humboldt River northwest, crossing into Humboldt County. East of Golconda the **Donner Party** suffered a tragedy that foretold the panic and fear setting in and even greater tragedies awaiting them in the future. On October 5, 1846, one of the Donner Party's leaders, James Reed, stabbed John Snyder to death during a dispute about driving the party's wagons over a steep, sandy hill approximately 10 miles east of **Golconda.** Reed pleaded self-defense but was contradicted by witness accounts reported to the council formed to investigate the matter. Some members wanted to hang Reed, but instead the council banished him from the party and, as a result, deprived the Donner Party of much-needed leadership.

Pull off the interstate for a brief tour through Golconda. The town originated as an ore-shipping station along the Central Pacific Railroad in 1868 but was a long-awaited stopping-off spot on the California Trail, due to the presence of refreshing hot springs. Around the turn of the century, Golconda's fashionable Hot Springs Hotel attracted travelers.

The town grew to a population of 500 by 1899, due to the discovery of gold and silver in the area and the construction of the Golconda and Adelaide Railroad to the Adelaide Mine, making Golconda the center of the Edna Mountains Mining District. Two Golconda mills (ninety-ton and one-hundred-ton) processed ore from nearby mines. Foundations of the mills remain. In addition to gold and silver, area mines have produced manganese and tungsten from time to time. Today mining activity has renewed in the area, but Golconda's glory days are gone. Take a picture of the **Golconda Community Hall** with the bright red roof (former schoolhouse) and browse around the streets for other historic structures and foundations.

Eight miles east of Winnemucca, you'll see a sign designating **Button Point.** Don't try to distinguish the shape of a button on the surrounding hills, because the name came from Frank and his uncle I. V. Button, of the famous Double Square brand. The Buttons raised thousands of horses on 4,000 square miles of ranchland.

Enter **Winnemucca** (population 6,134), the only Nevada town named after a Native American. The town began as French Ford, but Central Pacific Railroad officials renamed the community Winnemucca, in honor of the famous Chief Winnemucca of the Northern Paiute (called Winamuck by his people).

For several years Winnemucca laid false claim to another important figure and event in Western history. The story goes that on Wednesday morning, September 19, 1900, George Leroy Parker (Butch Cassidy), Harry Longabaugh (Sundance Kid), and Will Carver pulled their last U.S. bank job, robbing the First National Bank of Winnemucca and riding off with sacks filled with $32,640 in gold coins. Refreshed with a change of horses near Button Point, they escaped to Tuscarora, Nevada, and later Wyoming and Fort Worth, Texas, where they took the famous portrait they mailed back to the bank president with their sincere appreciation for his generosity. Although this makes for a wonderful story, it never actually happened. Butch Cassidy was never in Winnemucca, though residents told the story for decades before it was proven false. The bank building has been restored and now houses another business but can be viewed at the northwest corner of Bridge and Fourth Streets.

Twenty-two-year-old Charley Hymer owns the dubious distinction of being on the wrong end of Winnemucca's first hanging, for killing a man over a seating-arrangement dispute at a dance hall in 1880. According to legend, Hymer's dying wish was to have his "sad fate serve at least as an example for all wayward and non-law-abiding youth."

> **Trivia**
>
> It took the **Donner Party** two long months to cross present-day Nevada. Virginia Reed, whose entire family survived, gave this advice: "Never take no cut-offs and walk as fast as you can."

The Humboldt (Old French) Canal originated near Golconda and ran through Winnemucca at Bridge and West Fifth Streets. Several portions of the canal are still visible near Golconda, in Winnemucca, and at Rose Creek, south of Winnemucca. A grand scheme conceived in 1862 to supply water to more than forty stamp mills as well as to hold barge traffic, the canal was designed to run 66 miles and cost $160,000. French investors sunk $100,000 into the canal before severe seepage and other engineering problems halted construction.

About the same time as the canal construction was ongoing (1863), Winnemucca opened its first hotel, **Hotel Winnemucca,** on the banks of the Humboldt River. While renovated several times over the years, the building still stands on its original plot and operates as the Winnemucca Hotel & Bar, at 95 Bridge Street, the second oldest hotel in Nevada. Its restaurant serves Basque meals and American family-style dinners. Meal prices are moderate. For information call (775) 623–2908.

Take a walking or driving tour of these and other Winnemucca historical points of interest. Pick up a copy of the **Self-Guided Historical Tour of Winnemucca** at the Chamber of Commerce, at 30 West Winnemucca Boulevard (775–623–2225). In 1919 noted Nevada architect Frederic J. Delongchamps designed the **Humboldt County Courthouse,** located at 40 Fifth Street. Delongchamps employed a neoclassical design finished with buff-colored brick and cream terra-cotta and highlighted by Corinthian columns supporting the pediment. That same year Winnemucca missed becoming the state capital by one vote. The courthouse opened on January 1, 1921, and in 1983 joined the ranks of buildings on the National Register of Historic Places. For

Sarah Winnemucca

*C*hief Winnemucca's daughter, Sarah, was notable in her own right. She traveled to Washington, D.C., with her father to plead for improved conditions for their people. Their meeting with Secretary of the Interior Carl Schurz and President Rutherford B. Hayes produced promises but little action on the part of the U.S. government. She is credited with the first English book written by a Native American, Life among the Paiutes (1882), and frequently gave lectures on the conditions of Native Americans. She served as an interpreter in the 1860s at Fort McDermitt and founded an Indian school in 1884 near Lovelock.

Sarah was a Paiute Indian, one of the tribes that inhabited the Great Basin desert region comprising most of Nevada and parts of Utah, Idaho, Wyoming, Oregon, and California. At the time of the wagon trains, the

Paiutes thrived in a land that tested the heartiest emigrants. She began by telling of her grandfather, who greeted the wagon trains as a sign that the two sides (the dark-skinned and white-skinned) of a great family would at last be reunited. According to Paiute tradition, the Great Spirit, tired of their constant bickering, had separated the members of the family. She also talked about the men who came for her sister Mary, only ten years old but fair-skinned and pretty, when their father was away with the white ranchers. The men dragged her out of the barn and returned her in the morning. Mary, never the same, sat with the life gone out of her.

Sarah married twice, both times to soldiers she met when translating for the Army. Learn more about Sarah Winnemucca's life in her autobiography, Life Among the Paiutes.

additional information on Delongchamps, turn to the Lovelock discussion later in this section.

With its Spanish Mission–style architecture, *St. Paul's Catholic Church,* at the corner of Fourth and Melarkey Streets, was built in 1924 and is worth a look, as is the 1927 ***Winnemucca Grammar School,*** at Fifth and Lay Streets. The 1901 ***Shone House,*** at Bridge and Sixth, is an example of a splendid restoration. Unfortunately, all that remains of the town's pride and joy, the ***Nixon Opera House,*** is a plaque in the lot west of the Chamber of Commerce's office. The 1908 opera house burned down in 1992. The city of Winnemucca and the Friends of the Nixon Opera House posted a $21,500 reward for information leading to the conviction of the person or persons responsible for the fire. In its prime the opera house was the largest theatre between Salt Lake City and San Francisco.

On the corner of the spot vacated by the opera house stands a most unlikely sight in the middle of sagebrush country. The more-than-6-foot-tall slab of redwood represents the remains of what has to be one of the largest pieces of driftwood in history. The 1,477-year-old tree yielded in excess of 45,000 board feet of lumber. It drifted onto a Crescent, California, beach during the 1964 flood. It proclaims Winnemucca as the "Gateway to the Pacific Northwest" and marks the Winnemucca to the Sea Highway, via Highway 140, north of Winnemucca. The Humboldt County Library, at 85 East Fifth Street, maintains a Nevada Room, offering many interesting resources on Nevada and Humboldt County history.

> ## Name That Outlaw
>
> *Western legend **Butch Cassidy** was born George Leroy Parker in Beaver, Utah, on April 13, 1866. He took the name Cassidy after Mike Cassidy, a fellow cattle rustler in Utah and Colorado, and earned the nickname Butch while working as a butcher in Rock Springs, Wyoming.*

Enter the ***Buckaroo Hall of Fame and Western Heritage Museum*** through the Chamber of Commerce offices. A number of fine collections will keep you enthralled there for some time. Our favorite is the buckaroo clothing and gear used on the "96" Ranch in Paradise Valley. Learn about *tapederos* (stirrup covers used to keep snow and brush off the rider's boots and legs) and see fine-tooled leather cuffs to protect wrists from thorns and rope burns. Don't miss the collection of branding irons, saddles, Western bronzes, and artwork. Wrap up your visit with a look at the photo of Will Rogers at the 1930 Winnemucca Rodeo.

Buckaroo nominees must have been born before 1900, worked within a 200-mile radius of Winnemucca, made a living on horseback, and mastered the skills of a buckaroo. Viewing hours are from 9:00 A.M. to noon and from 1:00 to 5:00 P.M. Monday through Saturday and from 10:00 A.M. to noon and 1:00 to 4:00 P.M. on Sunday. Admission is free. For information call (775) 623–2225.

Winnemucca annual events include the following: Mule Show & Race and Winnemucca Basque Festival, both in June; Championship Team Roping, in July; 50s Fever (late July), Buckaroo Heritage Western Art Roundup, in September; and Winnemucca Vehicle Rally and Swap Meet, in October. Call (775) 623–2225.

Drive to the junction of Maple Avenue and Jungo Road for a peak at regional history housed in the former 1907 St. Mary's Episcopal Church, now the **Humboldt Museum.** Inside you will find a piano shipped from Europe to San Francisco and then overland to the Hotel Winnemucca in 1868. It provided piano music for the first time in the city. Other interesting displays include a 1903 Edison talking machine and Native American utensils, such as a mesh winnowing tray for sifting piñon nuts.

In the building behind the old church, more treasures await your arrival. There's an old sleigh and a collection of cars (a 1901 Oldsmobile, a 1907 chain-driven Schacht, a 1910 one-cylinder Brush, a 1911 CycleKar, and a 1916 Chevrolet). The piano here is of note—it's the piano from the Nixon Opera House and was restored after it plummeted through the floors during the fire that destroyed the opera house. Outside in the fenced area, you'll find a number of cigar store Indians. The Humboldt Museum is open Monday through Friday from 10:00 A.M. to noon and 1:00 to 4:00 P.M. and Saturday from 1:00 to 4:00 P.M. Admission is free. For information call (775) 623–2912.

The Smithsonian Institution in Washington, D.C., owns one of Ken Tipton's hand-tooled saddles. But you don't have to go east to see Tipton's handiwork. Stop in at **Tips Western** to peruse fancy horse bits, show spurs, custom chinks and chaps, and, of course, saddles. You can order any item with your own brand or initials tooled into the leather. For you city slickers, luggage canvas bags with leather trim, Pendleton blankets, Western audiocassettes, belts, and hats will fit the bill. Tips Western is located at 185 Melarkey Street, Winnemucca 89445. Call (800) 547–8477 for a catalog.

On the food front Winnemucca also comes in strong. To sample the Basque Sheepherder's Loaf, check in at **Hooft's Bakery,** a Winnemucca Bridge Street landmark (across the street from the Chamber of Commerce) for more than six decades. For premier Basque food and great atmosphere, try the **Martin Hotel,** at Railroad and Melarkey Streets. Pull up to the horsehead posts in front of the historic building, which has been a local gathering spot for more than a hundred years. Lunch is served Monday through Friday from 11:00 A.M. to 2:00 P.M. while dinner is served seven days a week from 5:00 to 9:30 P.M. Prices are moderate. Bring your appetite for the plentiful food served family style. For information call (775) 623–3197.

Moving to a new addition in the Winnemucca eating scene, the San Fermin, at 485 West Winnemucca Boulevard, is decorated in a black and white Art Deco motif. Enjoy the dramatic photos around the restaurant. Dinner is served from 5:00 to 10:00 P.M. Monday through Saturday. Prices are moderate to expensive. For information call (775) 625–2555.

Just on the northern outskirts of Winnemucca, on Highway 95, you will find **Pioneer Memorial Park** and **Veteran's Memorial Park,** complete with a cannon, tank, plane, and helicopter. Both are great places to have a picnic and let the kids run and crawl around.

As you head north on Highway 95, sand dunes will start to encroach upon the roadbed. Twenty-two miles north of Pioneer Memorial Park, you turn off Highway 95 onto Route 290 for a trip to **Paradise,** 18 miles away. Hudson Bay Company's Peter Skene Ogden passed through Paradise Valley in 1828. First settled in 1863, the fertile valley evolved into the granary and fruit-raising center for the central and eastern Nevada mining camps and fast-growing towns. The community of Scottsdale emerged in 1866 and took its name from nearby Camp Scott, established to ward off Indian attacks on valley ranchers. The name changed to Paradise City in 1869 and today is called Paradise Valley. By 1871 the Paradise Valley Post Office opened and one hundred people lived in town. Today a handful remain, along with some interesting historic buildings worthy of several photographs.

Founder of the famous "96" Ranch, William F. Stock first saw Paradise Valley in 1863 and homesteaded in 1864. The ranch is still owned and operated by his direct descendants. In town you pass an old stone church on the right before you reach one of the town's major social gathering spots, the post office, on the left. You cannot help but see the massive, gnarled 60-foot-high cottonwood tree stump reaching to the sky. A little farther along, on the right, you arrive at one of the other social hangouts, the **Paradise Saloon & Mercantile Company,** constructed out of granite block in 1910.

Inside you find the ceiling plastered with autographed dollar bills, overstuffed sofas, an antler chandelier, and a mounted wild boar "sipping suds." Excellent photographs of the town's early days cover the walls.

When asked about the dollar bills on the ceiling, the bartender explains, "It just kinda got to be a thing around here."

One of the other things that just got to be a thing around the saloon is the report of ghosts. Once a picture flew off the wall, and on frequent occasions the doors connecting the saloon to the back of the building sound like someone is opening and closing them without the benefit of anyone entering the saloon. Then there are the sounds of bartenders working late into the night, even though the bar is closed.

Adjacent to the saloon is a mercantile store with ice cream, food, and antiques. In fact, you don't have to leave the saloon to enter the store. It's worth a browse to see what treasure you might turn up. In any event, an ice cream cone will do your disposition wonders.

At the end of the main drag, turn right, but not before you get a look at the flying gas sign, a relic of earlier days. Get ready for some more photo opportunities. Historic buildings are lined up like a Hollywood movie set; the only thing missing is Gary Cooper strolling to his fate. When we pulled through town, a horse was tied up to the hitching post with a feed sack over its head at the last house before you veer left and leave Paradise. Across the road you can just barely make out the faded letters on the old blacksmith shed and stable.

That's all the exploring for today. It's time to return 5 miles south of town and turn left at the sign for the **Stonehouse Country Inn.** At the end of the drive, you pass under a welcoming arch and are greeted by a three-story ranch house with spacious rooms. Built in 1941, the ranch is surrounded by the beautiful Santa Rosa Mountains, which deliver wonderful sunset and sunrise vistas. All rooms have private baths for your convenience. Plenty of reading material makes for a relaxing evening. We recommend *Buckaroos in Paradise,* depicting life at the historic "96" Ranch. The book came about as a byproduct of the Smithsonian Institution's 1981 exhibit "Views of a Western Way of Life," on ranch life in Paradise Valley. Western art and historic photographs bring to life the real West. Ask to see the photographs of the ranch's original stone house structure, from which the creek takes its name. The inn's name comes from the creek. Notice how small the cottonwoods are in the picture compared with their current height.

Steve Lucas, the proprietor, and Maureen McClain specialize in tantalizing home-cooked meals, featuring prime rib, barbecued steak, lamb, pork, or seafood. If you still have room, a tempting dessert awaits you.

After a few of Maureen and Steve's meals, you will probably need to get some exercise. The Stonehouse Country Inn offers a variety of activities to get you active. Those in good shape or desiring to achieve that goal can enjoy hiking or biking along the Paradise Valley Trail or the Santa Rosa Mountain Trail. If you choose to relax near the ranch, an afternoon of pitching horseshoes can fill the day. For the more sedate, sit back in the solarium (the ranch hands call it the porch) and watch the birds and animals crisscross the meadow. No matter how you spend it, you will enjoy your stay in Paradise.

Room rates run from $50 to $60 on weekdays and from $60 to $85 on weekends and holidays. Those wishing to fly in can land at a ½-mile airstrip adjoining the Stonehouse property. For information and reservations contact Stonehouse Country Inn, P.O. Box 77, Paradise Valley 89426 (775–578–3530).

> **Trivia**
>
> *Northeastern Nevada is the prime grazing land for cattle such as Texas longhorns and sheep.*

On your way to McDermitt on the Nevada-Oregon border, take the scenic route out of Paradise Valley through the Humboldt National Forest. It's a well-maintained gravel road, although steep and winding. The road was constructed by the Paradise Civilian Conservation Corps in 1938. You will traverse Hinkley Summit, at 7,867 feet in elevation. The drive transports you through striated lava, interesting volcanic formations, rhyolite towers, and car-stopping views.

Creekside picnicking and camping can be had in the mountains at **Lye Creek Campground.** Turn left at road sign 087 and travel about 1½ miles past the U.S. Forest Service Station. Granite Peak, at 9,732 feet in elevation, towers over the remaining countryside. Ask the Forest Service ranger for guides to hiking trails to expand your mountain experience. The campground is typically open from late May through mid-October. A $4.00 overnight fee is charged. For more information on the Humboldt National Forest call (775) 738–5171.

The rest of the drive back to Highway 95 is just as enjoyable. You go over Windy Gap Summit, at 7,380 feet in elevation, and reach the blacktop 13 miles south of McDermitt. **Fort McDermitt** started out as Quinn River Camp, an outpost established in 1865 to protect travelers and area ranchers. That summer Lieutenant Colonel Charles F. McDermitt was killed in an Indian ambush, and later the fort was renamed in his honor. Twenty-four years of continuous operation made it the U.S. Army's longest active fort in Nevada. It also ranked as the last Nevada army post in service when it was converted into an Indian reservation school and incorporated into Fort McDermitt Indian Reservation in 1889. One original building remains on the reservation, 3 miles from town.

In March 1891 the post office moved off the reservation to McDermitt, Nevada, then to McDermitt, Oregon, and finally back to McDermitt, Nevada. The *Fort McDermitt Indian Powwow* takes place Father's Day weekend on the reservation. The oldest amateur rodeo in Nevada, the *Twin States Stampede,* runs every year during the Fourth of July weekend. The rodeo spun off from the 1920s street horse races held in McDermitt. For information contact the McDermitt Homemakers Club, P.O. Box 278, McDermitt 89421 (775–532–8742).

Pershing County

Miles of traveling through the desert and sagebrush take you to your next oasis, in the form of the living ghost town of Unionville. Retrace your tracks 71 miles on Highway 95 to Winnemucca, where you will pick up Interstate 80 going west. Exit at Mill City and turn south on Highway 400. Along the 21-mile route to the Unionville cutoff, you will pass the *Star City Historic Marker.* Star City bloomed with the discovery of a silver lode and the opening of the Sheba Mine. The town received its name because it rested in the shadow of Star Peak, at an elevation of 9,834 feet. The town rapidly grew to a population of 1,400 and in 1864 supported a Wells Fargo office and more than a dozen saloons. A short four years later, the boom collapsed and all but a few people deserted the town.

When the Sheba Mine company stock was listed on the volatile and speculative San Francisco Stock and Exchange, it immediately shot up to $400 per share. The stock price peaked at $600 per share, creating a market value of $60 million. During its years of operation, the Sheba Mine produced more than $5 million in silver.

At the Unionville cutoff take the dirt road to the right and head toward the mountains for 2 miles. Ironically, Southern sympathizers settling into the Buena Vista Canyon area prospecting for silver first named the town Dixie in 1861. Later that same year the more populous Northern partisans forced changing the town name to Unionville. Growth from mining activity helped the town garner the county seat, a distinction it held until 1873, when Winnemucca wrestled it away.

During the boom years, Unionville boasted fine houses and business establishments. Samuel Clemens (prior to arriving at Virginia City and taking on the name Mark Twain) arrived in Unionville in 1861. By

April 1863 approximately twenty stagecoaches arrived daily in the town. The Arizona Mine proved to be the most productive mine by far. In the early 1870s three ten-stamp mills treated its ore, producing wealth for the mine's owners. Underground, more than 17 miles of tunnels ferreted out veins of silver.

The 1870 census listed many Chinese laborers as part of the town population. Numerous interesting occupations showed up on the census records, such as blacksmith, hurdy dancer, tanner, candy store owner, and prostitute. A teamster's freight rig was valued at $300. A fire in 1872 and a lessening in ore quality contributed to the decline of Unionville. By the late 1870s most mining ceased and Unionville grew into a sleepy mining ghost town, with a few stalwart, self-sufficient residents remaining to keep the town alive.

Today some twenty people inhabit Unionville and keep it a charming place to live and visit. A true delight after a day on the backroads of Nevada or a hike in the canyons of the Humboldt Mountains is an evening or more at the **Old Pioneer Garden Country Inn.** Mitzi and Lew Jones are gracious hosts who make your getaway appear as if out of *Alice's Adventures in Wonderland.* For entertainment you can gather eggs for breakfast, milk the goats, or just listen to the geese honk up a storm. A magic stream passes by the old homestead and murmurs you to sleep at night as you are softly surrounded by a down quilt.

You have your choice of a variety of accommodations. The beautifully restored main house, named the Hadley House after a pioneer family, was built in 1864 and features many spacious bedrooms and a great room in which to visit with other guests. Local quilters come from Winnemucca and take over the Hadley House to stitch for several days

What Rolling Mountain Thunder Built

*R*olling Thunder Monument, dedicated to Native Americans, is found at Imlay, north side of Interstate 80, 42 miles north of Lovelock. This outdoor art installation, constructed mainly of found objects, was built in the 1970s by World War II veteran and Creek Indian Rolling Mountain Thunder. He attracted a small population that helped with the construction, using concrete and desert flotsam to erect this fascinating work of art. Visitors are welcome on self-guided tours. The experience has been described as "powerful, intriguing, as visionary as the Watts Towers." Contact the Pershing County Chamber of Commerce (775–273–7213).

in just the right vintage atmosphere. You can sit in the library in the older part of the house, where Mark Twain took his meals. Or opt for the 1860s Wagon Master's House, also called the Ross House, with room for six and a great period kitchen. Or sleep in the barn's refurbished Tack Room, close to your horse. Be sure to admire the hand-laid stone floor of the barn.

Everywhere you look, there's something to make you smile: a grouping of pictures, overstuffed easy chairs, a collection of antiques, or the Adirondack chairs by the creek. The grounds are covered with Mitzi's gardens and Lew's quality carpentry. After a small stroll or bike ride to Mitzi and Lew's Talcott House, get ready to partake of hearty homemade meals. Some of our favorites involved the innovative ways Mitzi prepares corn, whether in pancakes or in sweet side dishes. Take your breakfast on the lawn and your dinner in the gazebo down by the creek. Be sure to look at the gazebo's intricate detail and onion top that Lew created.

Rates run from $65 to $95 per night and include a full breakfast; other meals are available on request. The Wagon Master's House can also be rented by the month.

When you leave the Old Pioneer Garden Country Inn, it's like leaving home, because you know you'll be back again. For information and reservations call (775) 538–7585. To find the inn as you drive in to Unionville, watch for the inn's sign on the left or keep your car window down and listen for the geese honking.

Returning to Interstate 80, you'll find **Rye Patch State Recreation Area** at exit 129, 20 miles southwest of Mill City. The Rye Patch area is full of history. There are ancient petroglyphs to be found, a 12-mile stretch of trail taken by the Donner Party, and mill foundations from early mining efforts. Inquire about tours with park officials. Rye Patch includes a

The Lady Loves a Tramp

*C*harlie Chaplin's first leading lady, **Edna Purviance,** *starred in forty films with the good-hearted tramp. Edna helped out at her mother's boarding house in Lovelock, then moved to San Francisco. While living the life of a bohemian (she walked a duck on a leash), she was discovered by Chaplin, who described her as "quiet and reserved with large, beautiful eyes, beautiful teeth and a sensitive mouth." Edna became his lover and leading lady for ten years. He supported her until her death in 1958 from cancer.*

10,000-surface-acre reservoir perfect for boating, fishing, swimming, and waterskiing. Picnic during the day or stay overnight at the campground. Restroom and telephone facilities are available. For information call (775) 538–7321.

Moving on, 22 miles down the interstate brings you to Lovelock (population 2,310). Make it a point to stop at the Pershing County Courthouse, opened on June 21, 1921. It was designed by noted Nevada architect Frederic J. Delongchamps and contains one of only two round court chambers in use in the United States. If the court is locked, ask for the key in the City Clerk Office. Located adjacent to the courthouse are Bicentennial Park and a large swimming pool in which to cool off from all your sightseeing. The courthouse is located at the corner of Main Street and Central Avenue.

During Delongchamps's sixty-year career, he designed more than 500 buildings, including seven Nevada county courthouses. He apprenticed in San Francisco following the 1906 earthquake and returned to his native Nevada ready to put to use the design concepts he learned in San Francisco's reconstruction. Many of his creations serve as the cornerstones of Nevada's towns and cities. He also won awards for the Nevada buildings he designed for the 1915 Panama-Pacific International Expositions in San Francisco and San Diego. He also added the wings on the Nevada State Capitol in 1913.

Follow Cornell Avenue west to Marzen Lane and stop for a visit at the **Marzen House Pershing County Museum.** Outside you will find an excellent collection of agricultural and mining equipment. Inside view the Paiute Indian artifacts, such as baskets, beads, and arrowheads; typical period Western rooms and clothes, saddles, and brands; and an old dentist's office. You will learn that a dust storm forced Amelia Earhart to land in Lovelock on June 8, 1931, and that Edna Purviance, costar and love interest of Charlie Chaplin, was born in Paradise Valley and raised in Lovelock. The Lovelock Cave Decoys, created by a prehistoric people, were discovered in 1924 some 22 miles southwest of Lovelock. Admission is free. The museum is open May through December from 1:30 to 4:00 P.M., Tuesday through Sunday. For information call (775) 273–7213.

For a good time, schedule your visit to coincide with the Lovelock Frontier Days or the World Champion Fast Draw Competition, both in August. For information call the Chamber of Commerce at (775) 273–7213.

Leaving Lovelock, you follow the Humboldt River southwest until it disappears into the Humboldt Sink, never to reappear.

PLACES TO STAY IN COWBOY COUNTRY

ELKO
Stockmen's Hotel,
340 Commercial Street;
(775) 738-5141 or
(800) 648-2345.

Ruby Crest Guest Ranch,
HC 30 Box 197;
(775) 744-2277.

Once Upon A Time B&B,
537 14th Street;
(775) 738-1200.

JARBIDGE
Tsawhawbitts Ranch B&B,
P.O. Box 260090;
(775) 488-2338.

Outdoor Inn,
Main Street,
P.O. Box 260093;
(775) 488-2311.

LAMOILLE
Red's Ranch,
P.O. Box 1406;
(775) 753-6281.

Breitenstein House B&B,
P.O. Box 281381;
(775) 753-6356.

LOVELOCK
Ramada Inn Sturgeon's
Restaurant, Motel,
and Casino;
(775) 273-2971.

PARADISE VALLEY
Stonehouse Country Inn,
State Rte. 290,
P.O. Box 77;
(775) 578-3530.

UNIONVILLE
Old Pioneer Garden
Country Inn,
2805 Unionville Road;
(775) 538-7585.

WELLS
Cottonwood Ranch,
HC 62 Box 1300,
family-owned
working ranch;
(775) 752-3604 or
(800) 341-5951.

Starr Valley B&B,
Starr Valley Road,
P.O. Box 721;
(775) 752-3898.

Best Western-Sage Inn,
576 6th Street;
(775) 752-3353 or
(800) 528-1234.

WENDOVER
State Line/Silver Smith
Hotel-Casino,
100 Wendover Boulevard;
(775) 664-2221 or
(800) 848-7300.

WINNEMUCCA
Best Western-Gold
Country Inn,
921 West Winnemucca
Boulevard;
(775) 623-6999 or
(800) 346-5306.

Days Inn,
511 West Winnemucca
Boulevard;
(775) 623-3661 or
(800) DAYS-INN.

Holiday Inn Express,
1987 West Winnemucca
Boulevard;
(775) 625-3100 or
(800) HOLIDAY.

Red Lion Inn & Casino,
741 West Winnemucca
Boulevard;
(775) 623-2565 or
(800) RED-LION.

Val-u Inn,
125 East Winnemucca
Boulevard;
(775) 623-5248 or
(800) RED-LION.

PLACES TO EAT IN COWBOY COUNTRY

BATTLE MOUNTAIN
Donna's Diner (American),
West Front Street;
(775) 635-5101.

ELKO
Star Hotel (Basque),
246 Silver Street;
(775) 753-8696.

Biltoki (Basque),
405 Silver Street;
(775) 738-9691.

D'Orazio's Italian Gardens,
217 Idaho Street;
(775) 738-7088.

Mulligan's Bar & Grill,
Ruby Crest Gold Course,
2100 Ruby View Drive;
(775) 777-7279.

LAMOILLE
Pine Lodge Dinner House
(American) and display of
Ron Druck's collection of
North American big
game animals,
Lamoille Highway,
P.O. Box 281208;
(775) 753-6363.

LOVELOCK
Sturgeon's (American),
1420 Cornell Avenue;
(775) 273-2971.

MIDAS
Midas Saloon and Dinner
House (American),
Star Route Midas via
Golconda;
(775) 529-0203.

WELLS
Ruby Mountain Brewery,
Angel Creek Ranch,
tour and tasting,
award-winning brews. U.S.
Highway 93 south 8 miles
to Clover Valley,
HC 60 Box 100,
89835;
(775) 752-2337.

Wells Chinatown
(Chinese),
455 S. Humboldt Avenue;
(775) 752-2101.

WENDOVER
La Joya (Mexican),
the Plaza Mall West;
(775) 664-3966.

Peppermill (American),
680 West Wendover
Boulevard;
(775) 664-2900.

WINNEMUCCA
The Griddle (American),
460 West Winnemucca
Boulevard;
(775) 623-2977.

Winnemucca Hotel
& Bar (Basque),
95 Bridge Street;
(775) 623-2908.

Martin Hotel (Basque),
Railroad and Melarkey
Streets;
(775) 623-3197.

San Fermin (American),
485 West Winnemucca
Boulevard;
(775) 625-2555.

For More Information

Battle Mountain Chamber of Commerce
Box 333, Battle Mountain 89820, (775) 635-8245

Elko Chamber of Commerce
1601 Idaho Street, Elko 89801
(775) 738-7135 or (800) 962-2638

Elko Convention and Visitors Authority
700 Moren Way, Elko 89801
(775) 738-4091 or (800) 248-ELKO

Pershing County Chamber of Commerce
at the Marzen House Museum,
P.O. Box 821, Lovelock 89419
(775) 273-7213

Jackpot Recreation and Visitors Center
Box 627, Jackpot 89825, (800) 411-2052
Also provides information on the
Jarbidge Wilderness Area

Wells Chamber of Commerce
Box 615, Wells 89835, (775) 752-3540

Wendover USA Visitors/Convention Bureau
Box 2468, Wendover 89883
(775) 664-3414 or (800) 426-6862

Winnemucca Chamber of Commerce
30 West Winnemucca Boulevard, Winnemucca 89445
(775) 623-2225

Pony Express Territory

White Pine County

You enter Pony Express Territory from the east on Highway 50, then proceed to Route 487, gateway to one of the least visited national parks, **Great Basin National Park.** Only ten years old and Nevada's only national park, Great Basin National Park encompasses 77,000 acres full of camping, hiking, and exploring activities. Venture in the wonder of **Lehman Caves,** visit a desert glacier, gaze up to view the six-story-high Lexington Arch, and see the world's oldest living organism, the ancient **bristlecone pine** (*Pinus longaeva*). Living bristlecones are in excess of 4,000 years old; they predate the Egyptian pyramids by more than 1,000 years and the oldest giant sequoia by 1,500 years. Dead and fallen bristlecones trace back in time more than 9,000 years. Their gnarly shapes present wonderful photo opportunities, as does spectacular Lexington Arch in the southern part of the

Nevada Wilderness

Desert Survivors leads easy to strenuous hiking (car camping) and trekking (backpacking) trips through Great Basin National Park, Eastern Sierra sagebrush desert, the remote desert of western Nevada, and the canyons and mesas of the Massacre and Bitner Benches in the wild northwest. Many of these lands are designated Wilderness Study Areas where antelope, wild horses, and coyotes roam; where a moonrise and brilliant stars transform the night. Steve Tabor, president, invites you to experience, share and protect the Nevada wilderness. His organization is vigilant and active in its efforts to monitor and preserve them. Annual dues of $20 support wilderness preservation. Members receive a quarterly newsletter and seasonal trip schedules. Contact Desert Survivors at P.O. Box 20991, Oakland, CA, 94620. Activities Director Dave Halligan can be reached at (510) 528–3360; Steve Tabor at (510) 769–1706. Web site: www. desert-survivors.org/oasis. E-mail: bighorn@desert-survivors.org.

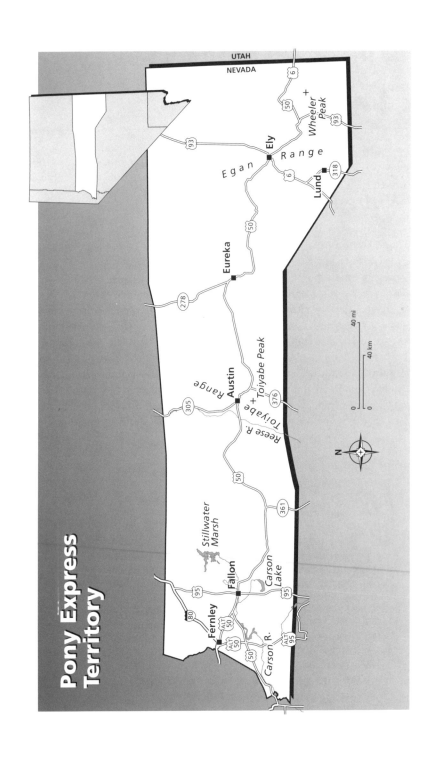

Pony Express Territory

park. The C. T. Rhodes Log Cabin, near the visitor center, was used as a guest house in the 1920s and is on the National Register of Historic Places.

Within the park are five distinct ecological environments. **Wheeler Peak,** the second highest in Nevada, boasts a permanent ice cap at 13,063 feet and intriguing glacial features. The 1,000-yard-long glacier remnant is Nevada's only known active glacier. In the depths of Lehman Caves, walk among giant limestone formations and through marble caverns on the ninety-minute guided tours. Flickering candlelight talks bring home the mystery of the caves. Look for the Parachute Formation. Absalom Lehman discovered the caves around 1885. Lehman Caves was designated a national monument in 1922 and became part of the national park in 1986. Tours are limited to thirty people and follow a paved trail for 6/10 mile. The temperature in the caves remains about fifty degrees all year, so wear warm clothing. While there is no entrance fee, tour prices range from $2.00 to $8.00 depending on the length of the tour. Tours operate seven days a week, year-round, from 7:00 A.M. to 6:00 P.M. except on New Year's Day, Thanksgiving, and Christmas. For information call (775) 234–7331.

Lower Lehman Creek Campground is open year-round, while three other campgrounds in the park operate on a seasonal basis. Overnight camping costs $10 and sites are on a first-come, first-served basis.

Lehman Caves

*B*ecause rivers and streams in the Great Basin have no outlet to the sea, they flow inland forming small lakes or soaking into the earth. This action produced the treasure of Great Basin National Park: **Lehman Caves.** Following a tour guide into the dark damp chill, I walked through caverns with names like Gothic Palace, Cypress Swamp, and the Grand Palace. The ceilings and walls were a literal art gallery of stalactites and stalagmites. Seeping water full of calcite crystals created amazing formations over hundreds of thousands of years. Open year-round. For information call (775) 234–7331.

Entrance to the park is free. Interpretive booklets are available at a reasonable cost at the visitor center. To reach the Great Basin National Park Visitor Center, travel 5 miles west of Baker on Highway 488. For information call (775) 234–7331.

Take Highway 893 north from Majors Place for 53 miles, until you reach the Route 2 junction, at which you will turn left (west) to reach Highway 93. At this junction you first encounter the original route of the Lincoln Highway (the nation's first transcontinental highway, which traversed the country from New York City to San Francisco) in Nevada, just after it crossed the Utah border near Ibapah.

The idea for the Lincoln Highway first took root in Indianapolis, at a 1912 dinner meeting of automobile industry tycoons. At the time, the nation's two million miles of roads were largely unconnected; railroads represented the only practical means of coast-to-coast travel. Within three years a patchwork made from existing roads wound its way across the country from Times Square in New York City via ferry to New Jersey and finally to Lincoln Park in San Francisco in time for the 1915 Panama-Pacific International Exposition, thereby creating the first U.S. transcontinental highway.

Bristlecone Pine

Later improvements made the Lincoln Highway one of the premier roads of its day. The federal government took over the road system in the 1920s. To mark the event, the Boy Scouts of America installed more than 3,000 Lincoln Highway markers along every mile of the route on September 1, 1928. A number of these Nevada markers can still be found. One is located in front of the courthouse in Eureka and another near the Nevada State Museum (old Carson City Mint Building) in Carson City.

In Nevada the Lincoln Highway route traveled through Ely, Eureka, Austin, Fallon, Fernley, Carson City, Sparks, and Reno taking one of two routes around Lake Tahoe into California. In Reno it went under the famed Reno Arch, which was erected in 1926 to celebrate the passing of the Lincoln Highway and the Victory Highway through Reno.

Top Annual Events
Eureka Opera House, *summer season;* *(775) 237–6006.*
Fallon Air Show, *Blue Angels, and Reno balloon race; for more information call (775) 423–4556.*
Ghost Train of old Ely, *14-mile round trip aboard vintage passenger train, spring and summer, Nevada Northern Railway Museum, Ely; (775) 289–2085.*
Gridley Days, *Austin, June; (775) 964–2200.*

Take this gravel section of the Lincoln Highway 15 miles, until you reach Highway 93 and the site of Schellbourne. In 1859 an Overland Stage stop and mail station was built at Schellbourne, and the Pony Express used the spot as a stop on its route in 1860. Turn right (north) on Highway 93 for 6 miles. Then take a left turn (west) and head approximately 8 miles for the hills and the *Cherry Creek Ghost Town.*

It may be hard to believe, but one of White Pine County's largest towns occupied this site, beginning in 1872 with the discovery of gold and silver. The construction of one of the first five-stamp mills in eastern Nevada took place here. Mining continued through several booms and busts into the 1880s and then quieted down until brief boomlets in the

Good Story but No Bones

*T*he disaster at **Chinaman Mine** occurred in 1872. An unstable mass of rock gave way, sealing the mine's entrance and trapping between eight and twelve Chinese miners who had been working underground. The mine owners decided not to reopen the pas- sage; since the mine had not been lucrative, they couldn't be bothered. Tragically, the Chinese men presumably died of suffocation. When the passage was recently mined, workers expected to find human bones. They found some ore carts, but no bones.

1905–1908 and 1935–1940 periods. Estimated gold and silver production through Cherry Creek's mills during its heyday ranged from $3 million to $20 million. Gold and silver mining gave way to tungsten in the 1950s, when the mills ran full force to handle production from ten operating properties. When the price of tungsten dropped from $63 to $12 a unit, the mines shut down once again.

Cherry Creek hangs on with a dozen or so residents, a far cry from the claimed 6,000 miners who once crowded its streets and gave the town a reputation for ripsnorting activity. One of the oldest remaining one-room Nevada schools (1872) now serves as the Cherry Creek Museum. To take a tour, honk your horn—if, that is, the museum curators are not out on a hike or a picnic. Otherwise, take a leisurely drive or walk around and visit with the friendly townsfolk. When asked what the museum held, one of the town residents paused a moment and then said, "It's kind of a hodgepodge museum." One of the more delightful displays consists of early photos of Cherry Creek schoolchildren.

Pay particular attention to the stone structure with a sod roof. Originally, it was the root cellar for the mercantile store, which has long since vanished. Down the street the Cherry Creek Barrel Saloon will quench your thirst while you look at old photographs of the town and mining activity. The dollar-bill-covered ceiling adds a new twist with the presence of a $1 million check.

The Cherry Creek Post Office opened in 1873 and operated for more than one hundred years. Today a dozen or so mailboxes line the corner near the saloon and serve the same function, as the local gathering spot. Mail reaches the town Monday through Friday.

Returning to the twentieth century, drive 45 miles south on Highway 93 to *Ely* (population 4,830). The BHP Copper Robinson operation near town first yielded copper in the mid-1880s, before being shut down by Kennecott in 1978. A change in ownership in 1991 and higher copper prices combined to put the copper property back to work temporarily in 1995.

Go to the north end of East Eleventh Street and pull up to the ***Nevada Northern Railway Museum*** to take a ride into Nevada's past. The rail station's unique architecture is worth a picture, but even more fascinating is the fact that it functions as a living history, operating railroad facility. The Ghost Train of Ely steams down the tracks on schedule from late May through early September. In addition, special-event train rides—such as an evening train ride with wine and hors d'oeuvres, a fireworks train, and a photographer's excursion. Rates run from $8.00

per child up to $16.00 per adult (depending on whether steam- or diesel-powered). Special-event train rides may have slightly different fares.

Don't forget to tour the general office, depot, dispatcher's office, round-house, and blacksmith shop. The Nevada Northern Railway Museum is located on Railroad Street at the north end of East Eleventh Street. For schedule information and reservations call (775) 289–2085.

Just up the street, at 220 East Eleventh Street, is the delightfully restored *Steptoe Valley Inn Bed and Breakfast,* where you can camp out for a few days while you tour the area sights. The building started out in 1907 as the Ely City Grocery and now sports elegant Victorian detail and five comfortable theme bedrooms for guests. Call for current rates. The Steptoe Inn operates a seasonal schedule from March through September. For information call (775) 289–8687.

To nourish your body, there are a limited number of food establishments. The Oriental wallpaper, ornate lamps, embroidery art, and painted booths set the tone for the colorful atmosphere of the *Orient Express,* at 562 Aultman Street, making for an enjoyable meal. Chinese dishes such as sweet and sour, chow mein, cashew chicken, ginger beef, and hot and spicy Szechuan shrimp fill the menu. Hours are from 11:00 A.M. to 9:00 P.M. Monday through Saturday and closed on Sunday. Prices are inexpensive to moderate. Call (775) 289–3313. Cappuccino, espresso, and Italian sodas are available at the *Flower Basket,* at 445 East Eleventh Street. Call (775) 289–2828.

Although small, the *White Pine Public Museum* houses a fine collection of White Pine County memorabilia and Great Basin Native American artifacts. Other interesting displays include a collection of young

Stephen King and *Desperation*

*E*ly residents won't soon forget the day novelist **Stephen King** rode into town. The sun glinted off the chrome of his Harley as he rumbled up Aultman Street to the Jailhouse Casino. The best-selling author from Maine made at least two trips to eastern Nevada in the fall of 1994. The result was Desperation, *another of King's* terrifying tales. In the book, Desperation *is the name of a Nevada mining town located near Highway 50 and just a couple of miles from the gates of hell. The setting is loosely based on the old copper-mining town of Ruth, five miles east of Ely. "He was very nice,"* said Ely resident Melody Hawkins, *"but he wouldn't give autographs."*

An Ely Hike

Ward Mountain Recreation Area/Murry Summit has a 4-mile trail and twelve loop trails perfect for cross-country skiing, snowmobiling, hiking, and mountain biking. The trail system meanders through high elevation piñon and juniper woodland, sagebrush, and grassland with excellent vistas of the vast basin and range country beyond. The trail head and parking lie 6 miles from Ely. A trail map is available at White Pine County Chamber of Commerce, 636 Aultman Street, Ely 89301; (775) 289–8877.

girls' delicate dresses; a large doll collection; an Ivers and Pond piano shipped by rail from San Francisco to Toana, Nevada, and by wagon freight to the Campbell Ranch in 1899; horsehair gloves; a barbed-wire collection; and a historical exhibit entitled "Nevada Women at Work and in Politics."

Here you will learn that Thelma Catherine Patricia Ryan (Pat Nixon) came from Ely. Outside are a homesteader's cabin with square logs and chinking and the railroad depot from Cherry Creek. The director is an archaeologist. Ask about the excavations at the Pony Express Station. The museum is located at 2000 Aultman Street. It is open year-round, from 9:00 A.M. to 5:00 P.M. Monday through Friday and from noon to 5:00 P.M. Saturday and Sunday. Admission is free. For information call (775) 289–4710.

Around town search out the 1928 City Hall, with old fire equipment, near the fire station; the fountain near the library, with swans and ducks paddling around; and the interesting architecture on East Eleventh Street. Plan a number of day trips. The ***Cave Lake State Park,*** approximately 15 miles southeast of Ely, delivers some of the best German-brown-trout and rainbow-trout fishing in Nevada. The 1,820-acre park includes a thirty-two-acre reservoir and thirty-six developed campsites. Two developed hiking trails are maintained. The Steptoe Creek Trail is an easy, 3-mile round-trip journey, while the 5-mile Cave Springs Trail involves moderately strenuous hiking. The park is open all year. Fees are $12.00 per vehicle for overnight camping and $3.00 for day use. To reach Cave Lake from the east end of Ely, take Highway 6/50/93 for 8 miles and turn left (east) on Route 486 (Success Summit Road) for 6 miles. Highway 486 dead-ends at Highways 6/50/93. Write to Cave Lake State Park, P.O. Box 761, Ely, 89301. For information call (775) 728–4460.

The ***Ely Elk Viewing Area*** begins 6 miles southeast of Ely, along Highway 6/50/93. A Bureau of Land Management map points out the best viewing areas during different seasons. For a brochure and map call the bureau office at (775) 289–1800.

Finish off your southeast Ely area sightseeing with a trip to the ***Ward Charcoal Ovens.*** These six beehive-shaped brick ovens were built around 1876 and produced charcoal for the smelters serving area mines. Among minerals mined at Ward were silver, lead, copper, manganese, and antimony. The 30-foot-tall, 27-foot-diameter ovens were filled with as many as thirty-five cords of wood at a time. A twenty-stamp leaching mill was built but never proved successful, due to the type of ore mined and the shortage of available water.

Many men were employed in the gathering and shipping of wood for the ovens. Piñon was used almost exclusively, and deadwood was preferred. The ovens contain a hole in the top and a window vent in the back. The entrances are large, but duck if you enter wearing a cowboy hat. The charcoal ovens were abandoned in the 1880s, after the smelters shut down.

For a time Sam Crowcroft used them for stables, housing twelve horses in one oven. Other local lore states that one of them was cleaned up and whitewashed as a prospective home for a gambler and his bride-to-be. The Ward Charcoal Oven apartment was never used, however, because the two lovebirds quarreled and never married. To reach the ovens, go east out of Ely on Highway 6/50/93 for about $5^{1}/_{2}$ miles, then turn right (west) and travel a little over 10 miles on a dirt road. The way is well marked with signs. Ward Charcoal Ovens, a State Historic Park since 1969, now has a campground, ranger talks, and guided tours in the summer. For a park brochure write to P.O. Box 193, Ely, 89301, or call (775) 728–4460.

During 1905–1906 the Nevada Consolidated Copper Company constructed a 150-mile rail line from Copper Flats ore mines west of Ely to the smelter at McGill and then to Cobre on the Southern Pacific line. During the first half of this century, the Ely area produced nearly $1 billion in copper, gold, and silver. Largest among the famed copper pits is the Liberty, which resumed operations temporarily in July 1995.

Rockhounds will delight in spending a few hours at ***Garnet Hill,*** with amenities such as picnic tables, barbecue grills, and shade trees. The Garnet Fields Rockhound Area is located in the Egan Mountain Range about 4 air miles from Ely. The major access road takes off from Highway 50 about $6^{4}/_{10}$ miles west ($^{1}/_{4}$ mile past the turnoff to Ruth) of the traffic signal at the junction of Highways 50 and 93 in Ely. Turn right and travel north a little over 3 miles. For a map contact the Bureau of Land Management Office north of Ely on Highway 93 (775–289–1800).

Now it is time to rejoin Highway 50 (the old Lincoln Highway route) heading west to Eureka. In 1986 *Life* magazine dubbed Highway 50 from Ely to Reno "The Loneliest Road in America." Rather than be insulted by the designation, Nevada and towns along the route took up the banner, erected loneliest road signs, and began a Loneliest Road campaign that turned the slam into a public relations bonanza. You won't sing the blues for 287 miles on Highway 50. Actually there's plenty to see. Driving east from Fernley to Ely, you cross nine mountain ranges—most more than 10,000 feet—pass through a farming oasis, the Fallon Top Gun Naval fighter pilot school, and historic Eureka, once an opulent mining town. Each of the towns issues a Highway 50 Survival Kit. Stop and pick one up at the Chamber of Commerce, get it stamped at each town you stop in, and send your verification to the Nevada Commission on Tourism.

Eureka County

The billboard on the eastern edge of Eureka (population 650) proclaims, THE LONELIEST TOWN ON THE LONELIEST ROAD IN AMERICA. That may have been true when the sign was erected a few years back, but as the county seat of Eureka County (population 1,500), the town is bustling with activity and plush with tax revenues from the boom in Eureka County mining projects. Today it is the happiest and friendliest town on Highway 50.

Eureka ranked as Nevada's second largest mineral producer. But instead of gold or copper, Eureka produced lead/silver. The town exploded to a population of 9,000 in the 1870s and 1880s. The 1879 *Eureka County Courthouse* is well worth a visit, as is the 1880 *Eureka Opera House,* which was restored for more than $1 million. Notice the courthouse's original tin ceiling, its chandeliers, and the Silver Party flag in the court chambers. The Silver Party advocated minting silver dollars, which in 1873 were outlawed in the United States, a move that severely damaged Nevada's mining industry and economy. Also, peek into the Treasurer's Office on the second floor and look at the vault adorned with a mountain scene. The Eureka County Courthouse is on the National Register of Historic Places.

Stop at the Chamber of Commerce in the *Eureka Sentinel Museum* and pick up a copy of the *Self-Guided Walking Tour of Eureka* brochure. The tour gives you a real flavor for the town and its history. We especially liked the buildings on Main Street where only the front walls were remaining. The museum itself is located in the restored *Eureka Sentinel* Newspaper Office, which dates back to 1879. Reproductions of the newspaper's historic front pages, along with the *Sentinel's* original printing equipment, fill the back of the museum. Printing equipment on display includes an 1887 Chandler & Price platen press, an 1872 Fairhaven flatbed cylinder press, a wire stretcher, and a paper cutter.

The newspaper operated in Eureka from 1870 to 1960. The Eureka *Sentinel* Building is on the National Register of Historic Places. The museum is 1 block north of Highway 50 at Ruby Hill Avenue. It is open April 15 through October 15 from 11:00 A.M. to 5:00 P.M. Monday through Saturday and from 10:00 A.M. to 3:00 P.M. Sunday. Admission is free. For information call (775) 237–5484.

The historic **Jackson House** dates back to 1877. The building was gutted by the fire of 1880 and rebuilt. In 1981, after many years of vacancy, it was restored as a historical building, and in 1994 present owner Robert E. Williams purchased the building and returned the apartments to guest rooms. He replaced the broken transoms with leaded stained glass reflecting the name of each room. A porch surrounds the second story for evening viewing of cars coming into town on Highway 50, and an upstairs parlor is a nice place to relax. Note the brass crib in the parlor. Rooms rent for around $80 per night and $120 for the Jackson Suite; rates vary depending on the season. In October 1994 Williams garnered the Governor's Award for Tourism and for Restoration of a Historical Building. The Jackson House is located on Highway 50 at its intersection with Ruby Hill Avenue and is right across from the courthouse. The present owner is Dr. Bartlett. For information or reservations call (775) 237–5577.

An interesting piece of Eureka history is the Charcoal War of 1879. It started when Italian charcoal suppliers to the smelters went on strike for higher prices, then 25 cents per pound. The armed workers virtually took over Eureka on August 11. The militia temporarily restored order. On August 18, a posse of miners (none Italian), headed by a deputy sheriff, engaged a number of charcoal burners at Fish Creek and attempted to arrest them.

The conflict climaxed with the shooting deaths of five charcoal burners and the wounding of six others. No one was convicted for the killings. With the strike broken, the owners reduced the price they would pay for charcoal by more than 20 percent. By the early 1890s the mines had played out and the smelters closed. In fifteen years Eureka produced in excess of $40 million in silver, $20 million in gold, and countless tons of lead. Brief mining operations spurted up over the years, but none lasted long. Today that picture is changing, with productive mines already operating in northern Eureka County and Homestake Mining Company poised to open a gold mine near Eureka.

The **Owl Club Steakhouse** serves more-than-ample good grub. Like almost everything else, the eatery is located on the main drag (Highway 50). The pine wainscoting and Western artwork on the walls give the place a comfortable feeling. Food prices are moderate. For information call (775) 237–5280. Farther east on Highway 50, **DJ's Diner** serves up burgers, yogurt, malts, and delicious peanut butter shakes. Call (775) 237–5356.

Before leaving, check out the **Perdiz Sport Shooting Inc.** range, just south of Eureka. It is open to the public and attracts shootists from near and far. Although relatively new, Perdiz Sport Shooting has garnered a number of distinctions. The club and Eureka County earned the Nevada Commission on Tourism Governor's Tourism Development Award in December 1993. Recently, Ducks Unlimited awarded its annual state sporting clays shoot to Perdiz Sport Shooting for five years. The fully automated range features ten shooting stations, each designed to simulate a certain species of game. The fee to use the range is $15 for fifty shots, not including the shells. The range is open on Saturday and Sunday and other days by appointment; there is no shooting after sundown. It is located in the Windfall Canyon, 2 miles south of town and just below majestic Prospect Peak. For information call the range at (775) 237–7027 or the Chamber of Commerce at (775) 237–5484.

Eureka lies in the Diamond Valley, first explored by Colonel John C. Frémont in 1845. Fourteen years later Captain James A. Simpson mapped a route through the north end of the valley. In 1860–1861 the Pony Express crossed the terrain. You can still see traces of the Pony Express route through the sagebrush as it crosses Highway 278 about 21 miles north of town. Early freight roads also crisscrossed the valley as mining camps boomed in the 1860s. The mining boom gave birth to an agricultural and dairy industry in Diamond Valley.

Lander County

ack on the Loneliest Road in America (Highway 50), head due west toward Austin. About 48 miles west of Eureka and 22 miles east of Austin, you come upon Hickison Summit, at 6,564 feet in elevation, and the **Hickison Petroglyph Recreation Area.** Turn right (north) and follow the well-graded gravel road to the campground, where shaded picnic tables, rest rooms, and twenty-one camping and trailer sites provide a refuge from the summer desert heat, which can easily rise above ninety degrees Fahrenheit. Make sure you bring your own water supply, since no drinking water is available.

Petroglyphs (ancient rock art) are located on the cliff at the edge of the picnic area. Estimates place their age between 1000 B.C. and A.D. 1500. A Bureau of Land Management brochure located in a box at the beginning of the trail provides an excellent tour guide, pointing out native plants as well as interesting petroglyphs on the cliff face. Archaeologists believe the horseshoe-shaped petroglyph symbolizes the female. Many of the glyphs may represent hunting or fertility magic. From the trail you can take a left fork to arrive at the Highway 50 overlook. The highway route roughly follows the routes taken by Frémont (1845) and Simpson (1859). Likewise, the Pony Express traveled through the area on the way to Austin and points west.

Continuing on the petroglyph trail, stop at site 11. The petroglyphs on this boulder are different from the others at the Hickison Petroglyph site, though they still resemble the curvilinear style. The petroglyph at the base of the boulder may be an animal, making it the only zoomorphic glyph at the site.

Take the following loop tour for a day trip to some intriguing places. Begin with a southeastern jog into Big Smoky Valley to **Spencer's Hot Springs,** which have eased the weary bones of travelers for more than one hundred years.

One of Nevada's best kept secrets is the abundance of geothermal springs. The earth's molten core comes close to the surface in parts of the western United States. Water passing through the core can push its way close to the surface and, finding a weak spot such as a fault, can burst out like a geyser, ooze out as a mud pot, or bubble up as a hot mineral spring. Spencer's Hot Springs near Austin is undeveloped, no more than a hot pool and a wooden bench. But you can sit in a toasty warm pool and enjoy the magnificent scenery of the Toiyabe Range. Access is easy from Interstate 50 east of Austin. Take State Route 376 south for 1/4 mile, turn left onto a gravel road. You'll see the Toquima Cave historic marker. After 5 1/2 miles turn left onto a dirt road and follow it to the springs.

Next, continue to the 7,900-foot Pete's Summit and **Toquima Cave.** The cave lies at the end of an easy 1/4-mile path from the picnic area. The paintings at the cave mouth were made by the ancient Shoshone tribe. To arrive at these refreshing spots, take Pete's Summit Road southeast off Highway 376 just south of the intersection with Highway 50, east of Austin.

Proceed through Sam's Canyon past Monitor Ranch. Notice the old mud and willow ranch buildings; they have stood for generations.

Approximately 8 miles past the ranch, a large white dome-shaped formation rises from the meadow. You have reached **Diane's Punch Bowl,** which is on private land. Eleven miles south turn west to enter **Northumberland Canyon** and proceed up to Northumberland Cave. A word of caution: This cave is for serious spelunkers with the proper equipment. Follow the road over Northumberland Pass, at 7,430 feet elevation. From here the road winds above the open pits of **Northumberland Gold Mine,** providing fantastic views. Wind downhill into Big Smoky Valley and spectacular formations and towering columns. When you reach Highway 376, turn right (north) and head back to Highway 50.

Before entering Austin (population 300), stop at **Scott's Summit,** at an elevation of 7,195 feet. At this spot you'll find the **Surveyors Historic Marker** and Bob Scott Campground with picnic tables, running water, and rest rooms. The historic marker commemorates the surveyors who plotted the West, laying out railway routes, water transport, and wagon roads. The Honey-Lake-to-Fort-Kearny wagon road was completed in 1860 by Captain Lander, after whom Lander County is named.

The Difficult Hanging of Rufus B. Anderson at the Lander County Courthouse

*R*ufus B. Anderson *was baptized into the Roman Catholic faith a few hours before his scheduled hanging for murder. The material for the scaffold had been brought to the jail the night before and was assembled and erected in front of the Lander County courthouse in Austin. Ten minutes before 1:00 P.M., Anderson was marched out and up the scaffold. He knelt in prayer with the priest, then rose and addressed the crowd, asking for forgiveness. Sheriff Sanborn read the death warrant; a deputy bound his arms, placed a black hood over his head, and slipped a noose around his neck. As the condemned man uttered the words, "I commend my soul to* thee," *the trap was sprung and he crashed to the ground. A cry went up from the crowd. Anderson was carried back up and once again the end of the noose slipped through the coil and he ended up on the ground. Men shouted, "For shame, for shame! It's butchery!" Unconscious, Anderson was tied in a chair where he soon revived and asked for a drink of water. The rope was adjusted a third time, and he and the chair swung free when the trap was dropped. The body and chair dangled for twenty minutes. The body was cut down, removed from the chair and placed on a bier and taken to the family home. —from Nevada Historical Society records, October 30, 1868.*

PONY EXPRESS TERRITORY

You cross one more summit, Austin Summit, at 7,484 feet, before twisting and turning into **Austin** (population 300) on a 6 to 7 percent grade. Make sure your brakes are in good condition. The final horseshoe bend drops you onto the main street. Early in 1862 an employee of the Overland Mail and Stage Company, William Talcott, discovered rich silver veins in Pony Canyon

and started a rush of prospectors to Austin. By 1867 the town boasted eleven mills to process ore and more than 10,000 people, making the fledgling city Nevada's second largest community. All in all, more than $50 million in silver was mined and processed at Austin.

Many of the brick buildings remain, giving the town a perfect setting for a period movie. It's one of the most photogenic of Nevada's small towns, with tall church spires, a large courthouse, and false-front buildings on main street. Through the years the Pony Express, Overland Stage, Transcontinental Telegraph lines, Lincoln Highway, and Highway 50 crossed right through the center of town, with very little change in scenery.

On your right a few blocks into town, stop at **Gridley Store,** the origin of a colorful bit of Austin history. The one-story stone structure was erected in late 1863 and operated as a general store by owner Reuel Colt Gridley. Mark Twain immortalized him in *Roughing It* after Gridley carried a fifty-pound sack of flour down Austin's main street after losing an 1864 election bet.

The sack of flour became even more famous after Gridley auctioned it off, with the proceeds going to the Sanitary Fund, a Civil War equivalent of the Red Cross. He auctioned the sack of flour many times throughout Nevada and California. It even made it to the 1864 St. Louis World's Fair, where it was auctioned off yet again. It raised more than $275,000 for the relief fund. You can see the original flour sack on display at the Nevada Historical Society in Reno. Ironically, Gridley died six years later, almost penniless.

Austin hosts Gridley Days every year in mid-June. Fun-filled activities include fiddle competitions, Nevada Civil War Volunteer demonstrations, and flour-sack races. For information call the Austin Chamber of Commerce at (775) 964–2200 or (775) 964–2418. It is located in the courthouse.

The first Austin commercial building, the **International Hotel,** ranks as one of Nevada's oldest hotels. It was originally built in Virginia City, later dismantled, and portions of it hauled board by board to Austin in 1863. Inside, the **International Cafe** serves good food at moderate prices. For information call (775) 964–9905.

Nevada's oldest newspaper, *The Resse River Reveille,* closed its doors in 1993 after having been published in the same location since 1863. Early dispatches were brought in by stage. Its files contain early news of the Civil War and the assassination of President Lincoln. The *Reveille* editor formed the "Sazarac Lying Club," named after the Sazarac Saloon and fertile ground for newspaper articles.

<table>
<tr><td>

Trivia

*The **International Hotel** is the oldest hotel in Nevada and perhaps the oldest in the West. A portion of the bar and east wall are from the original International Hotel, which was built in Virginia City in 1860. Wagons brought it to Austin where the sides were rebuilt and other sections were added over time.*

</td></tr>
</table>

The Lander County Court House cornerstone was laid in September 1871. The courthouse gained notoriety in the early 1880s when a man who murdered a popular local rancher was taken from the jail on the lower floor of the building by vigilantes and lynched from the balcony over the front door.

Austin contains a number of historic churches. St. Augustine's Catholic Church is the only remaining of the first four Catholic churches in Nevada. It opened its doors on Christmas Eve in 1866, and restoration plans are in the works. Erected in 1866, the Old Methodist Church (now Austin's town hall) housed a famous pipe organ that made the trip around the Horn and arrived in Austin from San Francisco via freight wagon. Donations of mining-company stock helped finance the church's construction. Some of the companies behind the mining stock went bust, causing the church consternation, not to mention cash flow problems.

On the western outskirts of town, **Stokes Castle** draws the curious. Modeled after a tower outside Rome, Stokes Castle is crafted from hand-hewn native granite stones raised into place by a hand-powered windlass in 1897. Anson Phelps Stokes, an eastern financier with substantial mineral interests in the Austin area, not only built the structure but also arranged financing for construction for the 92-mile Nevada Central Railroad from Battle Mountain to Austin.

The three-story castle with three fireplaces was used sparingly and eventually fell into disrepair. The remains are enclosed by a wire fence, but the site's view of up to 60 miles to the south and 35 miles to the north makes it a great place to picnic. To reach Stokes Castle, take Main

Street west to Castle Road and turn left. Follow the winding dirt road and signs to the castle, about 1 mile from the highway.

Austin had another connection with eastern culture. Emma Wixom, daughter of a pioneer Austin doctor, graduated from the Austin Methodist Choir to become the famous opera singer Emma Nevada. She trained in Vienna beginning in 1877, sang at the coronation of George VI, and was a favorite of Queen Victoria. During her triumphant tour of America in 1885, she ordered her managers to change her schedule so that she could travel to Austin and sing for her old friends.

While you are near the geographic center of Nevada, take a dip in the municipal swimming pool in Austin Park, at the east end of town. The other place to eat in town is *Toiyabe Cafe,* next to St. George's Episcopal Church (which was built circa 1878 and houses a pipe organ that came around the Horn and still works). Call the cafe at (775) 964–2220.

Churchill County

Twenty-five miles west of Austin you pass into Churchill County at New Pass Summit, at an elevation of 6,348 feet. The site also served as a stage station and freighter stop in the early 1860s. Completion of the first transcontinental railroad caused the eventual demise of the Overland Stage line.

Be sure to stop for a look at the *Cold Springs Pony Express Station,* one of the best-preserved Pony Express stations in Nevada. Nearby you can view remnants of freight and telegraph relay stations. A moderate 1$^1/_2$-mile hike takes you to the Cold Springs Pony Express Station. According to legend, an 1860 traveler noted that the station was "a wretched place, rudely built, and roofless and maintained by four rough-looking boys." Cold Springs is located 25 miles west of New Pass Summit.

Mountain biking along the Pony Express Trail is another option. Write for the Austin-Toiyabe mountain bike trail guide, Toiyabe National Forest–Austin Ranger District, 100 Midas Canyon Road, P.O. Box 130, Austin 89310; (775) 964–2671.

Traveling another 17 miles brings you to Highway 121. Go north to the Dixie Valley turnoff. For avid hikers seeking the fantastic views, consider a stop at the *Clan Alpine Mountains Wild Study Area.* At your disposal are 196,000 acres of roadless wilderness for the ultimate in backpacking. Travel over dissected ranges leading up to Mount Augusta, at 9,966 feet in elevation and 6,500 feet over the Dixie Valley below. Don't venture forth without proper maps, which you can obtain from the Bureau of Land Management.

Twenty miles east of Fallon delivers a natural wonder and recreational delight. Six hundred feet high, 2 miles long, and 1 mile wide, **Sand Mountain** captures the imagination when you consider that each grain of sand had to be blown separately from the desert floor into the corner of the mountains over millions of years. At the base of the mountain, you can explore the **Sand Springs Pony Express Station.** Self-guided interpretive trail signs provide you with the station history. For the more adventurous, choose from hiking, hang-gliding, and dune-buggy driving on and around the sand dunes. Wild horses also make the area their home.

Pony Express Riders

Strap on your chaps, cinch up your saddle, and put on your spurs. From April 1860 to October 1861, dozens of young men galloped the vast expanse of open range from St. Joseph, Missouri, to Sacramento, California. Despite sleet, rain, desperadoes, and fatigue, they delivered mail in an extraordinarily swift ten-days' time. With his mailbags slapping against the sides of his saddle, a rider would approach a **Pony Express** *station, where another rider awaited him. The next in line quickly mounted a fresh horse and raced away with the mailbags.*

Carrying on the "Loneliest" theme, the solar-operated public telephone at the Sand Mountain Road sports a sign declaring it as the LONELIEST PHONE ON THE LONELIEST ROAD IN AMERICA.

Be on the lookout for an unusual memorial on the flats near Sand Mountain. As you head west, look to the right (north) about 150 yards from the road shoulder for a wooden structure bordered by rocks. It marks the **graves of Le Beau children,** who died of diphtheria within three days of each other, around 1865. Over the years various Good Samaritans have periodically spruced up the grave site, adding a picket fence and a new cross after time and weather have taken their toll. The latest grave tender added a plaque that reads, DEDICATED TO THE MEMORY OF THE HUNDREDS OF MEN, WOMEN AND CHILDREN AND THOUSANDS OF ANIMALS THAT PERISHED ON THE OLD SIMPSON TRAIL TO CALIFORNIA 1846 TO THE 1880S.

Eight miles east of Fallon, **Grimes Point Archaeological Area** represents one of the largest and most accessible prehistoric petroglyph rock-carving sites. A 2,000-foot interpretive trail leads through a boulder-strewn area ripe with rock carvings at every turn. An informative Bureau of Land Management trail guide, available in the parking lot, discusses carvings at each station. Over a period of 8,000 years, the rock carvers left traces of their occupation of the area around the marshes of ancient Lake Lahontan.

Some 1½ miles north of Grimes Point lies **Hidden Cave.** The cave has provided important information on the chronology of the ancient lake and its inhabitants. The Churchill County Museum and Archive in Fallon sponsors free cave tours several times a month. Due to the fragile nature of the cave and the threat of vandalism, the cave is open only to guided tours. For information call (775) 423–3677.

The **Stillwater National Wildlife Refuge,** north of Fallon, has a rich history. In the mid-1980s record rain and snowfall swelled the Carson and Humboldt Rivers to record levels, flooding Stillwater Marsh. As a result, archaeologists discovered previously buried living and burial sites and bones dating back thousands of years. Stop at the U.S. Department of Interior Fish and Wildlife Service Office in Fallon for a copy of People of the Marsh, telling the story of these ancient people. During the fall waterfowl migration in October and November, more than 200,000 pintails, green-winged teal, shovelers, and other ducks arrive at the refuge. Whistling swans are frequent winter residents. More than 160 bird species can be seen at the refuge, as can many other types of wildlife. Stillwater, Nevada's largest bald eagle wintering site, has been named a Western Hemisphere Shorebird Reserve. Viewing of waterfowl and wading birds is exceptional at Stillwater, where birders can see birds of prey in fall and winter, tundra swans in early winter, pelicans from March to November, and shorebirds from spring to late summer. For more information visit www.nevadaaudubon.org or call (775) 423–5128. For information write Refuge Manager, Stillwater National Wildlife Refuge, 1000 Auction Road, P.O. Box 1236, Fallon 89407–1236, or call (775) 423–5128.

In **Fallon** (population 7,000) a must stop is the **Churchill County Museum and Archives,** located at 1050 South Main Street. Its 10,000 square feet house a fine collection of native artifacts, as well as historical Churchill County displays. Particularly interesting are the quilt display, the 1914–1930 amber glass collection, a variety of cameras from different periods, and telephone and telegraph equipment. Historical photographs show everything from a turn-of-the-century garage to a newspaper office to a sugar beet factory. Don't miss the display on one of Nevada's most respected photographers, Mary Walker Foster. The museum is open Monday through Saturday from 10:00 A.M. to 5:00 P.M. and Sunday from noon to 5:00 P.M. April through December; and Monday through Saturday from 10:00 A.M. to 4:00 P.M., Sunday from noon to 4:00 P.M., January through March. For information call (775) 423–3677.

Don't be alarmed by the fighter planes streaking across the sky at low altitudes. As of early 1996 Fallon became home to the U.S. Navy's Top Gun flight school. Naval Air Station Fallon is also home to the Naval Strike Warfare Center and is the only facility in the navy where an entire carrier air wing can train together. Therefore, it is not surprising that the spring Fallon Air Show features such top-notch crews as the navy's Blue Angels and the army's Golden Knights Parachute Team.

Other city festivals include the midsummer All Indian Stampede and Pioneer Days, Labor Day weekend's Hearts of Gold Cantaloupe Festival, and the Spring Wings Bird Festival in May. For information call the Chamber of Commerce at (775) 423–2544.

For a delightful lunch, stop in at the **Apple Tree,** at 40 East Center. Fresh hot and cold sandwiches, crisp salads, and homemade soups will restore your energy level, and the bright and cheery atmosphere will pick up any gloomy day. The walls are decorated with catchy quotes, such as "Looks can be deceiving . . . It's eating that's believing" or "Too much of a good thing can be wonderful—Mae West." Prices are inexpensive. Call (775) 423–4447.

Lunch with a Philippine twist is available at **Aniceta's Good Food,** at 70 South Main Street, inside the Fallon Nugget. Try the lumpia (small egg rolls) or pancit (thin noodle rice dish) for a welcome change from standard fare. Aniceta's serves breakfast and lunch only and is closed Monday. Call (775) 423–5440.

Fallon sits in the high desert at 3,965 feet above sea level. The city incorporated in 1908, six years after its founding. Its rich agricultural heritage stems from the Newlands Irrigation Project; the first land reclamation project in the country, this effort diverted water from the Carson and Truckee Rivers to reclaim the desert. Major crops include alfalfa, sugar beets, and cantaloupes. The irrigation project began in June 1903 under the authority of the Reclamation Act of 1902, signed by President Theodore Roosevelt. The first water from the Truckee River reached the Carson River in June 1905, when the Derby Diversion Dam was dedicated. The original scope of 400,000 acres of irrigated fields was never realized. The U.S. Reclamation Service (later called the Bureau of Reclamation) underestimated the acre-feet of water required to properly irrigate the sandy soils, and a shortage of water almost sank the project in its first years. The construction of the Lahontan Dam between 1911 and 1915 finally corrected the problem, delivering enough water to irrigate more than 75,000 acres of farmland.

The **Lahontan Recreation Area** around the 162-foot-high dam and 10,000-acre reservoir provides plenty of sporting and recreation activities for area residents and visitors. Lahontan features twenty-five picnic and camping sites, lots of beaches for swimming, and excellent fishing. Day-use permits run $3.00 per vehicle and $7.00 for overnight camping or those intending to launch a boat. To reach the Lahontan Recreation Area from Fallon, drive west 9 miles on Highway 50 and then turn south on main Highway 50 to Carson City. You'll find the ranger station and main entrance 8 miles from the Highway 50 cutoff. It is open year-round. For information call park headquarters at (775) 867–3500 or the Silver Springs Ranger Station at (775) 577–2226.

Buried under the water of the reservoir lies **Williams Station** (also called Honey Lake Smith's), the scene of a tragic event that triggered the Pyramid Lake Indian War. In 1860 one of the Williams brothers and some hired hands kidnapped two Paiute women. Tribe members trailed them to the station and burned it down, killing five of the men trapped inside. When word of the attack reached Virginia City, a volunteer army of 105 men was organized and trailed the Indians to Pyramid Lake. During the ensuing battle the volunteers suffered sixty-nine casualties, including the death of the group's leader, experienced Indian fighter Major William Ormsby. Calls for reinforcements went out to California, and a second battle resulted in substantial Indian casualties. As a result of the Pyramid Lake Indian War, the government constructed Fort Churchill. "Honey Lake" Smith rebuilt the station.

Lake Lahontan

*B*ecause Nevada sits squarely in the Great Basin desert region of the western United States, its boundaries seem artificial. Parts of this vast, empty land shoot straight past borders into Idaho, Wyoming, Utah, Oregon, and California. Dry and arid now but formerly an immense inland sea fed by Ice Age–induced rains, Nevada provided sanctuary to birds, animals, and the first humans. Paiute Indians called this inland sea **Lake Lahontan**. By the time wagon trains arrived, the Paiutes had retreated to camps at Pyramid Lake and Walker Lake, remnants of Lake Lahontan. Its dried-up alkaline surface snapped the strength of pioneers and livestock. Although rainfall was too scarce to support trees and woody plants, trading posts sprung up along the trail, then mining camps at rich ore deposits, then railroad depots and small towns. Remnants of this activity abound throughout the state—proud outdoor museums, slowly decaying into the ancient lakebed of Lahontan.

North of Fallon at the intersection of Interstate 80 and Highway 95 marks the beginning of the 40-mile desert, the most dreaded section of the California Trail. If possible, emigrants traveled the route at night to avoid the intense heat. As clearly pointed out in the diary of one 40-mile desert emigrant, Sarah Royce, traveling at night, although cooler, had its perils:

> Then the conviction, which had been gaining ground in my mind, took possession of the whole party. We had passed the forks of the road before daylight, that morning, and were now miles out on the desert without a mouthful of food for the cattle and only two or three quarts of water in a little cask.
>
> What could be done? Halt we must, for the oxen were nearly worn out and night was coming on. The animals must at least rest, if they could not be fed: and, that they might rest, they were chained securely to the wagon, for, hungry and thirsty as they were, they would, if loose, start off frantically in search of water and food, and soon drop down exhausted. . . .
>
> So there was nothing to be done but to turn back and try to find the meadows. Turn back! What a chill the words sent through one. Turn back, on a journey like that, in which every mile had been gained by most earnest labor, growing more and more intense, until, of late, it had seemed that the certainty of advance with every step, was all that made the next step possible.

Athough the Royces made it to California safely, the 40-mile desert was not so merciful at other times. The barren, waterless alkali wasteland claimed many an oxen team and its owners. According to an 1850 survey, more than 1,000 mules, 5,000 horses, nearly 4,000 cattle, and 953 graves marked the treacherous 40-mile stretch. An estimated $1 million in personal property was discarded along the route to lighten the load and save the animals. More than 3,000 wagons were abandoned in the desert, the heaviest use of which occurred from 1849 to 1869.

Lyon County

Silver Springs (population 420) and Stagecoach (population under 250), on main Highway 50 moving south toward Dayton, have been at the crossroads of the American West for more than a century. Explorer John C. Frémont camped near here in 1844. Later, prospectors on their way to California goldfields made their way through the area. They in turn were followed by emigrants along the California Trail or

Trivia

other trails that traversed the valley. Finally, with the Lincoln Highway and now Highway 50, motorized traffic continued the journey.

Stop at the **Desert Well Station Historic Marker,** opposite the fire station at Stagecoach. The station gained a bit of fame when mentioned in Mark Twain's *Roughing It.* Twain related a story of how he narrowly escaped death in the 1860s while caught in a desert snowstorm with two companions. They had been traveling in a circle for hours, following their own tracks. They finally settled down for the night. One of the companions attempted to start a fire with sagebrush, using sparks from his pistol; he succeeded only in scaring off the horses. At the pits of dispair, the men vowed reform, cast away their bottles of whiskey, and huddled together, awaiting death during the night. Morning found the eastern greenhorns camped not fifteen steps away from a stage station (reported to be the Desert Well Station). One of the wells was used exclusively by camels brought to the Nevada desert to haul salt to the mines on the Comstock.

The renaissance of Nevada's mining has been called the "Invisible Gold Era." Commercial gold is no longer found in nuggets or veins. Instead the exploration, assaying, extracting, and processing of precious metals relies heavily on technology. Nevada is the world's ninth-largest producer of gold and leads the nation in gold mining with over 64 percent of the nation's gold production.

Turning south off Highway 50 onto Break-a-Heart Road takes you down the alternate route used by early settlers on the California Trail. It also leads you to the site of the famous "mustang scene" from Clark Gable's last movie (with Marilyn Monroe as costar), *The Misfits.* Continue on Break-a-Heart Road until it dead-ends at Fort Churchill Road (Carson River Road). Head east to Fort Churchill. To take this route, make sure your car is sturdy. While the route is very scenic, it can be an endurance run for cars used to much smoother driving. An alternate route is to access the fort via a short, paved road from Highway 95A south of Silver Springs.

The U.S. Army constructed **Fort Churchill** in 1860 to protect against Indian attack in the wake of the Pyramid Lake Indian War. The fort guarded the Pony Express route and area settlers, and it served as the home post for hundreds of soldiers on excursions against the Indians. The military abandoned the garrison in 1869, and the remains of soldiers buried in the post cemetery were removed to Carson City in 1884. Over the years, the fort structures have served a variety of purposes. During the 1930s the National Park Service instituted some restoration plans that were carried out by the Civilian Conservation Corps. The Nevada Division of State Parks took over the site in 1957.

Start your tour at the visitor center. An excellent pamphlet on Fort Churchill and interpretive signs along the post pathway impart interesting knowledge about the fort and remaining structures. The 3-inch ordnance rifle (cannon) on display represents the first rifled cannon mass-produced for the U.S. Army. There are also a restored 130-year-old caisson (ammunition carrier) and a replica of a Pony Express Bible. Look over the fort schematic before embarking on the interpretive trail.

The fort was named after General Sylvester Churchill, then inspector general of the U.S. Army, who served the area well for more than a decade controlling Indian uprisings. Post strength averaged around 200 soldiers but held as many as 600 men at one time. It ranked as one of Nevada's first, largest, and most strategic military posts, also serving as a Union recruiting station. The buildings stood on a square, facing a central parade ground. The eerie, partly restored adobe buildings on stone foundations stand in stark testimony to the harsh life of soldiers in the Nevada West. Fort Churchill was declared a National Historic Landmark in 1964.

Time your visit toward the end of July and participate in the Fort Churchill Muster, a reenactment of the Civil War. A large tree-shaded area on the banks of the Carson River affords fine picnicking. Tables, cooking grills, and rest rooms are available. A twenty-site campground provides for overnight camping. Current fees are posted at the park. For information contact the Fort Churchill and Lahontan State Recreation Area, Nevada State Parks District 3, 16799 Lahontan Dam, Fallon 89406 (775–867–3500), or Park Supervisor, Fort Churchill State Historic Park, Silver Springs 89429 (775–577–2345).

Before finishing your tour of central Nevada at **Dayton,** take a brief detour to **Buckland's Station,** along the Carson River. Samuel S. Buckland settled here in 1859, began a ranching operation, and opened a station for the Overland Stage Company. He also constructed the first bridge across the Carson River downstream from Genoa. Buckland Station figured prominently in the Pyramid Lake Indian War, serving as the assembly point for the ill-fated volunteer units that rode off to defeat and death. In 1864 Buckland opened a store and sold goods to travelers along the California Trail. When the U.S. Army closed Fort Churchill, Buckland purchased the buildings at auction for $750 and used materials from the fort to build the large two-story hotel at present located at the Buckland's Station site. Sam and his family are buried in the cemetery at Fort Churchill. Buckland's Station is located on Highway 95A, a few miles south of Fort Churchill.

Fort Churchill

Retracing your steps to Fort Churchill, head due west, following the Carson River until you reach Highway 50. Turn left (south) and travel until you reach **Dayton Historic State Park,** off Highway 50 northeast of Dayton. Stroll along the nature trail, picnic, or set up camp for the evening. Within the park boundaries discover the remains of Rock Point Mill. It was constructed in 1861 and was one of the earliest large mills in Nevada to crush ore from the Comstock mines. Its forty water-powered stamps were arranged in eight batteries and could crush fifty tons of silver-bearing ore per day. An 1882 fire damaged the mill, but it was rebuilt in 1883. It continued operations until 1909, when another fire destroyed the mill.

The Nevada Mining Reduction and Power Company took over the original Rock Point Mill site in 1910, continuing ore crushing until the early 1920s, when the decline in Dayton area silver mining forced its closure. The mill was then dismantled, moved to Silver City, and rebuilt at the Donovan Mill site. Foundations, retaining walls, and the reservoir head gate remain at the Rock Point Mill site.

Tours of the mill are scheduled through the state park. For information write the Dayton State Historic Park, P.O. Box 1478, Dayton 89403, or call (775) 687–5678.

Washoe Indians frequently used the Dayton area as a base camp for fishing along the Carson River, for pine nut gathering, and as a winter village sheltered from the Sierra snows. When emigrants arrived on their way to California, the area took on the name Ponderers' Rest because wagon trains stopped here while the emigrants decided whether to continue westward or settle along the Carson River. One of the oldest Nevada communities, the town was originally called Chinatown, after the Chinese brought to the area in 1856 to build the Reese Ditch from the Carson River to the entrance of Gold Canyon. In 1861 the town took the name of Dayton, after early settler John Day. Day also surveyed the town, becoming Nevada's surveyor general in 1870.

Trivia

Famed for his music and knowledge of cowboy lore, Don Edwards appeared in Robert Redford's The Horse Whisperer. *He sings and plays guitar during the summer season at Eureka Opera House.*

Gold was found in Gold Canyon as early as 1849, but the 1859 silver Comstock Lode discovery transformed Dayton into a bustling mining and mill town with 2,500 people in its peak year of 1865. Unlike other Nevada mining towns, Dayton was the site of large-scale dredging operations by the Carson River Placer Mining and Dredge Company. The firm spent $2 million to erect a dredge in 1865, but the effort proved futile.

Be sure to stop in the historic district. The **Union Hotel,** built in the early 1870s, still stands, as do other historic buildings, making Dayton a charming place to visit. Next door is an original wall from the Pony Express Station. Visit the **Old Corner Bar** and listen to the jazz ensemble while you sip a sarsaparilla or plop down for a prime rib. Mosey on down to the 130-year-old **Odeon Hall & Saloon,** site of part of The Misfits filming, at 65 Pike Street, for American and European cuisine. Lunch and dinner is served weekdays, while only dinner is served weekends. For information call (775) 246–3993. Down the block you can enjoy ice cream at the **Grille.** Across the street is a unique junkyard with old fire trucks and military vehicles.

Among the firsts recorded at Dayton was the first dance at Hall's Station, on New Year's Eve in 1853. One hundred and fifty men attended, but only nine women. Every spring the Dayton Historical Preservation Society hosts an evening Cowboy Poetry and Western Art Show. For information write the Dayton Area Chamber of Commerce, 655 Highway 50 East, No. 4B, P.O. Box 408, Dayton 89403, or call (775) 246–7909.

Before your final departure, tour the **Dayton Cemetery,** at the top of the hill beyond the historic district. It dates back to 1851 and is one of Nevada's oldest cemeteries in continuous use.

PLACES TO STAY IN PONY EXPRESS TERRITORY

AUSTIN
The Pony Express House,
115 N.W. Main Street;
(775) 964–2306.

BAKER
Hidden Canyon Guest
Ranch, Cabins
teepees, campground,
2000 Big Wash
Canyon Road;
(775) 234–7267.

Silver Jack Motel,
1 Main Street;
(775) 234–7323.

ELY
Steptoe Valley Inn Bed
and Breakfast (open March
through December),
220 East 11th Street,
East Ely; (775) 289–8687
or (775) 435–1196.

Hotel Nevada &
Gambling Hall,
501 Aultman Street;
(775) 289–6665 or
(888) 406–3055.

Holiday Inn & Prospector
Casino of Ely,
1501 E. Aultman;
(775) 289–8900 or
(800) HOLIDAY.

Bristlecone Motel,
700 Avenue I;
(775) 289–8838 or
(800) 497–7404.

Elk Ridge Inn, 1550 High
Street; (775) 289–2512 or
(888) 866–8253.

Fireside Inn,
2 miles north of Ely, Highway 93;
(775) 289–3765.

EUREKA
Sundown Lodge,
60 N. Main Street;
(775) 237–5334.

Colonnade Hotel,
Clark and Monroe Streets;
(775) 237–9988.

Jackson House,
11 South Main Street;
(775) 237–5577.

Best Western Eureka Inn,
251 North Main Street;
(775) 237–5247.

FALLON
The 1906 House Bed
& Breakfast,
10 S. Carson Street;
(775) 428–1906.

Econo Lodge Downtown,
70 East Williams Avenue;
(775) 423–2194 or
(800) 55–ECONO.

FERNLEY
Rest Rancho Motel/
Wigwam Restaurant,
325 Main Street;
(775) 575–4452 or
(800) 682–6445.

Best Western–Fernley Inn,
1405 East Newlands Drive;
(775) 575–6776.

SILVER SPRINGS
Chestnut Inn,
1045 Truckee;
(775) 577–2162.

Piper's Motel-Casino,
1190 Highway 50 West;
(775) 577–2295.

PLACES TO EAT IN PONY EXPRESS TERRITORY

AUSTIN
Toiyabe Cafe
(International),
next to Episcopal Church;
(775) 964–2220.

International Cafe,
Highway 50;
(775) 964–9905.

BAKER
T & D's Restaurant
(American),
Highway 487;
(775) 234–7264

DAYTON
Odeon Hall & Saloon,
Mia's Swiss Restaurant
(Continental),
65 Pike Street;
(775) 246–3993.

ELY
Jailhouse Dining Hall
(American),
211 Fifth Street;
(775) 289–3033.

Economy Drug
(soda fountain),
696 Aultman Street;
(775) 289–4929.

Orient Express (Chinese),
562 Aultman Street;
(775) 289–3313.

Flower Basket (cafe),
445 East Eleventh Street;
(775) 289–2828.

La Fiesta (Mexican),
East McGill Highway, Highway 93 North;
(775) 289–4112.

EUREKA
Owl Club Steakhouse,
Highway 50;
(775) 237–5280.

DJ's
(hamburgers),
Highway 50;
(775) 237–5356.

Eureka Cafe (Chinese),
90 North Main Street;
(775) 237–7165.

FALLON
Apple Tree (American),
40 East Center;
(775) 423–4447.

Aniceta's Good Food
(Filipino),
70 South Main Street,
Fallon Nugget;
(775) 423–5440.

FERNLEY
Herrera's Tacos (Mexican),
20 North Center;
(775) 575–4433.

China Chef Restaurant
(Chinese),
45 West Main Street;
(775) 575–4939.

ALSO WORTH SEEING

McGill Drugstore,
12 miles north of Ely on
Highway 93. Call Dan Brad-
dock at (775) 235–7082.
Please call ahead. This is
one of the few places in
America you can order a
root beer float from a 1930s
vintage soda fountain. You
can sample other treats and
old-fashioned sodas and

explore a huge inventory of
Americana from the 1950s
and 1960s.

Jacobs Well Pony
Express and Overland
Stage Station.
Discovered in 1992, Jacobs
Well was an important link
on the Elko to White Pine
Stage Road, as well as the
Pony Express. To visit this
archaeology field school,
take Highway 50, 15 miles

southeast of Eureka, turn
north on the paved road at
the Strawberry Road sign,
State Route 892. The paved
road ends in 36 miles and
continues 5⁴/₁₀ miles to the
Pony Express Trail sign.
Jacobs Well Station is 1³/₁₀
miles east. Write to BLM for
a fact sheet and map:
Bureau of Land Manage-
ment, Ely District Office,
Ely 89301.

For More Information

Austin Chamber of Commerce
in the Courthouse Downtown, Box 212, Austin 89310
(775) 964–2200

Ely's Bristlecone Convention Center
150 Sixth Street, Box 958, Ely 89301
(775) 289–3720 or (800) 496–9350
www.elynevada.net

Eureka County Chamber of Commerce
Monroe and Bateman, Box 14, Eureka 89316
(775) 237–5484

Great Basin Chamber of Commerce
90 Main Street, Box 90, Baker 89311
(775) 234–7302

Fallon Convention & Tourism Authority
100 Campus Way, Fallon 89406
(775) 423–4556 or (800) 874–0903

Fernley Chamber of Commerce
485 Truck Inn Way, Box 1606, Fernley 89408
(775) 575–4459

White Pine Chamber of Commerce
636 Aultman, Ely 89301
(775) 289–8877

Pioneer Territory

Lincoln County

Enter Lincoln County on State Route 319, passing over Panaca Summit, at 6,718 feet in elevation. The road winds down into the Mormon farming community of **Panaca** (population 700), settled in 1864. During the 1870s coke ovens here produced charcoal for the smelters at Bullionville, now a ghost-town site. Panaca ranks as Nevada's second oldest town, second only to Genoa. Its name comes from a Southern Paiute word meaning "metal" or "wealth." The Panaca Spring, with a steady flow of water, makes the desert oasis of Meadow Valley possible.

From its dirt streets to its historic buildings, Panaca has changed little over the past 130-plus years. A short tour will give you a flavor of what

Lincoln County's Five State Parks

• *Cathedral Gorge State Park and Regional Visitor Center.* Trails abound in this long, narrow valley where erosion has carved dramatic patterns in the clay walls. Miller Point overlooks the canyon. Located 2 miles north of Panaca, west of Highway 93.

• *Beaver Dam State Park* is Nevada's most primitive park with piñon and juniper forest, deep canyons, a stream, and reservoir. Requires 28 miles on a graded gravel road.

• *Echo Canyon State Recreation Area* showcases eastern Nevada's abundant wildlife and native plants, and unique rock formations. Located 12 miles east of Pioche via State Routes 322 and 323.

• *Spring Valley State Park* at 65-acre Eagle Valley Reservoir offers water-oriented recreation, also hiking and touring the historic Ranch House Museum. Located 20 miles east of Pioche on State Route 322.

• *Kershaw-Ryan State Park* is situated at the northern end of Rainbow Canyon, an oasis to early settlers who planted grape vines, trees, and grassy lawns surrounding a spring-fed pond. Wild grape vines climb the sheer cliffs. The Kershaws homesteaded the canyon until the early 1900s when they sold it to James Ryan. Located 3 miles south of Caliente via Highway 93 and State Route 317.

Panaca Region Headquarters, P.O. Box 176, Panaca 89042; (775) 728–4467.

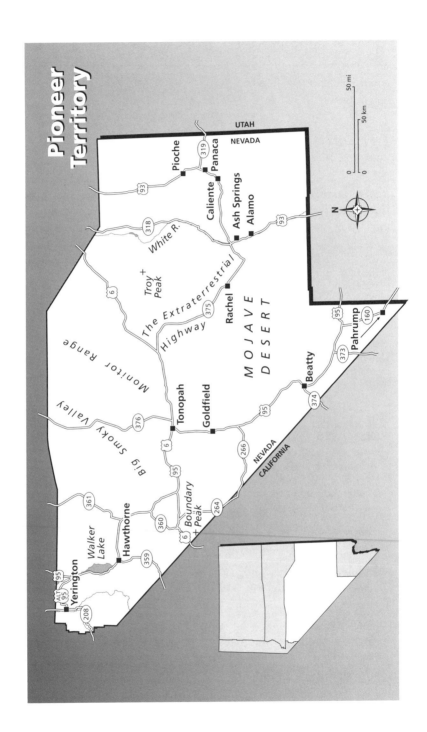

Pioneer Territory

Author's Top Picks

*Tonopah Historic
Mining Park,* Tonopah

Central Nevada Museum,
Tonopah

*Walker Lake Pine
Nut Festival,* Shurz

Extraterrestrial Highway,
Rachel

Rhyolite Ghost Town,
Beatty

Pahrump Valley Vineyards,
Pahrump

Mizpah Hotel, Tonopah

*Death Valley National
Monument/Scotty's Castle,*
near Beatty

Gold Well Museum, Beatty

it is like in this agricultural town on the edge of robust mining activity. The adobe *Panaca Mercantile Store* opened for business in 1868 with goods hauled in from Salt Lake City aboard wagons drawn by six-mule teams. The mercantile is located on the corner of Fourth and Main Streets.

The N. J. Wadsworth second home, composed of brick and natural stone and located at the corner of Fifth and Main Streets, features Victorian and Italianate styling. On Second and D Streets, the Henry Matthews property shows an evolution of shelters, from the dugout in the back to an adobe and lumber structure to a two-story brick/adobe Victorian home constructed in the late 1870s. Search out other unique structures and architecture on your own.

One mile west of Panaca, you bump into Highway 93. Take a right (north) and proceed another mile to the entrance of *Cathedral Gorge State Park,* on the left. Prepare yourself to view one of Nevada's real off-the-beaten-path treasures. Impressive outcroppings form picturesque spires that give the park its name and can keep you enthralled for hours. A brand-new visitor center will provide information on how the unusual formations evolved. As you drive through the park, notice the now abandoned 1930 Civilian Conservation Corps water tower.

Millions of years of erosion sculpted the churchlike formations and caverns. At various places you can walk between the crevices and venture through the labyrinth. While inside, peer up at the sky and see the jagged fingers reaching for the heavens. For a view from a different vantage, exit the main park entrance and head north about 1 mile to the *Miller Point Overlook.* The wife of a Bullionville mill superintendent in the 1890s, Mrs. W. S. Godbe, found the formations awe-inspiring and recommended calling the area Cathedral Gulch, which was later changed to Cathedral Gorge. It has been a state park since 1935.

The Panaca Formation is the remnant of a Pliocene-era lake bed. As the climate changed over the eons, the lake gradually dried up and erosion started its work on the sediments, creating the cathedral-like forms.

Picnic areas, showers, and campsites are available. The fee runs $3.00 per vehicle for day use and $9.00 for overnight stays. For information write Cathedral Gorge State Park, Box 176, Panaca 89042, or call (775) 728–4460 (use this number for Cove Lake and Ward Charcoal Ovens).

Head 9 miles north on Highway 93 to **Pioche** (population 830) and see one of the West's most ripsnorting towns ever. Guns were the only law, and Pioche made Bodie, Dodge, Tombstone, and other well-known towns pale by comparison. Pioche's rough-and-tough reputation put seventy-two men in Boot Hill by gunfire before anyone died of natural causes. When the early mine camp went for sixty days without a single murder, the newspaper congratulated its citizenry that Pioche was becoming a better place to live. One section of the cemetery was known as Murderer's Row. By 1875 more than 10,000 people flocked to Pioche and the area silver mines, and not a lawman in the bunch. The Territorial Enterprise in Virginia City reported in July 1873, "Pioche is overrun with as desperate a class of scoundrels as probably ever afflicted any mining town on this coast and the law is virtually a dead letter." The sheriff's office was reportedly worth $40,000 a year—in bribes. During 1871–1872, 60 percent of Nevada's killings took place in Pioche.

Trivia

*When **Pioche** was a frontier boomtown, mining companies employed professional fighters. Guns were the only law, and Pioche enjoyed more notoriety than Bodie, Tombstone, and other towns. It is claimed that seventy-two men were killed in gun fights and buried in Boot Hill before anyone died of natural causes. It's not surprising the word "gunfighter" entered the American usage with these words: "I'm Cemetery Sam, and I'm a gunfighter from Pioche."*

Real obituaries of people interned at the Pioche boot hill include Ad Rogers, who was shot and killed as he went out to examine some mining claims (May 1870); Richard H. Dodd, killed by William Dodds due to hard feelings between the parties (June 1870); Andrew Whitlock, killed by James Maxwell because Whitlock was to testify at a hearing over the title of a ranch (September 1870); Thomas Gorson, killed by Mike Casey because of a business settlement (March, 1871); and George M. Harris, shot and killed by D. A. Myendorff because Harris had slapped Myendorff across the face (August 1871). You get the picture. Enjoy your stay in Pioche but mind your manners.

Surveyed in 1869, Pioche maintains its authentic flavor with an abundance of historic buildings. The most notable, of course, is the famed ***Million Dollar Courthouse.*** The original estimate for the 1871 courthouse came in at $16,000 for the courthouse and jail combination. Design changes, construction cost overruns, and corruption pushed the tab up to $75,000 by the time the Classical Revival structure was completed in 1878. Closure of the principal silver mines caused Pioche to delay payments on the courthouse, and by 1890 the debt plus accumulated interest charges totaled

$450,000. The final payment was made in 1936, at an overall cost of $880,000.

Ironically, by 1935 the building started to come apart at the seams and the courthouse was all but abandoned when the final payment was made. Justice moved to a new Art Deco courthouse in 1938, after a mining rebirth. This time lead and zinc made government coffers flush with cash again. Since then the Million Dollar Courthouse has been restored, and it now houses a fine museum. Don't miss the opportunity to step into "The Tank," the jail with two-foot-thick rock walls, located at the rear of the courthouse on the second floor. The courthouse is located on La Cour Street. Hours are 10:00 A.M. to 1:00 P.M. and 2:00 to 4:00 P.M. daily, May through September. Admission is free. For information write Lincoln County Million Dollar Courthouse, P.O. Box 515, Pioche 89043, or call (775) 962-5182.

The **Lincoln County Historical Museum,** on Main Street, occupies the building constructed by A. S. Thompson around 1900. It has a fine display on area mining, local artifacts, and plenty of historic Pioche photographs. Admission is free. Hours are from 10:00 A.M. to 4:00 P.M. seven days a week. The mailing address is the same as that for the Million Dollar Courthouse, but the telephone number is (775) 962-5207.

Top Annual Events

Goldfield Days,
Goldfield, August;
(775) 485–6365.

El Capitan Fishing Derby,
Walker Lake, October to April; (775) 945–5896.

Walker Lake Pine Nut Festival,
Shurz, September;
(775) 945–5896.

Country Fair & Rodeo,
Hawthorne, September;
(775) 945–5896.

Jim Butler Days,
Memorial Day weekend, Tonopah; (775) 482–3558.

Jazz Festival,
Pahrump Valley Vineyards, June/July; (775) 727–5800.

Sand Drags and BBQ Celebration,
Amargosa Racing Association, October;
(775) 372–5658.

Labor Day Celebration,
Pioche, September;
(775) 962–5544.

Get a copy of the **Pioche Self-Guided Tour** pamphlet and map at one of the museums and put on your hiking boots. Our favorite spots included the newly restored Thompson Opera House, circa 1873, which has survived despite total wood construction; the 1909 Mission-style Pioche School; and the false-fronted Masonic St. John Lodge, in continuous operation since 1873.

No trip to Pioche would be complete without a drive up to the infamous Pioche **Boot Hill Cemetery,** situated at the end of Comstock Street. For a bit of graveyard humor, read the sayings on the wooden markers. Overhead the **Pioche Aerial Tramway** skims over part of the cemetery; it operated primarily by gravity, with buckets full of ore from the mine providing the momentum for the empty buckets to return to the mine for another load. Heading south out of town on Highway 93 provides other opportunities to stop and walk around abandoned mining structures such as headframes. Here it is important to remember that mine sites are dangerous places.

For a safer view of an ore train and mine entrance, stop at the park in Pioche as Main Street turns south onto Highway 93. Besides, it's a wonderful place for a picnic. With picnic tables and a gazebo, what more could you ask for?

To quench your thirst and fill your stomach, try the **Grubsteak Dinner House,** on Main Street. Food prices are moderate, and the decor will keep you busy until your food arrives.

Echo Canyon State Recreation Area lies less than a half-hour from Pioche. Take Route 322 (Mount Wilson National Backcountry Byway) east for 4 miles, then turn right (south) onto Route 86 and travel 8 miles southeast. Enjoy the scenery on the way while you contemplate catching some of the reservoir's rainbow trout or crappie for dinner. A boat ramp is available. Day-use fees are $3.00 per vehicle, while $7.00 will get you an overnight campsite. Hikers can explore the nearby canyons and hills. The recreation area is open from April through October. For information call (775) 962–5103.

Spring Valley State Park is open year-round and also offers hunting opportunities. To reach the state park, stay on Route 322 after leaving Pioche and travel approximately 20 miles to the park entrance. At the Eagle Valley Reservoir you can fish for rainbow and cutthroat trout. The park includes a 750-acre ranch where you can horseback ride and use the corral overnight; bring your own horse, and contact the park ranger to arrange corral use. Fees are $12.00 per vehicle in-season; $4.00 off-season. For information call (775) 962–5102.

Stop next at the railroad town of **Caliente** (population 1,111), the largest town in Lincoln County. To reach Caliente, proceed south from Pioche on Highway 93 for 25 miles. Across the tracks you will locate the highlight of Caliente, the 1923 **Caliente Railroad Depot.** The Mission-style building was once an Amtrak station and it is one of only two Mission-style buildings in Lincoln County; you saw the other one in Pioche. Enter the depot and learn about southern Nevada history from 1864 through 1914 depicted by the large mural painted on the wall. The depot is open year-round from 10:00 A.M. to 2:00 P.M. Monday through Friday. Admission is free. For information call (775) 726–3129.

The building has been adapted for reuse; the upstairs area includes the distance education classrooms for the Community College of Southern Nevada, a library off the waiting room, and the offices for the city of Caliente. Stop here for directions and brochures to state parks and campgrounds.

The railroad did not come easy to Caliente. A bitter battle and legal fight between E. H. Harriman's Union Pacific Railroad and William Clark's San Pedro, Los Angeles & Salt Lake Railroad waged over rights-of-way in the late 1890s culminated in a federal court order in favor of Harriman. Rail construction resumed in 1903 with Caliente as a division point; however, railroad engineers ignored the advice of a local Native American and laid the track through a flood plain. Ravaging floodwater washed out miles of the track in 1907 and again in 1910 before the railroad raised the roadbed.

Caliente originated in 1901 and took its name from the area hot springs. Also testimony to its railroad heritage is the row of company houses on Spring Street (Highway 93) north of the railroad tracks. The first eighteen houses were constructed in 1905. At one time the town's population topped 5,000. On Culverwell Street stop at the stone Methodist Church, built in 1905. It began its life as the Caliente School and exhibits the Classic Box style of architecture popular at the turn of the century.

Stop for a bite to eat at the **Brandin Iron** on Clover Street, on the same side of the tracks as the railroad depot. For less than $6.50 you can get breakfast for two, and the French toast is delicious. The restaurant is open from 6:00 A.M. to 8:00 P.M. Tuesday through Thursday and Sunday and from 6:00 A.M. to 9:00 P.M. Friday and Saturday; it is closed Monday.

Caliente Railroad Depot

Pay particular attention to the Brandin Iron front counter, whose decorative, colorful inlaid tiles of greens and yellows depict a pioneer scene and other designs. It was originally a soda fountain counter and came from Pioche. On Highway 93, you can grab a cup of coffee, some grub, and lively conversation at the *Knotty Pine* from 7:00 A.M. to 9:00 P.M.

Beaver Dam State Park, located nearly 40 miles from Caliente (drive north on Highway 93 for 6 miles, then turn right) on gravel and dirt roads, is well worth the trip. (Trailers and motor homes are not recommended). It is as far as you can go without leaving Nevada and entering Utah. Beaver Dam Reservoir provides some of the best rainbow-trout fishing in Nevada. Nonmotorized boating is allowed. Hiking trails through juniper and piñon forests bring peacefulness, while the 5,000-foot-high campgrounds deliver refreshing coolness at night. Thirty-five campsites are available. For information call (775) 728–4467.

Go south of Caliente on Route 317. The entrance to Kershaw-Ryan State Park is located 2 miles south of Caliente on the Rainbow Canyon Road. The park is situated in a colorful, narrow canyon at the northern end of Rainbow Canyon. Wild grapevines climb up the sheer rock cliffs, and Gambel oaks, cottonwoods, and elms provide shade. The Samuel Kershaw family homesteaded the canyon in the 1870s and sold it to James Ryan in the early 1900s. Ryan donated the "Kershaw Garden" as a public park in 1934. The park was closed for more than a decade following a flash flood. Facilities were rebuilt and now have hiking trails and shaded picnic areas. A campground is scheduled to open this year. Next, you will pass through *Rainbow Canyon,* with its tinted cliffs and unique geologic formations. A dirt road and a short walk will take you to Etna Caves for a closer look at the canyon and some petroglyphs. Ask in town for directions. You will travel through flood plains and alongside railroad trestles for an enjoyable drive. Go 15 miles farther south for a closer look at Grapevine Canyon and some petroglyphs at the end, of a 1-mile dirt road. Directions are listed on the Rainbow Canyon brochure which you can pick up at the Depot.

Caliente Hot Springs Motel has three private family pools. Five of the eighteen rooms offer in-room, natural mineral baths. If you stay in the motel, a hot mineral bath is included in the room fee. Pools are open daily year-round from 8:00 A.M. to 10:00 P.M. Call (775) 726–3777.

In the late 1890s *Delamar* outproduced every other Nevada gold mine. All materials arrived at Delamar via mule teams from a railhead 150 miles away at Milford, Utah. Most of the $15 million in gold bullion departed in the same manner. The main mine shaft descended 1,300 feet, and underground tunnels snaked for a combined length of 36 miles. The town's boom lasted from 1894 to 1909, with a brief revival in the 1930s. At one time up to 3,000 residents walked its streets and the town boasted a hospital, a newspaper, a school, a theater, churches, saloons, and a stockbroker. Current mining activities in the area limit access to the Delamar site, which is located on private property 16 miles west of Caliente on Highway 93 and then 15 miles south on a gravel/rock road not recommended for passenger cars.

In addition to being famous for its peak gold production, Delamar gained notoriety as "The Widow Maker." The dry milling processes used prior to the introduction of wet methods created a fine silica "death" dust, causing the premature death of many miners, mill workers, and town residents. Legend has it that at one time there were 500 widows in town. While other Nevada mines fought against the flooding of mines, Delamar had the opposite problem. Drilling for water proved unsuccessful, and water had to be transported by pipeline to the town and mill site from Meadow Valley Wash, 12 miles away. Three pumping stations were required to lift the water 2,000 feet in elevation to Delamar.

Joshua trees, yucca flowers, and shadowy ghosts on distant mountain ranges accompany the trip west on Highway 93. *Crystal Springs* enjoyed a brief moment in the sun when the discovery of silver in the Pahranagat Valley made the community the provisional county seat in 1865. It was determined, however, that too few legal voters existed in the county. Formal establishment of Lincoln County took place in 1866, and the county seat moved to Hiko in early 1867, sounding the death knell for Crystal Springs.

Talk about off the beaten path. *Rachel* (population 105 and counting) is the lone community along the entire stretch of Route 375 from Crystal Springs to the junction at Highway 6 near the Warm Springs site. All of fifty cars pass through Rachel on any given day. Despite this remote location, Rachel receives quite a bit of publicity and more than its share of visitors from faraway places. For those interested in other-worldly creatures, venture straight west for 25 miles on Route 375 to arrive at Rachel and another world.

Disregarding (or taking into account) its location due north of the Nevada Test Site and due east of the Nellis Air Force Bombing and Gunnery Range, Rachel plays host to a number of UFO sightings. In fact, not to take matters such as these lightly, the Nevada Department of Transportation in April 1996 officially dedicated Route 375 as the *Extraterrestrial Highway.* The new EXTRATERRESTRIAL HIGHWAY SIGN depicts several flying saucers. Nearby the speed limit sign warns you to reduce your approach to WARP 7. The event put Rachel on *Inside Edition* and in *Newsweek*.

One local hang-around known only as Ambassador Merlin II pointed out that Rachel will be a destination point for intergalactic tourists. "Now that it is official, they will be here in three years," he predicted. Other celebrities reported sighted at the dedication ceremony include Darth Vader and Elvis.

The dedication took place exactly thirty-four years after the most notable UFO sighting in Nevada history, making it kind of an anniversary event. That sighting consisted of a fireball visible across Nevada and in several neighboring states.

While in town, stop in at the **Little A'le'Inn** (pronounced *alien*). The tiny cafe and UFO seminar headquarters features racks of UFO T-shirts, caps, and books. You can't miss it—look for the building with a picture of an alien and an EARTHLINGS WELCOME sign on it. Owners Pat and Joe Travis will serve you up an Alien Burger or some other out-of-this-world fare. For more information call (775) 729–2515.

UFO sights abound. In the center of town is a large bronze plaque and time capsule placed by Twentieth Century-Fox Studios, maker of the film *Independence Day*. Rachel activist Glen Campbell's Area 51 Research Center (Area 51 is the secret base reputed to be nearby) tracks

Aliens Have Landed?

*T*he **Roswell Incident** of 1947 continues to provide wonderful entertainment for believers and skeptics alike, as any X-Files fan knows. The July 8 edition of the Daily Record in Roswell, NM, reported that a "flying disc" had crashed on a nearby ranch and that soldiers from the 509th Bomb Group, stationed at Roswell Army Air Force Base, had recovered the remains.

In 1994 Air Force investigation confirmed that the debris at the crash site wasn't an alien spaceship: It was debris from Project Mogul, a secret experimental listening device that used balloon-borne detectors to monitor Soviet nuclear tests. The Pentagon issued a 231-page report explaining what really happened at Roswell. The report argues that the humanoid corpses Roswell residents claimed to have seen were probably humanoid crash-test dummies that were used in high-altitude impact tests, dropped from airplanes to test parachutes. These dummies were bald, had no eyebrows, no hair, no ears, bluish skin, and were between 5 feet 3 inches and 5 feet 6 inches tall.

mysterious movements locally, but is always willing to warn visitors of strange goings-on around Rachel.

To fully partake of the ET Highway experience, call the Nevada Commission on Tourism at (800) 237–0774 to request an ET Highway travel package. It provide maps, information, and itineraries. When you complete your journey and furnish proper verification, you'll receive an ET Highway bumper sticker and a glow-in-the-dark license plate frame that says, "I was out there." Before you pull back onto the highway, be especially careful in case one of those fifty cars may be whizzing by in excess of WARP 7 speed.

Due to the government facilities (real and imagined), no direct route exists to get from Rachel to Pahrump (assuming no "Beam me up, Scotty" tactics). Therefore, you need to backtrack to Highway 93 and head south through the outskirts of Las Vegas to Route 160 (Blue Diamond Road) headed west. Before embarking on the long trip, stop off at Ash Springs, north on U.S. 93. Springs are abundant in the Pahranagat Valley. The waters at Ash Springs are very warm, indicating a lime formation underground. Stream channels have been built to carry this water to the numerous ranches in the valley below the springs. Finish

Tips for Area 51 Sleuths

*A*rea 51, Dreamland, Groom Lake, the Ranch, the Box—all these names refer to the top-secret research installation, located 100 miles north of Las Vegas, that has prompted speculations about captured alien spacecraft and hidden bodies of extraterrestrial beings. The facility and surrounding areas are also associated with UFO and conspiracy stories.

You cannot intrude into **Area 51** because you can't cross the 13 miles of open desert between public land and the Groom Lake base. The guards along the military border are used to tourists but don't annoy them. Drive past the Restricted Area signs and you'll be captured and fined about

$600. You can only see the Area 51 base from Tikaboo Peak, a ninety-minute drive from Vegas, followed by an hour drive on dirt roads and an hour hike up a mountain. You will need binoculars or a telescope to see anything of the base; hangars are 26 miles away.

David Darlington details the history, legends, and characters involved with Area 51 in his book Area 51: The Dreamland Chronicles.

Write for a copy of the Area 51 Viewer's Guide for tourist information, highway logs, Tikaboo Peak instructions, and maps.

off your stay in Pahranagat Valley with a picnic at the **Pahranagat National Wildlife Refuge,** a favorite stopping-off spot for ducks, geese, whistling swans, great blue herons, and bald eagles.

Nye County

Traveling into southern Nye County transports you to a California-like environment, one that lies less than 10 miles away as the crow flies. A climate with four distinct seasons, lush green valleys, and the sight of a Mediterranean-style winery send you checking the map to see if you made a wrong turn back down the road. Nevada's only winery, **Pahrump Valley Vineyards,** washes away the weariness of a long day on the road with a selection of fine wine, gourmet food, and quiet elegance.

For a delicious lunch try the mesquite chicken Caesar salad. For dinner select tournedos St. James (tender filets sautéed in olive oil, served in a lobster sherry cream sauce, and topped with mushroom caps and scampi), or lobster Wellington from the seafood side of the menu. Top it off with a fresh-baked torte or peach melba. Take owner Jack Sander's invitation to dress casually and dine lavishly. The restaurant is open from noon to 3:00 P.M. for lunch and from 5:00 to 9:00 P.M. for dinner. Meals, by Nevada standards, are moderate to expensive. Tie your evening in with a winery tour or wine-tasting event. For information or reservations call (775) 727–6900 or (800) 368–WINE.

Pahrump Valley Vineyards teams up with Helicop-Tours for a dining adventure that begins with gliding over nearby Red Rock Canyon and the ruggedly beautiful Spring Mountains in the comfort of an air-conditioned executive helicopter, then landing at the winery for an informative tour and masterful wine tasting before settling in for an elegant meal. The return trip gives you a bird's-eye view of Mount Charlestown and Calico Canyon rock formations. For information and rates write Helicop-Tours, 135 East Reno Avenue, Las Vegas 89119, or call (702) 736–0606.

Currently, the winery produces its selection from grapes brought in from California while it waits for its Nevada vines to produce high-quality commercial grapes. In the meantime, enjoy one of the award-winning vintages. In its first five years of production, Pahrump Valley Vineyards has garnered twenty-nine gold, silver, and bronze medals in domestic and international competitions. If you desire, the winery will personalize your label. You will easily spot the cobalt blue roofs of the winery at the base of the western slope of Mount Charleston; turn right onto Winery Road from Route 160.

The name **Pahrump** comes from the Paiute, who harvested pine nuts and seeds and hunted wild game in the area. The Paiutes discovered an abundance of water in the valley coming from natural springs; they named the valley Pah (water) Rump (rock). The Native Americans cultivated corn, melons, and wild grapes. Ever since, Pahrump Valley's fertile fields have fed emigrants, settlers, and miners. Irrigation in the 1930s turned cotton into a very profitable crop and the main cash crop into the 1980s.

The distance of Pahrump (population 15,000-plus) from Las Vegas and the mountain pass kept the town isolated well into the twentieth century. The first paved road arrived in 1954, but not until nearly a decade later, in 1963, did electricity make it over the hill from civilization. The road to the Nye County seat in Tonapah did not get paved until 1966.

For excitement try a few turns around the dance floor at **Peg Leg's Saloon & Dance Hall,** at 621 South Linda. Live entertainment on Friday and Saturday nights is followed by Sunday jam sessions. The bartenders are reportedly the friendliest around. For information call (775) 727–5032.

Set your toes tapping to the **Country Music Festival** (June) or the **Jazz Festival** (September). The **Biggest Little Rodeo** in Nevada (Professional Rodeo Cowboys Association rodeo) takes place during the **Pahrump Harvest Festival,** in October. For information and dates contact the

Nevada's Volcanic Past

*T*wo million years ago volcanic activity began in the desert region between Tonopah and Ely. Molten lava surfaced along a fault line in the earth's crust forming a 100-square-mile landscape of fantastic cinder cones, lava flows, and craters. **Lunar Crater,** the area's most outstanding phenomenon, is almost 4,000 feet across, 430 feet deep, and more than 400 acres in size. Because of its appearance—a bowl-shaped depression almost devoid of vegetation—it looks more like a meteor impact than a collapsed cinder cone. The Shoshone avoided the place, leaving it to the powerful spirits that resided there. First mapped by Lt. George M. Wheeler's surveying party in 1869, it was named to the National Natural Landmark Register in 1973. The turnoff to the Lunar Crater Volcanic Field is 77 miles east of Tonopah on Highway 6. Four miles south on the graded road is Easy Chair Crater and 7 miles farther is Lunar Crater. No services are available at this remote site, so fill your tank and check your spare tire in Tonopah. The road into the area is graded but quite narrow. Contact the Bureau of Land Management, Tonopah Resource Area, Box 911, Tonopah 89049; (775) 482–7800.

Pahrump Valley Chamber of Commerce, Highway 160, P.O. Box 42, Pahrump 89041 (775–727–5800 or 800–633–9378).

The *Pahrump Valley Speedway's* 1/4-mile dirt track attracts racers from across the country. After days or weeks on the road, let someone else do the driving. Sit back and watch the Street Stocks battle for position in the cool night air of Pahrump Valley. Volunteers built the track several years ago. It is located off Basin Avenue east of Highway 160, and the season runs from March to the fall. For information call (775) 727–7172.

About 16 miles northwest of Pahrump on Route 160, be on the alert for a small sign with the word JOHNNIE on it and an arrow pointing to the left. Like most other Nevada mining ghost towns, Johnnie sprang up overnight after the Montgomery brothers, using directions from Indian Johnnie, discovered a large quartz ledge. By 1893 the shallow veins had run dry. In 1898 Utah investors acquired the Johnnie and Congress Mines. A title dispute at the Congress Mine raged, and a gun battle of several hours' duration left one man dead and three wounded. Another dispute between lessees and mine owners killed two more men and ended up with the ten-stamp mill being torched and burned to the ground. Dynamiting of the mine office resulted in the safe, minus its door, landing 200 feet away.

Johnnie's post office opened in 1905, and by 1907 the town had 300 residents. The Johnnie Mine and sixteen-stamp mill operated steadily until 1914, after which production became more sporadic through the late 1930s. While prevailing wisdom believes that Butch Cassidy died in South America after he and his gang fled the country following the Winnemucca Bank robbery, people in these parts subscribe to the story that Butch lived for years in seclusion at Johnnie, dying of injuries resulting from a mining accident there around 1940.

Proceed on Route 160 until you reach Highway 95. Turn left (west) and drive 46 miles farther to Beatty (population 1,500), gateway to Death Valley National Monument. Founded in 1904, Beatty served as the rail transportation hub of the bustling historic Bullfrog Mining District. By 1907 Beatty supported three railroads, a bank, and more than 1,000 people. Ash deposits from some of the world's largest volcanic eruptions provide a colorful backdrop for the town. For information on area ghost towns and Death Valley National Park, stop at the Beatty Visitor Center on Route 374 (Death Valley Highway), or call (775) 553–2200.

The *Rhyolite Ghost Town* is an honest-to-goodness ghost town, with the remains of a number of historic town structures and only ghosts remaining from the past, the last living resident having departed in the 1950s. Fortunately, Rhyolite is easily accessible: From Beatty drive 4 miles west on Route 374 and turn right at the Rhyolite sign. There is active mining going on in the area, so be on the alert for large mining trucks crossing the roadway. First stop at the **Gold Well Museum,** on your left as you approach Rhyolite.

When open, the museum provides information on the history of Rhyolite and area mining activities. Even if the museum is not open, the outdoor artwork will capture your attention. *The Ghosts of the Last Supper,* by Belgian artist Albert Szukalski, creates an appropriately haunting scene. Other intriguing pieces of art include *Szukalski's Desert Flower,* crafted out of car bumpers; a ghost with a bicycle; and *Homage to Shorty Harris,* by another Belgian, Fred Bervoets, depicting a miner with a lonely and out-of-place penguin (you'll have to interpret that one yourself). Every summer since 1984 a new installation has gone up here, with the Mojave outback as the dramatic backdrop. Szukalski returns each summer to oversee the installation, often bringing another Belgian artist with him. For more information call (775) 553–2424 or write Gold Well Museum, P.O. Box 53, Beatty 89003. As you walk among the art, be prepared for chukars and rabbits to scurry out of the underbrush.

Rhyolite boomed after the 1904 discovery of gold by two penniless prospectors, Eddie Cross and Frank "Shorty" Harris. The resulting Bullfrog Mining District derived its name from the green-stained rock holding the veins of gold. Assays of $3,000 per ton drew more than 6,000 people to Rhyolite, and the town quickly established a newspaper, a post office, several hotels, two stock exchanges, ice plants, and forty-five saloons to serve its residents. Three railroads (Las Vegas & Tonopah Railroad, Tonapah & Tidewater Railroad, and Bullfrog Goldfield Railroad) hauled in supplies and shipped out gold-bearing ore.

Five-term Nevada senator William Stewert retired from politics and opened a law office in Rhyolite in 1905. The 1906 San Francisco earthquake, coupled with the 1907 financial panic, dried up the inflow of investment money into Rhyolite. By 1910 the city streetlights went out and the water company announced it would no longer service the town's remaining 600 residents. A decade later only a few diehards called Rhyolite home.

Ahead, on the right, *Tom Kelly's Bottle House* consists of in excess of 20,000 discarded bottles. There are even a miniature village constructed

The Ghosts of the Last Supper

of glass chips and a fence with bottle necks strung on wire. Built in 1906, the bottle house gives mute testimony to the quantity of beverages consumed in Rhyolite during its heyday. The house was reconstructed in the 1920s for the filming of Zane Grey's *Wanderers in the Wasteland.*

Informative U.S. Department of the Interior and Friends of Rhyolite markers at each building site contain photographs of the town and buildings when Rhyolite thrived. They bring the town alive again as you study the ruins. Among the downtown ruins, find the H. D. and L. D. Porter Store (1906); the three-story John S. Cook & Company Bank, built for the grand sum of $90,000; the Overbury Building and Bishop Jewelry Store; and the 1906 Corrill Building.

The **Rhyolite Depot,** up the hill at the end of town, features Mission-style architecture with terra-cotta trim. The Las Vegas & Tonapah Railroad Depot cost $160,000, and its railyard had a capacity of one hundred freight cars. Listen closely for sounds of accordion music drifting in the wind—it is reportedly the musical talent of one of the town's last residents, Tommy Thompson.

The Friends of Rhyolite organization raises funds to restore the town's ruins. In addition to selling T-shirts and booklets, the nonprofit organization hosts a Rhyolite Resurrection Festival in March each year. Historic vignettes, Rhyolite descendant reunions, and other activities fill the weekend. For information write Friends of Rhyolite, P.O. Box 85, Amargosa Valley 89020.

Ash Meadows, a wildlife refuge in Amargosa Valley, has the greatest concentration of endemic species, including the Devil's Hole Pupfish. This tiny, transparent fish lives only in Devil's Hole, a narrow, deep pool of spring water. Once a large alfalfa ranch, then a cattle ranch, and

PIONEER TERRITORY

now part of Death Valley National Park, this 24,000-acre refuge is accessible from U.S. Highway 95. Turn south onto State Route 373. For information call (775) 372–5435 or Death Valley National Park at (760) 786–2331.

Death Valley National Monument, a National Monument since the 1930s, achieved National Park status in 1997. Native Americans called it Tomesha (ground fire), while the forty-niners dubbed the sun-blistered terrain Death Valley. Though seemingly lifeless, the desert yields an amazing variety of life, from desert tortoises to lizards to cacti. Death Valley's unique geologic formations and other features give one plenty to ponder. It is famous for great, shifting sand dunes. Within its borders lies Badwater, the lowest spot in the United States, at 282 feet below sea level. The highest ground temperature sent the mercury boiling at 201 degrees Fahrenheit at Furnace Creek on July 15, 1972. The most unusual year in Death Valley occurred in 1913 when 4.54 inches of rain fell, the maximum temperature reached 134 degrees Fahrenheit, and the minimum temperature fell to 15 degrees Fahrenheit. In 1974 for 134 consecutive days the maximum temperature was posted at more than 100 degrees Fahrenheit, while in the summer of 1994 for 31 days it was recorded at more than 120 degrees Fahrenheit.

When storms roll across Death Valley, rains flood a wide, flat dried lakebed. The clay, hard as ceramic tile, melts into mud. After the rain, winds roar in from the southwest and barrel along the surface of the clay, sometimes up to speeds of 100 miles an hour—just the right conditions to skid rocks across the slick area known as the Racetrack.

*In 1948 James F. McAllister, a geologist at the United States Geological Survey, published the first scientific paper about the **sliding rocks of Death Valley.** Rocks weighing less than a pound up to more than 700 pounds leave deep tracks on the slick lakebed.*

One must-see attraction in Death Valley can be reached from Route 267 off Highway 95 about 36 miles northwest of Beatty. *Scotty's Castle* dates back to the turn of the century when flamboyant Death Valley Scotty built an elaborate Mediterranean-style hacienda with Spanish tiling and a 56-foot clock tower. National Park rangers dress as characters from 1939 and bring the castle's heyday back to life. Tours of Scotty's Castle interior take place daily from 9:00 A.M. to 5:00 P.M. Tickets are sold on the day of the tour on a first-come, first-served basis; the ticket booth opens at 8:30 A.M. Tours are limited to nineteen people at a time. For information write Castle Curator, Death Valley National Park, Death Valley, CA 92328, or call (760) 786–2392, ext. 26. Castle tours cost $8.00 per adult and $4.00 for children under age twelve; half-price discounts are offered for adults over age sixty-two and adults or children with disabilities. In addition, there is a Death Valley National Monument entrance fee of $5.00 per vehicle. Scotty's Castle is located approximately 25 miles from the junction of Route 267 and Highway 95, just across the Nevada-California border.

Esmeralda County

Crossing over into Esmeralda County leads you to another boom/bust mining town. Like Rhyolite, *Goldfield* contains many remaining historic buildings, giving one a feel for the town's fleeting prosperity. Harry Stimler and William Marsh staked their gold claims in December 1902, but the real influx of people did not begin until late 1903. The Tonopah & Goldfield Railroad reached the town in September 1905. By 1907 Goldfield sported a population of around 20,000, larger than that of either Reno or Las Vegas. From 1904 to 1918 the Goldfield Mining District was Nevada's most important gold-producing region, with $85 million mined during that time frame. The Goldfield Consolidated Mining Company constructed a huge, hundred-stamp mill northeast of town.

The mining town boasted an opulence not normally found in frontier towns, earning Goldfield distinction as "Queen of the Camps." The 1908 four-story, luxurious *Goldfield Hotel,* built at a cost of $450,000, still stands, patiently awaiting a revival in the town's fortune. It closed in

Visiting Nevada's Ghost Towns

Trading posts along the emigrant trail, gold and silver mining towns, and railroad towns all suffered a similar fate. In fact, so many settlements have been temporary that for every living town in Nevada there is a ghost town. Even the biggest, most flamboyant towns were abandoned when the rich ore gave out. Goldfield, Nevada's largest city in 1909 with a population of 20,000 and daily output of $10,000, is seeing a revival as a tourist attraction. While buildings in Goldfield are restored, Gold Point, 30 miles south, belongs to another category of ghost town: "arrested decay." Gold Point and

Belmont are watched over by "guardian angels," the last remaining residents who fend off souvenir hunters and greet visitors with a friendly "you can look all you want, but don't touch anything." Rhyolite, near Beatty, was abandoned in 1930 but a house made of bottles and the railroad depot have been restored. Delamar, too, was empty by the 1930s, and many of its buildings transported on wagons to Pioche. You can explore the ruins, mainly walls and foundations, but the dirt road, 25 miles southwest of Caliente and 15 miles south of Highway 93, requires a four-wheel-drive vehicle.

Trivia

The Santa Fe Saloon in Goldfield is one of the oldest (1905) and most famous structures in Nevada. It preserves the frontier character of the days when Jim Casey, Virgil Earp, Wyatt Earp, and Death Valley Scotty strolled its streets.

1936, then reopened in 1942 only to shut down again in 1945 after housing soldiers during World War II. An attempt to renovate the hotel in 1986 failed, leaving a nightmare for some investors and a partly restored dream for yet some future investors.

Boxing promoter Tex Rickard heavily advertised the town and arranged for the world lightweight championship bout between champion Joe Gans and challenger Oscar "Battlin" Nelson to be held in Goldfield on September 3, 1906. Gans won the bout on a technicality, due to a low blow by Nelson in the forty-second round. Tex Rickard's 1906 Victorian house stands at the corner of Crook and Franklin Streets.

Intense labor disputes in late 1907 forced Nevada governor Sparks to call in federal troops to restore order. This action broke the back of the fledgling International Workers of the World. Double disasters of the 1913 flood and the 1923 fire dealt the town crippling blows from which it never recovered. Adding insult to injury, a flash flood in 1932 and another fire in 1943 nearly finished the job. A few stalwart residents still keep Goldfield's flame burning.

The following other historic sights should be a part of your walking tour. The **Esmeralda County Court House** beckons. If the front door is locked, enter through the back door used by the sheriff's dispatcher. Be sure to look at the brand display on the ground floor of the courthouse; more than 145 brands trace back to the 1870s and are seared into pieces of leather. Upstairs in the courtroom, original Tiffany lamps grace the judge's bench.

Across the street and down the block stands the dilapidated high school, condemned in the 1940s. Search out the firehouse and the offices of the Consolidated Gold Mining Company on your own. Before leaving town, stop in for a sip at the **Sante Fe Saloon,** in business since 1905 and one of the oldest remaining saloons in the state. As you depart Goldfield, notice the collection of antique mining equipment on the left. For information on Goldfield write the Chamber of Commerce, 115 Columbia, P.O. Box 219, Goldfield 89013, or call (775) 485–3560.

Nye County

North of Goldfield on Highway 95, you venture through 20 miles of a wind-sculptured basin sprinkled with Joshua trees before climbing over Tonopah Summit, at 6,255 feet in elevation, and dropping down into *Tonopah* (population 2,500), on the edge of central Nye County. Scattered skeletal remains of mine headframes punctuate the hills around Tonopah, and dozens of historic structures and interesting ruins give visitors plenty to view during their stay.

Jim Butler kicked off Tonopah's boom with his May 1900 discovery of silver in "them thar hills." According to local lore, Butler picked up a stone to throw after his recalcitrant burro and discovered the rock to contain fine-grained quartz. An assay reflected 395 ounces of silver, plus $15^{1}/_{2}$ ounces of gold to the ton, sparking Nevada's first twentieth-century mining rush and great mining camp, with a population of 10,000 people.

Tonopah's peak production years occurred during 1910 and 1914 with an annual yield averaging $8.5 million. Unlike other boom towns, the majority of which disappeared almost overnight, Tonapah prospered for many years. After World War I its mines continued to produce until the Great Depression interrupted production. Today the rebirth of mining activity includes copper, gold, and molybdenum mines.

The *Central Nevada Museum,* at Logan Field Road, will keep you occupied for hours. Its yard is full of intriguing displays, such as antique mining equipment, a blacksmith's shop, a miner's cabin, a 1934 Mack fire truck, horse-drawn freight wagons, and a 1927 Universal Power Shovel. An old mining ledger serves as the sign-in sheet. Inside, displays and collections will teach you about central Nevada Native Americans,

Tee Time in the Desert

*E*ven though "green" might not be the first thing that comes to mind when you think about the desert, check out these desert golf opportunities. **Tip:** Local duffers bring pieces of indoor-outdoor carpeting for a clean hitting surface.

- **Burning Sands Golf Course,** Downtown Empire; (775) 557-2341. Course was built over the years by gypsum-mine employees. The course crosses some streets and features a 420-yard par five that has a 320-yard dogleg.

- **Lucifer's Anvil Golf Course,** Black Rock Desert north of Gerlach; (775) 574-0140. Site of the annual Self-Invitational Black Rock Desert Classic. Informal layout of more than 7,000 yards in the desert.

- **Sandy Bottom Golf Course,** Gabbs; (775) 285-2671. Laid out on a dry lake bed, Sandy Bottom is Nevada's oldest clay course. Built at the rodeo grounds, 3,010 yards, par thirty-five.

- **Pioche Golf Course, Pioche;** (775) 962-5544. This old mining town has a nine-hole course that was carved from the sagebrush and dirt in the flat below town.

Trivia

*Boxer **Jack Dempsey**
once worked as a bouncer
and bartender at the
Mizpah Hotel.*

Nevada boom towns, area railroads, and the region's Asian population. The museum is open April through September from 9:00 A.M. to 5:00 P.M. daily and October through March from 11:00 A.M. to 5:00 P.M. Monday through Saturday. For information write Central Nevada Museum, 1900 Logan Field Road, P.O. Box 326, Tonopah 89049, or call (775) 482–9676.

The newly opened **Tonopah Historic Mining Park** allows visitors to see original mining claims. Another favorite attraction is the Miner's Cemetery. For information write the Tonopah Chamber of Commerce, P.O. Box 869, Tonopah 89049, or call (775) 482–3859.

By far one of the most colorful buildings left from the boom times, the **Mizpah Hotel,** currently under restoration, has generated its share of history since construction in 1907. Five stories of turn-of-the-century elegance returns you to the glory days of yesterday.

The dining room, named after Jack Dempsey, refers to the young man who worked in the historic Mizpah Hotel before his rise to fame and glory. Dempsey also worked in the Tonopah mines and participated in the drilling and prizefighting contests popular in those days. The Manassa Mauler (originally from Manassa, Colorado) left the West to win the heavyweight championship on July 4, 1919, in three rounds over defending champion Jess Willard. He fought four championship bouts, each grossing more than $1 million. Dempsey earned more money than any previous boxer in history.

On September 23, 1926, Dempsey lost the crown to Gene Tunney. In a rematch bout a year later, Dempsey again lost but only after the controversial long count in the seventh round, when Dempsey knocked down Tunney but the referee refused to start the count until Dempsey went to a neutral corner. More than 145,000 people attended that match, which grossed a record $2.6 million in gate receipts.

Dempsey returned to Tonopah in the 1920s, breezing in to the Ace Club on Main Street to see the proprietor, an old friend. Upon leaving, Dempsey turned and punched the proprietor's son, sending the young boy reeling but not to the ground. "Now you can say you took a punch from Jack Dempsey and didn't go down," said Dempsey.

Dempsey may be long gone, but some of the others associated with the Mizpah Hotel's early days remain. Guests have reported strange goings-on, such as encountering a ghost dressed in a red gown or finding their own red shoes moved or missing. One of the housekeeping

Trivia

In 1989 **Bob Lazar** claimed on a Las Vegas television station that he had worked with alien spacecraft at Papoose Lake, south of Area 51. For the whole story, check out www.ufomind. com/people/1/lazar.

staff, a levelheaded woman as far as we could tell, periodically catches glimpses of people in old-fashioned clothes and hears doors mysteriously opening and closing. According to legend, a local prostitute was stabbed to death at the Mizpah Hotel by a jealous lover years ago.

Then there's the ghost of Senator Key Pittman, who died in the hotel of natural causes on Election Night, before the final votes were tallied. His political cronies put the senator on ice until after he was declared the winner, in order to save the victory for the party. After his election they announced that he died during the victory celebration.

Partake in Jim Butler Days with Nevada championship mining events; a rock, gem, and bottle show; historic mining park tours; stock-car races; and the children's tall-tales contest. It takes place near the end of May. For information write Jim Butler Days, Tonopah Convention Center, Box 408, Tonopah 89049, or the Chamber of Commerce, 301 Brougher Avenue, P.O. Box 869, Tonopah 89049, or call (775) 482–3859.

A brief sidetrip takes you to another fascinating Nevada ghost town. Travel 5 miles east on Highway 6, turn north on Route 376 for 13 more miles, and then take the right fork for 27 additional miles to reach **Belmont.** The town was the county seat from 1867 until 1905, when upstart Tonopah took over those honors; prior to that Ione served as the county seat. Declining ore quality and White Pine County finds around 1868 depleted Belmont's population, but rich discoveries at Belmont in 1883 brought another round of prosperity until 1887, when most mines were shut down. The post office departed in 1911. The mines lay dormant until the Monitor-Belmont Company built a flotation mill in 1914 to treat old mine dumps. Several years later all mining activity ceased.

All but a handful of Belmont's 2,000 residents have long since departed, but in their haste they left behind some well-preserved, picturesque historic ruins. Workers built the *1876 Nye County Courthouse* for $22,000, using bricks manufactured in nearby kilns and locally quarried stone for the foundation. Partial restoration implies that the fine structure should be in use today. The building became a historic state monument in 1974. The town cemetery is on the west end of town with a few weathered, hand-carved wooden markers remaining. If you're lucky, the Belmont Saloon will be open for a chat and a refreshment. Its bar originally came from the deserted Cosmopolitan Saloon, down the street.

In the true tradition of mining camps, the Belmont Catholic Church, built in 1874, uprooted itself in 1908 after being vacant for seven years and moved the distance to **Manhattan,** becoming the Manhattan Catholic Church. The Manhattan Mining District first came into being in 1867. A discovery of gold at the foot of "April Fool Hill" in 1905 reactivated the boom, with 4,000 people flooding into the region. The San Francisco earthquake of 1906 and the financial panic of 1907 dried up investment money and curtailed mining activities. In 1909 another boom started, with thirteen mine and sixteen placer operations producing ore. Dredging operations started in 1939 and continued for eight years.

Besides the Manhattan Catholic Church, old wooden headframes and dilapidated buildings remain. To reach Manhattan, take the gravel road west out of Belmont for 13 miles. Along the way you'll pass the large stack from the Belmont-Monitor Mill.

Retrace your steps to Tonopah, this time going west on Route 377 from Manhattan and then south on Route 376. Three miles west of Tonopah, turn right onto the gravel Gabbs Cutoff Road, headed northwest. Sixty-seven miles later you will intersect Highway 361 pavement, 6 miles south of Gabbs. Proceed through Gabbs and turn right (east) on Highway 844; travel 17 miles farther to the well-preserved mining site of **Berlin.**

Nevada state senator T. J. Bell first discovered silver here in 1895. At its peak Berlin supported a post office, a store, a stage line, and 250 people. The mine and thirty-stamp mill shut down in 1909; however, between 1911 and 1914 a fifty-ton cyanide plant worked the Berlin tailings. Demand for steel during World War II resulted in salvage of the mill equipment.

The impressive shell of the mills remains, as do a number of town buildings, such as the blacksmith shop, the mine foreman's house, a bachelor's quarters, a store warehouse, an assay office, a stagecoach stop, and a machine shop. As you enter Berlin, stop at the ranger shed—the mine supervisor's home, on the left—for a map of the mining site and ghost town. An extensive trail marker system provides the history and historic features of Berlin and the mining area. Tours are given from Memorial Day to Labor Day beginning at 10:00 A.M. on Saturday and Sunday; otherwise, you are on your own. The ghost town also operates as the entrance to the **Berlin-Ichthyosaur State Park.** There is a $3.00 entrance fee.

Two miles out of Berlin, past the large mill, you step back into prehistoric time. The **Ichthyosaur,** a giant fish lizard, archaeological dig has produced some of the largest known fossils of the prehistoric reptile. Scientists place the ichthyosaur in time more than 240 million years ago. For more than 135 million years, these 50-foot-long sea lizards dominated the inland sea, weighing up to forty tons.

The fossils were first discovered in 1928, with large-scale excavation beginning in 1954. The bones were covered by thousands of pounds of mud and petrified over millions of years. Later geologic activity fractured and uplifted the former shore area and eventually formed Nevada's mountains. Aeons of erosion carved out canyons and unearthed the fossils.

A large structure houses the fossil archaeological dig area. Tours are given daily from Memorial Day to Labor Day at 10:00 A.M., 2:00 P.M., and 4:00 P.M. The rest of the time, you'll have to peak through the windows on either end of the fossil shelter or study the large cast of the ichthyosaur located to the right of the main entrance to the fossil shelter. Other tour schedules are available during the off-season. For information on Berlin, the ichthyosaur dig, and tours, write Berlin-Ichthyosaur State Park, Route 1, Box 32, Austin 89310, or call (775) 964–2440; alternatively, call the State Park District III Headquarters at (775) 867–3001.

Seven miles north of Berlin, you come upon *Ione,* which grew out of an 1863 silver discovery. An 1865 population of 600 people dwindled rapidly as the silver veins proved less productive than originally thought. Ione lost the county seat to Belmont in 1867. Periodic revivals and busts occurred up to 1880. The post office closed in 1882. In 1907 Ione revived with the discovery of mercury and regained a bit of respectability with the reopening of its post office in 1912, only to lose it again in 1914. Then in the 1920s quicksilver mining brought yet another period of prosperity before a final slowdown.

As you drive into Ione, you see a sign proclaiming a population of forty-three; however, when you talk to the barmaid in the *Ione Ore House Saloon,* she confesses that forty-three is the town's goal—its real population is eight. The saloon operates as the local watering hole plus a general store, where you can pick up a few groceries, and as the town gas station. It is the original one-stop shop. After I changed my flat tire in front of the saloon in one-hundred-degree heat, we were extremely grateful for their ice cream freezer.

Inside there's a long bar and gunnysack-covered walls, giving the bar flavor. Enjoy a game of pool and crack open a can of sardines or smoked oysters while you sip a cool one. What more could you ask for after a busy day of touring ghost towns and gazing at fossils millions of years old?

Mineral County

Retrace your tracks to Gabbs and then head southwest 32 miles on Route 361 to Highway 95, where you'll turn right and head due west to Hawthorne (population 4,162), the gateway to Walker Lake and ample recreational opportunities. **Boundary Peak,** at an elevation of 13,140 feet and the highest in Nevada, lies on a distant horizon as you head south on Route 361.

Hawthorne's roots are tied to the Carson & Colorado Railroad, when railroad president H. M. Yerington chose the spot as the division and distribution point for the railroad. The first train arrived on April 14, 1881. Two years later Hawthorne became the Esmeralda County seat but later lost it to Goldfield after the Southern Pacific Railroad purchased the Carson & Colorado and realigned the tracks, bypassing Hawthorne. Area mining booms returned prosperity to Hawthorne, and in 1911 Mineral County was carved out of Esmeralda County, with Hawthorne regaining county seat honors. Appropriately named Mineral County has provided the nation with borax, copper, gold, iron, limestone, mercury, silver, and uranium over the years.

A 1926 catastrophic munitions explosion in the East convinced the government to move its munitions operations to Hawthorne, a move that has provided a relatively stable economic base for the town. The population increased to 680 people after establishment of the Hawthorne Naval Ammunition Plant (now the Hawthorne Army Ammunition Plant) in 1927. It reached a peak population of 14,000 during World War II. As you drive past the outskirts of Hawthorne, observe the row after row of government munitions facilities, concrete bunkers, and ammunition magazines.

To learn more about Mineral County and Hawthorne history, visit the **Mineral County Museum,** at Tenth and D Streets in Hawthorne. Special collections include fire, mining, and railroad equipment; rocks and minerals; horse-drawn vehicles; and vintage clothing. Be sure to view the early 1880s mission bells and period pharmacy. The museum is open during the summer Tuesday through Saturday from 11:00 A.M. to 5:00 P.M. Off-season hours are Tuesday through Saturday from noon to 4:00 P.M. Saturday and Sunday tours can be made by appointment. Call the Mineral County Museum at (775) 945–5142.

Mineral County is also home to the nation's first formally recognized wild burro range, consisting of 68,000 acres. Look out for wild burros as you journey across the county.

Walker Lake

For a day of relaxation, stop at **Walker Lake State Recreation Area,** 11 miles northwest of Hawthorne on Highway 95. Jedediah Smith passed through here in 1827, followed by Peter Skene Ogden in 1829 and John C. Frémont in 1845 with his guide, Joseph Walker, for whom the lake is named. You can imagine the surprise when explorers first sighted this grand ancient lake with its clear blue waters in the middle of the desert. Mount Grant towers 11,245 feet over Walker Lake's 36,000 acres. Watch for bighorn sheep on the sharp cliffs around the Sportsman's Beach area. There are numerous picnicking and camping facilities at both Sportsman's Beach and Tamarack Point Beach.

The lake is an angler's paradise, with year-round fishing and more than 360,000 native cutthroat trout to provide you with hours of pleasure and test your angling skills. Other activities include boating, canoeing, hang-gliding, hiking, jet-skiing, parasailing, sailboarding, and wildlife viewing. Year-round festivals, such as the annual Fishing Derby in February and Walker Lake's Paiute Tribe Pinenut Festival & Rodeo in September, make Walker Lake a great destination. For information on Walker Lake events, write the Mineral County Chamber of Commerce, P.O. Box 1635, Hawthorne 89415, or call (775) 945–5896.

Walker Lake also serves as headquarters for the Walker River Paiute Indian Tribe and the 300,000-acre Walker River Indian Reservation. Be respectful of tribal hunting and fishing regulations. North of Walker Lake take the opportunity to see Native American crafts at the Schurz service area, where Highway 95 and alternate Highway 95 split.

Lyon County

Take the left fork of Highway 95 and travel 24 miles to **Yerington,** in the lush Mason Valley. The agricultural town started out with the unflattering name of Pizen Switch, taken from the poor quality of liquor served in a small willow thatch hut saloon. Reportedly, as fresh liquor supplies ran low, the proprietor added a few plugs of chewing tobacco and water to the mix. Local cowboys and ranchers considered the switched mixture poison, and the Pizen Switch moniker stuck.

The town changed its name to Greenfield in 1879 and to Yerington in 1894. Some accounts contend that the name was changed to Yerington to influence Henry M. Yerington to extend his Carson & Colorado Railroad into the valley near Yerrington. The strategy did not work; however, Yerington has kept its new name to this day.

John Frémont's expedition made its way through Mason Valley in January 1844. In the snow-clogged terrain on the western edge of the Sweetwater Mountains, he abandoned the expedition's French-made howitzer, which had made the journey all the way from St. Louis, Missouri, to Oregon and into Nevada. Over the years, some claim to have found the missing howitzer, while others contend it is still out there, awaiting discovery.

The *Lyon County Museum,* at 215 South Main Street in Yerington, displays several historical buildings including a 1910 Baptist church, a blacksmith shop, and a late-1800s schoolhouse on the property. An old country store brings back memories of simpler times and features a working crank telephone. You are welcome to try it. The museum is open during the summer from 1:00 to 4:00 P.M. Thursday through Sunday; winter hours are November through March from 1:00 to 4:00 P.M. on Saturday and Sunday. Tours during the week are by appointment only. For information call (775) 463–6576.

Next door, the Information Center also has some interesting displays and data on the area. A sweeping mural on the outside wall next to the parking lot illustrates pioneers with their visions of the valley. Especially informative is the display on Wovoka, an area Native American spiritual leader who interpreted visions that told him the Indians should fight no more and live in peace with the whites. Ironically, misinterpretations of his visions led to the 1890s Ghost Dance Religion Movement that tragically culminated in the Wounded Knee Massacre. Wovoka (also known as Jack Wilson) preached peace until his death in September 1932.

Yerington's *Grammar School No. 9* represents a cherished piece of history and a look to the future. The pressed-brick school opened in 1912. Reno architects McDonald and Beatty employed the Italian Renaissance Revival style. Frederic DeLongchamps designed the 1935 edition. The building's grammar school days ended in 1980. A fund-raising program began in 1988 to turn the historic school into the Yerington Cultural Center, with a 250-seat theater, meeting rooms, and studio space. It is a perfect example of creative reuse of public buildings. For information on the Yerington Culture Center, contact the

Yerington Grammar School No. 9 Restoration Group, Inc., 22 Highway 208, Yerington 89447, or the Mason Valley Chamber of Commerce, 237 South Main Street, Yerington 89447 (775–463–2245).

The Spirit of Wovoka Days Powwow, held in late August, features Native American dancers in their colorful regalia. For information call (775) 463–2245.

Moving on from Mason Valley, take Route 208 south of Yerington to reach the **Smith Valley Bed & Breakfast** in the quaint farming community of Smith Valley, nestled in the foothills of the Sierra Nevada. Dr. Mary Fulstone's 1879 home also contained her office. She practiced medicine longer than any other doctor in Nevada, delivering more than 6,000 babies during her sixty-year medical career. Dr. Mary's in-house office has been preserved as a museum for you to enjoy.

Still in the Fulstone family, the home now operates as a B & B run by Amy and Georgia Fulstone. The two-story house has been part of the Fulstone family's working cattle and sheep ranch since 1903. The recently renovated home provides a choice of king, queen, and twin bed accommodations, starting at $65 per night. To relax, sink into the chintz-covered couches around the living room fireplace and 1860s piano. At breakfast you can look out at the rustic barns and the backdrop of the Sierra Nevada from your dining room vantage point.

Easy access to the surrounding Sierras provides endless biking, hiking, skiing, and wildlife viewing treks. Kennels and stabling are also available on the premises. The B & B is located right on Route 208 between Smith and Wellington. Reservations only; for information and reservations write Smith Valley Bed & Breakfast, Box 21, Smith 89430, or call (775) 465–2222.

Try the **C&G Bar** in Wellington or the historical **Heyday Inn** for a traditional Basque meal. The Heyday was built around 1875 by Zadok Pierce as Pierce Station. Stagecoach travelers arrived from the Virginia & Truckee train station in Minden. The next day either the stagecoach or a spring wagon would take the passengers and mail the rest of the journey. Specialty entrees include beef Wellington, orange roughy, shrimp scampi, and New York steak and lobster. Prices are moderate to expensive. The Heyday Inn is open for dinner Monday through Saturday from 6:00 to 9:00 P.M. and Sunday from 5:30 to 8:30 P.M. It also opens early for breakfast. The pancakes are hubcap-size, so order the short stack unless you have a tremendous appetite.

When I inquired at the post office about Wellington, the lady there said,

"I just arrived here from California; please don't tell anyone else about this wonderful place."

The barn red building on the left as you proceed through Wellington is the *1867 Wellington Mercantile Company.* Climb up the broad board porch and enter another era. Inside you will find all sorts of tools on the wall, homemade pies, deli sandwiches, and pleasant conversation. The mercantile was built by John and Mary Hoye, Irish emigrants who settled in Smith Valley and formed a solid trade business. Later they built what is now called the Hoye Mansion, which served as an inn for travelers.

Longtime transplants from California are the proprietors of the *Hoye Mansion Bed & Breakfast Inn* next door, Frank and Judy McBryde. Judy says that "Wellington isn't a town—it's a happening." Frank and Judy have beautifully and lovingly restored the Hoye Mansion back to its original purpose as an inn. Five theme rooms bring forth Frank's background as a film projectionist and their love of Western heritage. The Southwestern Room gives you a striking view up Hoye Canyon and features southwestern colors. The Mark Twain Room includes a selection of Twain reading materials and a big portrait of the writer. The John Wayne Suite is adorned with photos and posters of Wayne, plus a video room in which to enjoy old John Wayne flicks. Rose, blue, and white lace accents the large antique-furnished Tara Room. Our favorite, the Jean Harlow Room, combines white wicker furniture with a blue bedspread. Several photos of the star highlight the room, as does a stunning charcoal portrait. To complete the scene, a blue feather boa drapes across a wicker screen.

Wake up to your juice and coffee on the back second-story enclosed porch. For a more substantial breakfast, Judy provides a complimentary slip for use at the Heyday Inn a few blocks down the road. The front of the inn is flanked by Reach-for-Heaven trees and a wooden bench that goes round and round a massive mulberry bush.

Jeep tours are available to surrounding mines and ghost towns, or you may want to hike up Hoye Canyon a spell, or just sit in the parlor and listen to Frank's fascinating stories about the movie business in the good old days. He grew up in Culver City, California, where many of the studios were located.

Rates run from $70 to $85 per night and include breakfast at the Heyday Inn. For information or reservations write the Hoye Mansion Bed & Breakfast Inn, 2827 Highway 208, P.O. Box 85, Wellington 89444, or call (775) 465–2959.

PLACES TO STAY IN PIONEER TERRITORY

BEATTY
Burro Inn Hotel & Casino;
(775) 553–2445 or
(800) 843–2078.

Stagecoach Hotel & Casino;
(775) 553–2419 or
(800) 4–BIG–WIN.

CALIENTE
Caliente Hot Springs Motel;
(775) 726–3777.

GABBS
Gabbs Motel,
100 S. Main Street;
(775) 285–4019.

GOLDFIELD
Santa Fe Saloon & Motel,
9000 N. Fifth Avenue;
(775) 485–3431.

HAWTHORNE
Best Western–Desert Lodge,
1402 East Fifth Street;
(775) 945–2660 or
(800) 528–1234.

Cliff House Lakeside Resort,
331 Cliff House Road,
Walker Lake 89415;
(775) 945–5253.

Covered Wagon Motel,
1322 Fifth Street
and Highway 95;
(775) 945–2253.

Monarch Motel,
1291 Fifth Street;
(775) 945–3117.

Sand 'n' Sage Lodge,
1301 East Fifth Street;
(775) 945–3352.

El Capitan Resort Casino,
540 F Street;
(775) 945–3321.

PAHRUMP
Pahrump Station–Days
Inn, State Route 160
Loop Road; (775) 727–5100
or (800) 329–7466.

PIOCHE
Motel Pioche,
100 La Cour Street;
(775) 962–5551.

TONOPAH
Jim Butler Motel,
P.O. Box 1352;
(775) 482–3577.

For More Information

Amargosa Chamber of Commerce
HCR 69-2 Box 401W, Amargosa 89020
(775) 372–5459

Beatty Chamber of Commerce
Box 956, Beatty 89003
(775) 553–2424

Caliente Chamber of Commerce
Depot Building Box 553, Caliente 89008
(775) 726–3129

Goldfield Chamber of Commerce
Box 2225, Goldfield 89013
(775) 485–9957

Mineral County Chamber of Commerce
932 East Street, Box 1635, Hawthorne 89415
(775) 945–5896

Pioche Chamber of Commerce
Box 127, Pioche 89043
(775) 962–5544

Pahrump Valley Chamber of Commerce
P.O. Box 42, Pahrump 89041
(775) 727–5800 or (800) 633–9378

Tonopah Chamber of Commerce
301 Brougher Avenue, Tonopah 89049
(775) 482–3859

Greater Smoky Valley Chamber of Commerce
P.O. Box 2020, Round Mountain, 89045-2020
(775) 377–2490

Station House
Hotel/Casino,
1100 Erie-Main Street;
(775) 482–9777.

RACHEL
Little A'Le' Inn,
Route 375;
(775) 729–2515.

SMITH
Smith Valley Bed
& Breakfast,
2400 Highway 208;
(775) 465–2222.

YERLINGTON
Arbor House B&B,
39 North Center Street;
(775) 463–2991.

WELLINGTON
Hoye Mansion Bed &
Breakfast Inn,
2827 Highway 208;
(775) 465–2959.

PLACES TO EAT IN PIONEER TERRITORY

BEATTY
Exchange Club Casino
(American);
(775) 561–2333.

CALIENTE
Brandin Iron (casual),
Clover Street;
(775) 726–3129.

HAWTHORNE
McDonald's,
1055 F Street;
(775) 945–1200.

Pizza Factory,
Highway 95 by Safeway;
(775) 945–9866.

Happy Buddah (Chinese),
570 East Street;
(775) 945–2727.

Dos Amigos (Mexican),
825 East Street;
(775) 945–9019.

PAHRUMP
Break Time (casual),
930 South Pahrump
Valley Boulevard;
(775) 727–1622.

TONOPAH
Station House/Mary's
Kitchen (American),
1100 Erie Main Street;
(775) 482–9777.

WALKER LAKE
Cliff House (American),
Cliff House Road;
(775) 945–5253.

YERINGTON
China Chef Restaurant
(Chinese),
415 North Main Street;
(775) 463–7112.

WELLINGTON
Heyday Inn (Basque),
Highway 208;
(775) 465–2424.

ALSO WORTH SEEING

*Walker River runs from
the Sierra Nevada to
Walker Lake. It supports
threatened fish and hun-
dreds of thousands of
breeding and migrating
water birds, including
1,400 common loons. In
spring and fall at Walker
Lake you also see western
grebe, eared grebe, red-
heads, ruddy ducks, and
American white pelicans.
Birdwatching information
is available from three
sources: Great Basin Bird
Observatory, 440 Hill Street,
Suite D, Reno 89501,
(775) 348–2644; Lahontan
Audubon Society, P.O. Box
2304, Reno 89505,
(775) 324–BIRD; and
Sierra Club, Toiyabe Chapter, P.O. Box 8096, Reno
89507, (775) 323–3162.*

Reno-Tahoe Territory

Douglas County

Leaving Wellington, you take Route 208 westward, following the churning Walker River as it twists and turns through the rugged gorge. Stop for a picnic or overnight stay at one of the riverside campgrounds. When you are ready to continue, turn right at Holbrook Junction onto Route 395 headed northwest to Gardnerville, Minden, and Carson Valley. The pine-covered rolling hills give way to flat lush farmland. Just as in emigrant days, Carson Valley offers a respite for weary travelers plus a time to stock up on good food. More recent are the variety of activities that draw people to the area for recreation.

Home in the Hills

*In the juniper-covered hills north of Reno is the **Animal Ark**, a nature center and wildlife sanctuary that houses cougars, black bears, wolves, bobcats, kit foxes, peregrine falcons, burrowing owls, and other native species. The animals are spaced along the hillsides amid the sagebrush and juniper, in enclosures built around existing terrain and vegetation. I climbed a trail that led to a peregrine falcon named Whoopi. Diana Hiibel, who opened the Ark to the public in 1994, brought Whoopi from her enclosure to show me the falcon up close. I wandered around and read about each resident on plaques. Three wolves, Annie, Raven, and*

Nischa, are stars of the Ark's Wolf Howl Nights, when they holler and howl. The focus at Animal Ark is on non-releasable wildlife like Whoopi, but Hiibel says her group occasionally takes in orphaned animals and later places them back in the wild. A young black bear found near Topaz Lake recuperated from a broken hip at Animal Ark. When they took him out and opened his cage, the bear bounded across a meadow. The sanctuary is 10 miles north of Reno on Highway 395. Exit at Red Rock, then drive 12 miles. Open from 10:00 A.M. to 4:30 P.M. Tuesday through Sunday and closed on Monday; (775) 969–3111.

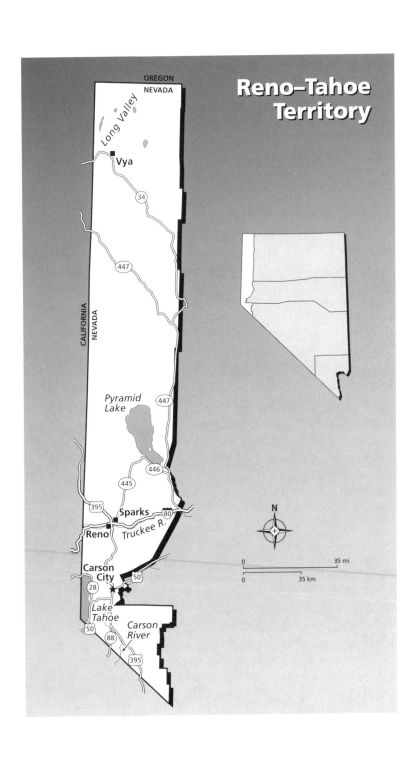

RENO-TAHOE TERRITORY

AUTHOR'S TOP PICKS

Lake Tahoe's 72-mile shoreline

Nevada Historical Society, Reno

Nevada State Museum, Carson City

Shakespeare Festival, Sand Harbor

Horse Drawn Carriage Rides, Virginia City

Here's just a smattering of exciting activities that will keep your days in Carson Valley filled. *High Country Soaring,* at the Douglas County Airport, boasts the most complete and finest soaring facility in the United States. See beautiful Carson Valley, the Sierras, and Lake Tahoe from a new perspective. For information call 782–4944. Likewise, *Aero Vision Balloons, Inc.,* in Gardnerville, delivers hours of panoramic vistas beyond your wildest imagination. For information call (775) 265–5177 or (800) 468–2476.

The more sedate or less adventurous may prefer some learning experiences. A self-guided walking tour through the *Lahontan National Fish Hatchery,* on the outskirts of Gardnerville, will teach you the fish-hatching business from the arrival of eggs at the hatchery to incubation to fry (young fish up to 1 inch long) to fingerling (young fish between 1 inch in length and one year of age) to release in Nevada lakes. The hatchery began operations in 1967. Daily visiting hours are from 7:30 A.M. to 3:00 P.M. Recreational fishing information and educational material on fish culture is available at the hatchery. For information contact the Lahontan National Fish Hatchery, 710 Highway 395, Gardnerville 89410; (775) 265–2425.

Laurie and Shannon Hickey, operators of *Heritage Tours* and fifth- and fourth-generation Carson Valley natives, live on one of the valley's oldest ranches (in the family since 1863). This is one way to sit back, relax, and have the history of the area delivered to you at a leisurely pace. Tours operate year-round and can be arranged to meet your schedule. You will see Pony Express trails, "Snowshoe" Thompson's homesite, the emigrant trail, historic Genoa, and other sights—the tour can be tailored to fit your desires. Four-hour tours run $35 and you ride in the comfort of a minivan that seats seven people. For information write Heritage Tours, 1456 Foothill Road, Gardnerville 89410, or call (775) 782–2893 or (800) 949–4286, PIN 2893.

You'll encounter the work of Frederic Delongchamps once again, this time in the design of the 1916 former Douglas County High School, whose red brick is accented by classic white columns leading to the front entrance. The building is on the National Register of Historic Places. Today the *Carson Valley Museum and Cultural Center* occupies most of the building, which it shares with the visitor center of the Carson Valley Chamber of Commerce.

Among the interesting collections are early day newspaper and telephone displays, medical tools from when doctors still made house calls, agricultural history items, Native American basketry, and an art gallery of local artists. Don't miss the Animal Room, with exhibits from all over the world. History marches by when you study the timeline display. The museum is located at 1477 Highway 395, Gardnerville 89410. For information call (775) 782–2555.

After a fun-filled day, prepare yourself for some royal treatment at the **Nenzel Mansion,** built in 1910 and now splendidly restored. As you enter the large front porch into the foyer, you will look upon the gracefully arched moldings of the entranceway to the parlor. The matching arched doors open in welcome.

Your hosts, Chris and Virginia Nenzel, will greet you with an afternoon glass of wine, accompanied by cheese and crackers. Other niceties include bowls of chocolate and other candies spread around the house and an evening decanter of Bailey's Irish Cream in your room. From early morning, coffee is available, and a hearty country meal with fresh breads sets the scene for great conversations. Breakfast is served in the formal dining room with original chandelier.

Four theme rooms each have their own charm. Learn tales of a countess owning the home during the 1930s. Some of her remodeling remains in the dramatic raspberry tiled bath of the Honeymoon Suite. If you choose the Wicker Room or the Brass Room, look forward to a great soak in the large claw-foot tub. For you nostalgia buffs the Antique Room awaits. Take time to relax on one or more of the porches. A large parlor with a magnificent marble fireplace provides a splendid place for guests to congregate and talk or play some games. An antique player piano with more than seventy rolls of music will keep you entertained all night.

Room rates range from $90 to $110 per evening. Discounts are given for midweek stays, winter stays, and stays of three or more nights. For information or reservations write the Nenzel Mansion, 1431 Ezell Street, Gardnerville 89410, or call (775) 782–7644.

Basque sheepherders came to Carson Valley in the 1890s. The **J. T. Basque Bar and Dining Room,** at 1426 Highway 395, brings you Basque family-style dining, a Gardnerville tradition for more than thirty-six years. Featured entrees include top sirloin steak, lamb shoulder steak, roasted rabbit, and shrimp Basquaise. The restaurant is open for both lunch and dinner Monday through Saturday. Prices are moderate to expensive. For information call (775) 782–2074.

RENO-TAHOE TERRITORY

A few miles north of Gardnerville on Route 395, turn left on Genoa Lane and travel the 2 miles into history. This is where it all began. Nevada's first white settlement, **Genoa,** grew out of a post established by Mormon traders in 1851, a full ten years before Nevada Territory existed and thirteen years before President Abraham Lincoln declared Nevada the Union's thirty-sixth state. The original **Mormon Station** burned in 1910, but a reconstructed trading post still holds a prominent position in historic Genoa. In addition to historical photos and displays such as the telegraph, the Mormon Station State Park facilities include shaded picnic areas and outdoor grills. The park is open daily May through mid-October from 9:00 A.M. to 4:30 P.M. Admission is free. For information call (775) 782–2590 or (775) 687–4379.

Directly across the street, the **Genoa Courthouse Museum** contains displays on the Pony Express, "Snowshoe" Thompson, first-day canceled envelopes, a courtroom, and a beautiful Apache wedding shawl. Pay particular attention to the snowshoes for horses in the Buckaroo Room. Legendary "Snowshoe" Thompson (John A. Tostensen) earned his reputation carrying mail and supplies across the Sierra Nevada from Placerville, California, to Genoa for more than twenty years. Born in the Telemark district of Norway, he became the human link between the eastern and western slopes of the Sierra Nevadas. He died in 1876 and rests in the Genoa Cemetery north of town.

The 1865 Douglas County Courthouse operated until 1916, when the county seat moved to Minden. The building was sold at auction for $150 and served as an elementary school for forty years. The museum is open daily from 10:00 A.M. to 4:30 P.M. May through the beginning of October. Admission is free. For information call (775) 782–4325.

Be sure to pick up a copy of the **Walking Tour of Genoa** pamphlet at the museum. It contains a detailed location map and a description of each historic site. The tour is a pleasant way to spend an afternoon.

Top Annual Events

Candy Dance, Genoa, September; (775) 782–8696.

Thunder on the Mountain Civil War Encampment, Virginia City, August; (775) 847–0311.

Mountain Oyster Fry, Virginia City, March; (775) 847–0311.

Pow Wow & Arts and Crafts Festival, Stewart Indian Museum, Carson City, June; (775) 882–1808.

Nevada Day Parade & Celebration, Carson City, October 31; (775) 882–1565.

Silver & Snowflake Festival of Lights, Carson City, December; (775) 882–1565.

Artown, Reno, July; www.RenoIsArtown.com.

Great Reno Balloon Race, Reno, September; (775) 686–3030.

Camel Races, Virginia City, September; (775) 847–0311.

Kit Carson Rendezvous, Carson City, June; (775) 687–7410.

Step across Nixon Street and down Main Street to the south to bend your elbow at the **Oldest Bar in Nevada.** The Genoa Saloon traces its lineage back to the 1850s. Across Main Street the **Pink House Restaurant** has been sending customers away happy for decades. Colonel John Reese, the wagonmaster who led the Mormons to the valley, built the historic Gothic Victorian Pink House in 1853. It was painted pink in 1870 by merchant J. R. Johnson. Named after this beautiful home, the Pink House Restaurant serves dinner from 5:00 to 9:00 P.M. Sunday through Thursday and from 5:00 to 10:00 P.M. Friday and Saturday. Medallions of beef, steak teriyaki, and rack of lamb are a few of the delicious choices. Prices are moderate to expensive. For reservations call (775) 782–3939.

When it's time to settle in for the evening, you have several options. The **Wild Rose Inn,** at 2332 Main Street, provides all the modern comforts of a new Queen Anne Victorian home decorated in antique oak furniture.

Take a Cruise

- **M S Dixie II.** *Lake Tahoe's largest cruise boat was launched in May 1994. It offers champagne brunch cruises and Emerald Bay dinner cruises. It is 151 feet long, has three enclosed decks, can carry 550 passengers, and serve dinner for 200. P.O. Box 1667 Zephyr Cove; (775) 588–3508. Adults $23–$49.*

- **Sierra Cloud.** *This 55-foot long and 30-foot wide catamaran seats up to forty-nine passengers. Operating out of the Hyatt Regency, it departs three times a day and offers nightly champagne cruises during the summer, weather permitting. Hyatt Regency Activities Desk, Incline Village; (775) 832–1234.*

- **Tahoe Gal.** *This 70-foot sidewheel boat offers two-hour cruises along the West Shore and three-hour cruises to Emerald Bay for 150 passengers. Continental breakfast and an optional lunch are served depending on the cruise and time of year. P.O. Box 7913, Tahoe City, CA; (530) 583–0141 or (800) 218–2464.*

- **Tahoe Queen.** *An authentic Mississippi paddlewheeler, 144 feet long and capable of carrying 500 passengers. Features Emerald Bay cruises and evening dinner-dance cruises. Also provides a morning winter cruise for skiers from South Lake. Hornblower Lake Tahoe, 900 Ski Run Boulevard, South Lake Tahoe, CA; (530) 541–3364 or (800) ON–THE–BAY.*

- **Woodwind II.** *In the afternoon the skipper unfurls the sails and lets the winds push it across Lake Tahoe. Passengers can peer into the lake's clear waters through two underwater observation windows aboard this 55-foot catamaran. Book in advance. P.O. Box 1375, Zephyr Cove; (888) 867–6394 or (775) 588–3000.*

Many of the antique pieces are for sale, so if one catches your eye, put in your bid. Hosts Sandi and Joe Antonucci start off your stay with complimentary afternoon wine and send you on your way in the morning, your stomach warmed by a scrumptious breakfast—Sandi's creations will bring you back for more. A fireplace sitting area is a great place to catch up on the news or just relax with a magazine.

Overnight rates from $100 to $140 (depending on the season and day of the week) the Gables third-floor suite has a wet bar, fridge, and private dining area; the extra day and twin bed make the suite ideal for a family stay. Your other choices range from the elegant Cameo Rose, romantic Cottage Corners, and nostalgic hand-stenciled Stage Stop to the Garden Gate. The Wild Rose Inn is the perfect romantic getaway. For information write the Wild Rose Inn, P.O. Box 256, Genoa 89411, or call (775) 782–5697.

Ask about the Wild Rose Inn's graveyard. Resting amid the trees lies Elzy H. Knott, who was shot and killed in 1859 during an argument over a bridle. He came from one of the first families to settle in Carson Valley.

Over on Nixon Street the *Genoa House Inn,* operated by Linda and Bob Sanfilippo, beckons you to stay a spell. The Victorian home has been restored and placed on the National Register of Historic Places. Newspaper publisher A. C. Pratt built the house in 1872. Ask about the intriguing stories of former owners. A stone walkway leads you to the lilac-framed front entrance. A wraparound porch gives you plenty of seating options for a relaxed afternoon or enjoyment of the evening coolness. We opted for the wicker swing.

Enter the front parlor, where you'll enjoy a glass of wine and a nibble of cheese. The library offers plenty of reading material on Genoa and the historic area. Choose among the Rose Room, the Blue Room, and the Garden Room, each with its own charm. Our favorite is the Rose Room, adorned with Gothic stained-glass windows from New Zealand, letting in the morning light. What a glorious way to awaken. The artistically handmade barn-wood bed will give you a great night's sleep. The Blue Room's private bath comes with a Jacuzzi tub. A gentle path leads to the private entrance to the Garden Room, with grand old tub. All rooms are decorated with Victorian antiques.

Partake of your full breakfast either in the formal dining room downstairs or in the comfort of your room. During our stay Linda was kind enough to share her recipe for her delicious beehive banana bran muffins. Room rates range from $120 to $150 per night. For information or reservations write the Genoa House Inn, P.O. Box 141, Genoa 89411, or call (775) 782–7075.

Dr. Eliza Cook (1856–1947), Nevada's first woman doctor, practiced in Carson Valley. She wrote a letter stating eleven reasons why she supported women's suffrage. Reason 4: "Because being a woman, I can see things from a woman's viewpoint. Hence, no man, however willing he might be to suppress his own view on my behalf, could represent me fully at the ballot box or anywhere else."

Nevada women began voting in 1915 before the national referendum.

If you can time your visit to coincide with the **Candy Dance** in the fall, you won't be disappointed. The gala event originated in 1919 as a way to raise funds for Genoa streetlights. Townspeople made candy and hosted a dinner dance. Carrying on the tradition, a buffet dinner precedes a dance in the Town Hall from 8:00 P.M. to midnight. More than 3,000 pounds of candies and cookies are gobbled up by willing Candy Dance participants each year. Treats range from dipped chocolates and divinity to mints and turtles. For information on the annual festival, ask your hosts.

Brigham Young recalled the Mormons in 1857, but not before probate judge Orson Hyde placed a curse on Genoa. For a time the town declined, but the discovery of silver in the Comstock Lode revived Genoa as an important commercial center for the bustling mining district. Genoa did, however, lose its pioneer newspaper, the *Territorial Enterprise,* to Virginia City, where it became famous throughout the nation.

Both the Wild Rose Inn and the Genoa House Inn include a complimentary visit to **Walley's Hot Springs Resort** as a courtesy to their guests. Make time to experience the healing waters. David and Harriet Walley invested $100,000 in 1862 to develop a lavish hot springs resort, with eleven baths, exquisite gardens, and a grand ballroom. It sold for $5,000 in 1896 and operated as a hotel until 1935, when it burned down. Over the years, Walley's hosted such dignitaries as President Grant, Mark Twain, and Clark Gable.

The resort was rebuilt in the late 1980s. Soothe your body in the hot mineral baths while you soothe your mind by gazing at the Sierra Nevada under a starlit sky or over Carson Valley. The six mineral pools range in temperature from 96 to 104 degrees Fahrenheit. Or take advantage of the swimming pool, steam and dry sauna, or fitness room. Massage is available for an extra fee and by appointment only. Walley's is open seven days a week from 7:00 A.M. to 10:00 P.M. Daily visits for those without a complimentary pass run $20. Children must be at least twelve years of age. Walley's is located at 2001 Foothill Road, just 1½ miles south of Genoa. Take Main Street out of town to the south. Historic cabins are also available at rates ranging from $90 to $350 per night. For information write

Walley's Hot Springs Resort, P.O. Box 158, Genoa 89411, or call (775) 782–8155 or (800) 628–7831.

Carson City

Take Genoa Lane back to Highway 395 north to Nevada's capital, **Carson City.** The **State Capitol,** at the corner of Carson and Musser Streets, represents the appropriate place to begin your tour. Of course, oil portraits of Nevada governors over the ages grace the capitol walls. More interesting is the mural commemorating precious minerals, Nevada's 125th Birthday Quilt, and a violin gift to Billy Lynch, President Lincoln's body servant.

The "Story of Our Capitol" exhibit provides a history of the building, and photographs show early construction and expansions. The capitol was completed on May 1, 1871, with free building stone from the state prison quarry. The capitol annex dates to 1906, and the extension of two wings took place in 1914.

Stop by another historic Carson City building, **Nevada State Museum (Carson City Mint),** for a delightful and informative tour. The building was constructed in 1870 and minted coins with the famous "CC" mint mark from 1870 to 1893. Before you enter the building, take a look at the Lincoln Highway Marker on Carson Street, to the left as you face the entrance. The museum includes a number of excellent exhibits, including the history of the Carson City Mint, an underground mine, and Native American culture and lifestyle. Be sure to see the famous Washo basket display of Dat-So-La-Lee, the last of the great Washoe basket weavers; she died in 1925 and her pieces, which cost the state of Nevada $75 each are now each worth $25,000. The museum also has the USS *Nevada*'s silver service, America's largest exhibited imperial mammoth (found in the Black Rock Desert, north of Gerlach, Nevada), and North America's oldest known mummy (Spirit Cave Man).

> ## More Reno-Tahoe Territory Trivia
>
> 1. What item of clothing was invented by a Reno tailor?
>
> 2. Who is Reno named after?
>
> 3. Who is Carson City named after?
>
> 1. Blue Jeans. 2. Civil War hero Jesse Lee Reno. 3. Explorer Kit Carson.

The museum is located at 600 North Carson Street. Admission is $3.00 for adults, $2.50 for seniors, and free for children under eighteen. Hours are from 8:30 A.M. to 4:30 P.M. daily. For information call (775) 687–4810.

Up the block at 813 North Carson Street, children can delight in the *Children's Museum,* located in the old civic auditorium. Nearly thirty hands-on exhibits challenge minds and impart knowledge. Kids can walk on the "Walking Piano" keyboard and make music, use a computer mouse to travel from continent to continent, or study a replica of an Egyptian tomb discovered by Napoleon. The Children's Museum is open from 10:30 A.M. to 4:30 P.M. Tuesday through Saturday. Admission runs $5.00 per adult and $3.00 per child. For information call (775) 884–2226.

Climb aboard a steam train at the *Nevada State Railroad Museum* and ride a bit of history. The railroad museum maintains some sixty pieces of railroad rolling stock, including six steam engines and a number of restored passenger coaches and freight cars. Much of the rail equipment came from the famous Virginia & Truckee Railroad. Weekend train operations depart from Memorial Day through Labor Day, with limited schedules in September and October. Admission to the museum is $2.00; train fares run $2.50 for adults and $1.00 for children age six to eleven. Museum hours are from 8:00 A.M. to 4:30 P.M. Wednesday

Physical Pleasures: Hot Springs and Spas

- *Carson Hot Springs Resort.* This private hot springs spa offers private indoor baths, an outdoor pool and patio, and an adjoining restaurant and bar. 1500 Hot Springs Road, Carson City; (775) 885–8844 or (888) 917–3711.

- *Cho-Cho.* Offering "European thalassotherapy," which involves body polishing and scrubbing, a seaweed bath, a massage, and a thermal wrap. Appointments are required. At Caesar's Tahoe, Stateline; (775) 586–3515 or (800) 367–4554.

- *Euro Spa.* Cal-Neva Lodge's in-house spa, featuring massage therapy, body and skin treatments, scalp massage, manicures, pedicures, a fitness facility, Jacuzzi, steam-sauna, and relaxation lounge. Robes, slippers, towels, and hair dryers are provided. Once owned by singer Frank Sinatra, this historic casino is on the state line of California and Nevada, on the North Shore of Lake Tahoe. P.O. Box 368, Cal Neva Resort, 2 Stateline Road, Crystal Bay; (775) 832–4000 or (800) CAL-NEVA.

- *Massage Therapy Cottage.* This facility features Swedish, Shiatsu, reflexology, sports massage, stress relief, Reiki, lymphatic drainage, aromatherapy, and creative visualization. 1169 Ski Run Boulevard #4, South Lake Tahoe, CA; (530) 541–4269.

- *Walley's 1862 Hot Springs Resort.* This outdoor hot springs was originally built more than a century ago. The resort has several outdoor pools at varying temperatures. 2001 Foothill Road, Genoa; (775) 782–8155 or (800) 628–7831.

through Sunday. The Nevada State Railroad Museum is located at 2180 South Carson Street. For schedule information call (775) 687–6953.

Stop in for a drink at the restored **St. Charles Hotel,** built in 1862 and the oldest remaining commercial building in Carson City. It was the place to stay, with important politicians and mining executives filling the guest ledger. The St. Charles Hotel is located at 304 South Carson Street. Call (775) 882–1887 for more information.

Carson City sports a number of prestatehood structures, including the Roberts House (1859), the oldest home in town, and the Nye House (1860). To find these and other historic sites, pick up a copy of the **Historic Carson City Walking Tour** and **Carson City: The Blue Line Trail** guides, available at the Carson City Chamber of Commerce, located at 1900 South Carson Street, Suite 100, Carson City 89701 (775–882–1565).

Trivia
The **Carson Street Beautification Project** resulted in historic lampposts, iron railings, and trees lining Carson Street from Fifth to Caroline Streets.

Carson City restaurants provide a wide variety of dining experiences. Lunch at the **Wild Scallion,** at 318 North Carson Street, includes not only such favorite standbys as Caesar salad and French dip but innovative dishes such as Two Time Loser Chili and Thai Chicken Satay. Prices are moderate. For information or reservations call (775) 883– 8826. **Adele's,** at 1112 North Carson Street, features seafood and is located in one of the few remaining Second Empire–style buildings in Carson City. Notice the mansard roof. The house was built in 1875 and owned by M. A. Murphy, a Nevada attorney general and Nevada Supreme Court justice. Specialties include lobster Jeremiah and veal and prawns Marsala. Prices are moderate to expensive. For reservations call (775) 882–3353.

We suggest **Silvana's** for the ultimate Carson City dining experience. Silvana's specialty is her ability to make heaven-sent sauces, such as her whiskey pear sauce, accompanying veal scaloppine Silvana, and her rosemary sauce, served with medallions of lamb. Silvana's is open from 5:00 to 10:00 P.M. Tuesday through Saturday. It is located at 1301 North Carson Street. For reservations call (775) 883–5100.

Carson City's premier annual celebration, **Kit Carson Rendezvous** in June, kicks off the summer season. A two-day wagon train trip, an Indian village, gunfighter competitions, and the Mountain Man Encampment provide plenty for the whole family to do and see.

Nevada State Railroad Museum

Storey County

The rush to the Comstock Lode started as a trickle in 1859 and turned into a flood of prospectors in 1860. Despite the vastness of the Comstock Lode mineral deposit, separating the wealth from the earth was not easy. Milling methods prevalent in other parts of the world did not work on the Comstock. Two of the most productive early Comstock mines, the Ophir and the Gould & Curry, spent more than $1.4 million combined on mills that were later abandoned. By 1863 mill construction costs mounted to $5 million per mill.

Likewise, frequent cave-ins required elaborate timbering systems designed specifically for the Comstock. It is estimated that more lumber was underground in Comstock mine shafts and tunnels than was in all the buildings in Nevada at the time. Both timber and scarce water were transported from the Lake Tahoe area to Virginia City via flumes. V-flumes sent logs flying down to the valley floor. Mule teams hauled them to the mines until the Virginia & Truckee Railroad took over that chore. Gravity flumes carried water 25 miles from Marlette Lake to Virginia City at a cost exceeding $2 million.

Despite all the expense to mine the Comstock, it was well worth while. An estimated $1 billion in silver and gold helped build San Francisco and structures in other cities. Virginia City riches built the elaborate

Sutro Baths, Fairmont Hotel, and Flood Home (later the Pacific Union Club) in San Francisco; Lucky Baldwin's Tallac House at Lake Tahoe; and Harbor Hill on Long Island. The price of Comstock mining-company stock fluctuated wildly. For example, in 1860 Ophir stock sold for $60 per share and in 1863 rose to $2,500 per share, only to drop to $800 per share. Fortunes were made and lost overnight.

Elaborate saloons, ornate gambling establishments, and houses of prostitution, all looking to separate the miners from their fortunes, replaced the tent cities of the Comstock by the middle of the 1860s. Comstock Lode miners, working in 170-degree-Fahrenheit heat below the surface, earned the highest wages paid anywhere in the world—$4.00 per day—and more than twice the prevailing wage earned by other miners. The area prospered for more than twenty years before the boom ended. At its peak Virginia City boasted more than 30,000 residents. Today the entire area composes the largest National Landmark.

To get to the Comstock Lode, take Highway 50 northeast out of Carson City, turn left on Route 341, and then take Route 342. You will pass through Silver City, which boasted of eight mills with 95 stamps by 1871. The town also served as the boarding area for animals used in hauling ore-laden wagons between the Comstock Lode and mills on the Carson River.

Continue on to Gold Hill and stop at the **Gold Hill Hotel,** Nevada's oldest hotel. Browse through the great bookstore in the office area—it carries tons of material on Virginia City, the Comstock Lode, and other Nevada places of interest. The patio affords a good view of the surrounding hills, and the great room's fireplace area invites you to sit and chat. The stone 1859 hotel carries on the tradition of fine dining from the gold and silver rush days in its Crown Point Restaurant. Choose from roasted duck, pheasant, medallions of venison, calamari, steak almondine, and a host of other delicious entrees. Prices are moderate to expensive.

The hotel sponsors a historic lecture series covering such topics as superintendents of the Comstock; Paddy's and Cousin Jack's, Irish and Cornish miners on the Comstock; and Lucius Beebe, the flamboyant railroad enthusiast, gourmet, gadabout, and resurrector of the famed *Territorial Enterprise* in the 1950s. For information and rates write The Gold Hill Hotel, P.O. Box 710, Virginia City 89440, or call (775) 847–0111.

Stroll the boardwalks of Virginia City or take a carriage ride to historic mansions, the old cemetery, and mines.

Virginia City's silver days may be history, but they remain captured in a wealth of museums. Start at the **Fourth Ward School Museum,** at the corner of C Street and Highway 431. The stately 1876 Second Empire four-story school produced graduating classes for sixty years before closing in 1936. Erected at a cost of $100,000, the school encompassed sixteen classrooms capable of handling more than 1,000 students. The fourth floor held the gymnasium. Today the school educates the public on the history of the Comstock Lode. Museum hours are 10:00 A.M. to 5:00 P.M. daily from May through October. Admission is free. For information call (775) 847–0975.

Continue on C Street and take a right on Flowers to 129 South D Street for a tour of the oldest home on the Comstock, the **Mackay Mansion,** built in 1860 for the Gould and Curry Mining Company. The original old mine office, vault, ore samples, and company records still occupy the house for your viewing. George Hearst, the father of famous newspaper baron William Randolph Hearst, lived in the house first. Fortunately, the Mackay Mansion escaped damage from the disastrous 1875 fire that destroyed most of the town. John J. Mackay, one of the richest men on the Comstock and founder of the *Postal Telegraph,* acquired the house in the 1870s.

Beautiful lawn and garden areas surround the Mackay Mansion. The original 1878 Tiffany sterling silverware and original elegant furnishings give you a taste of the opulent life led by the "Silver Kings." Tours are conducted daily during the summer and on weekends during the off-season. Admission is free for children under twelve and $4.00 for adults. For information write the Mackay Mansion, 129 South D Street, P.O. Box 971, Virginia City 89440, or call (775) 847–0173.

The town rebuilt quickly after the fire, but production dropped rapidly after 1876. By 1880 the population had dwindled to 11,000, and at the turn of the century it plunged to 3,000, a far cry from the booming town of the 1860s when Samuel Clemens (Mark Twain) worked at the *Territorial Enterprise* and prowled its streets for stories.

Twain once wrote, "Virginia City was no place for a Presbyterian, and I did not remain one very long."

The **Virginia & Truckee Railroad Company** delivers sights and sounds of historic steam locomotives in the heart of the Comstock while it transports you between Virginia City and Gold Hill. Long-term plans are in the works to extend the track to Carson City. Trains operate from late May through early October. Take D Street right to Washington and then turn right onto F Street to get your train tickets. Fares run $5.50 for adults and $2.75 for children for the thirty-five-minute round-trip or $10.00 for an all-day pass.

Jackpot!

The conductor gives you a narration of the many historic sights along the route. On the way you travel through Tunnel No. 4. The lore of the Virginia & Truckee Railroad makes it the most famous of the short line railroads. Dignitaries from all over the world rode its rails, and more than forty-five trains a day arrived and departed at Virginia City during the boom. For current schedules write the Virginia & Truckee Railroad Company, P.O. Box 467, Virginia City 89440, or call (775) 847–0380.

"Just once I'd love to do what San Francisco Muni repairman Reynald Herren did after hitting the $14-million jackpot in Reno. He stayed home from work and called in rich." —noted in Scott Ostler's column, San Francisco Chronicle, September 23, 1998.

Go up Washington Street and take the stairs up to C Street. Moving down the block, you come upon numerous museums. The **Comstock Firemen's Museum** resides in the 1864 Liberty Engine Company No. 1 Building, on C Street between Flowery and Taylor. The volunteer firemen maintain the museum and present the Comstock Firemen's Muster with a parade of antique fire equipment and fire department competitions. Check out the hand-pumpers. The museum is open Saturday through Wednesday from 10:00 A.M. to 5:00 P.M. May 31 through November 1. Admission is free. Call (775) 847–0717 for more information.

Inside the Ponderosa Saloon, at the corner of C Street and Taylor, you can arrange for an **underground mine tour,** guided by experienced miners. Learn about complete underground workings, such as cross-cuts, drifts, slopes, raises, and winzes. For information call (775) 847–0757. Mine tours cost $4.00 for adults and $1.50 for children ages eleven and under. The mine tours are open from 10:00 A.M. to 6:00 P.M. daily.

Next stop in at the **Nevada Gambling Museum,** on C Street between Taylor and Union, for a glimpse of rare gambling artifacts from the 1880s, antique slot machines, innovative cheating devices, and a display of old $500 and $1,000 bills. The museum is open daily from 10:00 A.M. to 5:30 P.M. during the summer season. Admission is $1.50; children ages eleven and under enter free.

At 18 South C Street, the 1875 Delta Saloon's museum area includes a 1909 L'Organda music player, old photos, and the infamous **Suicide Table:** Reportedly three of its owners committed suicide. Peek into the 1876 Silver Queen Casino Hotel, at 28 North C Street, for a look at the **Silver Dollar Dress,** made with more than 3,000 silver dollars. The **Julia C. Bullette Museum,** at the corner of C Street and Union, commemorates Virginia City's most famous madam. It is open Monday through Friday

Trivia

Territorial Enterprise features the real newspaper office of author and reporter Mark Twain, along with his desk and the newspaper's printing facility.

from noon to 8:00 P.M. and Saturday and Sunday from 11:00 A.M. to 7:00 P.M. Admission is $1.00.

Don't miss *The Way It Was Museum,* at the corner of C Street and Sutton, for the world's most complete collection of Comstock artifacts. See Jim Fair's personal stamp mill, Sutro Tunnel mule-train mine cars, early Comstock maps, a working model of a water-powered stamp mill, and historic photos and litho prints. The entrance fee is $3.00 per adult; children under age eleven are admitted free. For information call (775) 847–0766.

Silver Terrace Cemeteries is a good place to stop. Take a right on Carson Street and then a left on Cemetery Road to reach the parking lot. Notice the ornate ironwork and Mason symbols. Elaborate monuments stand next to caved-in crypts. Search out the monument to Captain Edward Faris Storey (1828–1860), after whom Storey County was named. *Hint:* It's on top of a hill. The headstones illustrate the draw Virginia City and the Comstock Lode had on people who had traveled from places as far away as England, France, and Scotland to seek their fortune.

Charlotte Antonia Kruttschnitt, the wife of the Storey County assessor, was buried here in 1867 after she died in a stagecoach rollover. According to legend, her funeral was "well attended with sixty carriages and many more on horseback." Modern burials are still conducted at Silver Terrace Cemeteries. Please be respectful as you tour the grounds. For more information call the Virginia City Chamber of Commerce at (775) 847–0311 or visit their Web site at www.virginiacity-nv.org.

On B Street, next to the courthouse, you'll find the most significant vintage theater in the west. *Piper's Opera House* has been undergoing restoration to preserve its nineteenth-century appearance and ambience without interrupting performances. The stage once hosted famous singers and sustained culture in the Comstock. Call for a current schedule; (775) 847–0311 or visit www.virginiacity.nv.org.

Wind up your museum tour at the *Western Historic Radio Museum,* at 109 South F Street. More than one hundred wireless antique radios are on display, including Hoot Gibson's 1929 Victor radio-phonograph. The museum is open daily April through October and by appointment the rest of the year; hours are 11:00 A.M. to 5:00 P.M. Admission runs $1.50 for adults and 50 cents for children under twelve. For information call (775) 847–9047.

"Luscious Lucius" Beebe rejuvenated the **Territorial Enterprise** in the 1950s, restoring the Enterprise Building to its former grandeur and boosting circulation to more than 5,000 across the nation. He was widely regarded as the best-dressed overdressed man in America. When spotted carrying a bucket of champagne early one morning in Virginia City, Beebe responded to the inquiry whether he was drinking champagne for breakfast, "Doesn't everyone?"

Bob Richards, editor of Beebe's *Territorial Enterprise,* started an enduring Virginia City tradition as a jest. In a tongue-in-cheek article, Richards wrote a fictitious account of Virginia City's camel races in 1957. Camels were introduced to the Comstock Lode in 1861 as pack animals, but the rocky terrain proved too difficult for them. Richards continued the spoof, reporting that the races had to be canceled for a variety of reasons in 1958 and 1959 but declaring that the races would be held the next year. The *Phoenix Gazette* and the *San Francisco Chronicle* challenged the *Territorial Enterprise* to sponsor a real race. In 1960 *The Misfits,* directed by John Huston and starring Clark Gable and Marilyn Monroe, was being filmed in the Virginia City area during the scheduled camel races. John Huston joined the fun and entered the race on a camel borrowed from the San Francisco Zoo. Huston crossed the finish line first, and the rest is history.

The *Virginia City Camel Races* take place in early September. Other Virginia City events include the Way It Was Rodeo, in July; and All the Arts Art Faire, in August. For information write the Virginia City Chamber of Commerce, P.O. Box 464, Virginia City 89440, or call (775) 847–0311.

Choose from among several historic B & Bs for your own elegant accommodations. The *Chollar Mansion* dates to 1861. It is on the National Register of Historic Places and once housed Isaac Requa, superintendent of the Chollar Mine, one of the Comstock's most productive mining properties. Twelve-foot ceilings, a spacious parlor filled with shelves of books on Virginia City, and portraits of former owners all add to the charm of this B & B.

A surprise feature, tucked out of sight, is the 164-square-foot arched ceiling vault. During the heyday of the Comstock, millions of dollars of bullion rested safely here. Also ask to see the paymaster's booth. Outside, an 1870s cottage provides additional privacy. Sarah and Isaac's son Mark used the cottage as his personal playhouse. In later years Mark followed his father's footsteps in mining, becoming a "Copper King."

Breakfast is served in the formal dining room and features fruit, breads and muffins, and egg dishes. Take time to enjoy the gardens around the yard and the view down Six Mile Canyon from the porches. Overnight rates run from $75 to $125. For reservations write the Chollar Mansion, 565 South D Street, P.O. Box 889, Virginia City 89440, or call (775) 847–9777.

Trivia

Samuel Clemens arrived in Virginia City after trying his hand at mining for three weeks in 1862. He began writing under the pen name of Mark Twain for the town newspaper, Territorial Enterprise.

Down on F Street, Patrick Gilmore invites you to settle in to the *Crooked House Bed & Breakfast* and let yourself be pampered. Originally built in 1870 as the home of Virginia & Truckee Railroad superintendent Henry M. Yerington, the structure was destroyed in the 1875 fire. A year later it was rebuilt as a boardinghouse.

Step out onto the second-story verandas for a beautiful vista of the Nevada landscape and Virginia City. Later sink into the depths of a large claw-foot tub to end a perfect day. Room rates run from $75 to $125, depending on the room and the season. Coffee is served from 7:00 A.M., and you can enjoy a continental breakfast at 9:00 A.M. For reservations write Crooked House Bed & Breakfast, 8 South F Street, P.O. Box 860, Virginia City 89440, or call (775) 847–4447 or (800) 340–6353.

As you depart Virginia City, ponder the foresight of Mr. Forman, manager of the Eclipse Mill and Mining Company. Wise in the boom-and-bust fortunes of mining towns, Forman erected his house using wooden pegs instead of nails and spikes. When the mines played out and his mill closed, he dismantled his house, loaded the pieces onto the Virginia & Truckee Railroad, and shipped it to Los Angeles for reassembly.

Washoe County

You will discover seclusion at the *Deer Run Ranch Bed & Breakfast.* Proprietors Muffy and David Vhay have created a peaceful retreat from life's everyday pressures. Sit back in the evening and watch the deer come out to play or watch the blue heron swoop down to the pond at dusk. Across Washoe Lake the Sierra Nevadas provide spectacular views. Listen for coyotes or mountain lions as they prowl around in the dark. It's hard to believe, but a drought in the 1980s completely dried up the sprawling Washoe Lake now before your eyes.

The B & B is located on an operating 200-acre alfalfa ranch. Muffy's parents purchased the land, then called the Quarter Circle JP, for back taxes in 1937 for $2,400. Muffy attended the one-room schoolhouse in Franktown, directly across the lake. During Prohibition, moonshiners used the natural springs on the ranch to brew their poison. Before repeal of Prohibition in 1933, government agents blew up the stills. You can consider this while you sip your welcoming glass of wine. In your room you will find a basket full of tasty snacks and fresh fruit.

Contractor Dave built the ranch with a passive solar system, providing warmth in the winter and coolness in the summer. Winter visitors can curl up next to the fireplace with a good book or venture outdoors to ice-skate on the frozen pond. For an added treat ask Muffy to show you her pottery studio and some of her work.

The private guest wing has two comfortable bedrooms and a spacious common area. Perch yourself in the window seats and keep a vigil watch on the Sierra Nevadas. Wall after wall of bookshelves will delight any bibliophile. Navaho rugs and paintings give warmth and a feeling of home to your guest quarters. A television, VCR, and refrigerator provide all the comforts of home.

A full ranch breakfast with Muffy's homemade jellies and muffins topped with omelets Florentine or Provençal prepares you for the coming day. You will hate to leave, but further Nevada adventures await you. Nightly rates run $80 to $105. To reach Deer Run Ranch Bed & Breakfast from Carson City, take Highway 395 to the top of Lakeview Hill. Turn right off the freeway at exit 42 (Eastlake Boulevard). At the bottom of the freeway ramp, turn right again onto Eastlake Boulevard. Travel $3^9/_{10}$ miles and turn right, over the cattle guard. Just up the road on the left, you will see a cluster of buildings. Turn left here and enter Deer Run Ranch Bed & Breakfast. For information or reservations write the B & B at 5440 Eastlake Boulevard, Carson City 89704, or call (775) 882–3643.

Left over from the riches of the Comstock Lode days, the **Bowers Mansion** was built in 1864 by millionaires L. S. "Sandy" (one of the early Comstock wealthy) and Eilley (boardinghouse owner) Bowers. They combined their fortunes through marriage but Sandy died only three years after the house was built. His widow tried to earn money by adding a third floor to the home for more rooms and turning her home into a hotel and resort. Eilley's fortune disappeared, and she eventually died destitute in San Francisco in 1903 but not before she had been reduced to telling fortunes to earn a meager living. To the day she died, she insisted that she could tell fortunes and locate new mines.

The two-story granite structure contains sixteen rooms and cost $200,000 to construct and furnish. The Bowers Mansion is located in Bowers Mansion Regional Park. Tours are given several times per day, seven days a week, between Memorial Day and Labor Day and also on weekends in the spring and fall; call (775) 849–0201 or (775) 849–1825 to check schedules. After the tour take advantage of the park's swimming pool and picnic area. Pool fees are $2.50 per adult and $1.50 per child. The twenty-minute mansion tours cost $4.00 per adult and $2.00 per child under age twelve. To reach Bowers Mansion Regional Park, take Eastlake Boulevard back to Highway 395 North almost past Washoe Lake on the right and turn left onto Route 429.

Go north on Highway 395 and take Highway 431 (Mount Rose Highway) to Incline Village and "The Jewel of the Sierras," Lake Tahoe. Along the way you'll pass over Mount Rose Summit, at 8,933 feet in elevation. Incline Village was named after a railway that operated here between 1879 and 1896, hauling an estimated 200 million board feet of lumber and more than 1 million cords of wood to Washoe Valley.

Settle comfortably into Old World charm in a mountain setting at *Haus Bavaria Bed & Breakfast Inn,* a European, Alpine-style B & B built in 1980. Each of the five guest rooms opens onto a balcony with views of the magnificent Sierra Nevadas. Your host, Bick Hewitt and his two cats, Bosco and Whiskers, will make you feel right at home. A full breakfast in the cozy dining room will entice you with cornmeal pancakes (Bick's grandmother's recipe), fresh baked goods, and fresh fruit. Sit down in the upstairs lounge and enjoy the many German collectibles or read from Bick's extensive library. Later explore the Lake Tahoe area. As an added bonus, Bick provides free passes to two private beaches on Lake Tahoe: Spend a day at the beach with heated pool and volleyball court.

Bick also puts on some special catered dinners, such as Christmas Dinner, New Year's Eve Buffet, and Mother's Day Dinner (when Bick's mom is in town). Room rates range from $99 for a single to $255 for a double. For reservations write the Haus Bavaria Bed & Breakfast Inn, 593 North Dyer Circle, Incline Village 89450, or call (775) 831–6122 or (800) 731–6222.

Since you've come this far, you may prefer lodging on the lake. The *Lakeside Cottages at the Hyatt Regency* are worth the splurge, especially if you are splitting the cost with another couple or family members. From the lodge nearest the Lake you can see opal-colored Lake Tahoe and Canadian geese descending on the sand. $350 a night. Lakeside Cottages,

Hyatt Regency Lake Tahoe Resort & Casino, 111 Country Club Dr. At Lakeshore Boulevard, Incline Village; (702) 832–1234 or (800) 233–1234.

One of my favorites is **The Shore House,** a bed and breakfast with a lakeside hot tub, fireplace, and full breakfast. Owners Marty, Barb, and Jake Cohen have lived at Lake Tahoe for twenty-five years and are happy to recommend the best places to ski and snowshoe. Room rates start at $160 and include breakfast and wine reception. 7170 North Lake Boulevard, Tahoe Vista, CA; (530) 546–7270 or (800) 207–5160; www.inntahoe.com.

Spend one or two days experiencing **Lake Tahoe.** The best way to get the lay of the land, and in this case water, lies in driving the 72-mile rim of Lake Tahoe. Pick up a handy brochure entitled *The Most Beautiful Drive in America* at the Incline Village/Crystal Bay Visitor's & Convention Bureau, 969 Tahoe Boulevard, Incline Village 89451 (775–832–1606).

Lake Tahoe ranks as the highest alpine lake of its size in the country, with a surface elevation of 6,225 feet. It earns its name honestly, *Tahoe* is Washo for "big water," with a length of 22 miles and a width of 12 miles. Its crystal-clear waters have enthralled visitors for more than a century. In some places objects can be seen to depths of up to 75 feet. Lake Tahoe's depth of 1,645 feet makes it the third deepest lake in North America and the tenth deepest in the world. Its forty trillion gallons would cover a flat area the size of California to a depth of 14 inches but would take 700-plus years to refill. Freel Peak rises to 10,881 feet, while Mount Tallac on the shoreline rises to 9,735 feet.

> ### Trivia
>
> *Lake Tahoe is the third deepest lake in North America, containing over 39 trillion gallons of water. The lake's pure, crystalline water owes its intense blue to the thin mountain air, which allows the water to reflect the blue sky above. During sunsets it appears pink-orange or red, during storms a seething gray-black.*

One of the more interesting landmarks is Cave Rock on the east side of Lake Tahoe in the Highway 50 stretch. The highway passes through 25 yards of solid stone. The original Lincoln Highway route passed around Cave Rock where only a thin ledge exists today. Washo Indians consider Cave Rock a sacred spot, one where they put their deceased to rest in the cold waters below the outcropping. A magnificent estate on the shore of Lake Tahoe, built in 1936 by wealthy San Franciscan George Whittell, Jr., and listed in the National Register of Historic Places, is open for business as a site for conferences and other gatherings. The buildings were designed by architect Frederic DeLongchamps. The Thunderbird Lodge Preservation Society was formed in 1999 to preserve 6.6 acres that include the main house, which Whittell had named Thunderbird

Trivia

Bill Cosby, one of the richest men in show business, comes to Lake Tahoe once a year to Harrah's. He stays at the villa built by the late Bill Harrah and is sometimes seen snacking on pizza or a burger at Sam's Place in Zephyr Cove.

Lodge. At one time Whittell controlled 27 miles of Lake Tahoe shoreline, from Crystal Bay to Zephyr Cove, and 5,300 acres became Lake Tahoe State Park. After Whittell's death in 1969, the 140-acre estate was first purchased by investor Jack Dreyfus, then by the Del Webb Holding Corporation. For information call (775) 832–8750; www.thunderbirdlodge.org.

Farther south past Zephyr Cove, you will come upon Round Hill. John Frémont and Kit Carson were among the first white men to gaze upon Lake Tahoe, in 1844. Continue on around the lake and discover more special places. More energetic visitors can leave their vehicles and traffic behind and travel by foot or horseback on the **Tahoe Rim Trail.** A number of trailheads offer a variety of hiking and riding experiences. For a brochure on the trails, write Tahoe Rim Trail, P.O. Box 4647, Stateline 89449, or call (775) 588–0686.

Hikers, mountain bikers, and skiers love **Sorensen's.** After a snowstorm, this cluster of cabins presents the perfect winter tableau. Sorensen's is nestled in an aspen grove in Hope Valley thirty minutes from Lake Tahoe traffic. The sauna cabin offers great camaraderie in the evenings as does the dining room, renowned for its beef burgundy stew and house specialties. Ask them to send their newsletter and map, which shows the location and charms of each cabin. Across a footbridge on a small rise, Sierra House is the newest cabin. Rates range from $125 to $225. Sorensens, 14255 Highway 88, Hope Valley, CA; 96120, (530) 694–2203 or (800) 423–9949.

Myriad excursions offer new perspectives from which to view Lake Tahoe. The *MS Dixie II* paddlewheeler cruises the surface while the captain points out historic sites along the shoreline. Start out your day with a breakfast cruise, or opt for the champagne brunch cruise or the sunset dinner dance cruise. The boat provides underwater videos and glass-bottom viewing to enhance your trip. Seeing the lake from the lake is truly an unforgettable experience. Rates run from $23.00 to $49.00 for adults and from $7.00 to $29.00 for children, depending on your cruise selection. The boat leaves from Zephyr Cove, 4 miles north of Stateline, Nevada, on Highway 50. Reservations recommended. For schedule information and reservations, call (775) 588–3508.

Also in Zephyr Cove, **Woodwing Sailing Cruises** depart five times daily from April 15 through October 15. Don your deck shoes and climb aboard a 41-foot, three-hull sailboat for a close-to-the-water delight. Rates for the daytime cruise are $24 per adult and $12 per child; a sunset champagne cruise includes all beverages for $30 per adult. Write Woodwind Sailing Cruises, Box 1375, Zephyr Cove 89448, or call (775) 588–3000.

Nine Stops Along the Scenic Drive Around Lake Tahoe (from South Lake Tahoe)

1. *North on Highway 89,* **Fallen Leaf Lake** *is a large alpine lake where* The Bodyguard *was filmed with Kevin Costner and Whitney Houston.*

2. **Emerald Bay** *is Tahoe's most photographed site, a glacier-carved bay surrounded by magnificent granite peaks. The bay is 3 miles long by 1 mile wide, and you can find impressive vantage points along Highway 89, or by taking a lake cruise through the bay.*

3. **Eagle Falls** *is a series of three waterfalls that pour into Emerald Bay. You can hike to the foot of the lower falls, or hike up to Eagle Lake and Desolation Wilderness. Parking is scarce.*

4. **Sugar Pine Point State Park.** *Ehrman Mansion, a three story rock and wood estate, was designed by well-known architect Walter Danford Bliss. Tours provide views of the spacious living and dining rooms with their oak floors and polished wood ceilings. Free tours are held daily. One mile north of Meeks Bay Lake Tahoe.*

5. *Side trip to* **Squaw Valley.** *The site of the 1960 Winter Olympics, and one of the great ski destinations in the world. In addition to skiing, you can ice skate, mountain bike, bungee jump, and play tennis.*

6. *Side trip to* **Emigrant Trail Museum & Pioneer Monument,** *12593 Donner Pass Road, Donner, CA. A monument to the tragedy of the Donner Party stands 22 feet high (the depth of the snow they were trapped in). The museum offers a thirty-minute film that details the ordeal of the trek, and has several exhibits on the history of Truckee.*

7. **Sand Harbor.** *Over a mile of white, sandy beaches on the North Shore of Lake Tahoe, Sand Harbor is arguably the most popular beach on the lake. In summer it is the site of the Shakespeare Festival. Because of its popularity, arrive early for parking. Highway 28, 4 miles south of Incline Village.*

8. **Ponderosa Ranch.** *Anyone who grew up with Bonanza will enjoy a nostalgic visit to the Cartwright Ranch. This open-air museum and theme park offers guided tours of the original ranch house where the 1960 series was filmed. The ranch features a complete town and shops. 100 Ponderosa Ranch Road, Incline Village; (775) 831–0691. Adults $8.50; children $5.50.*

9. **Heavenly Ski Area Tram.** *Take a trip up 2,000 feet to monument peak, where you can really appreciate the grandeur of Lake Tahoe. While you're there have lunch and spend some time on the spacious outdoor deck. End of Ski Run Boulevard, South Lake Tahoe, CA; (775) 586–7000. Adults $11; children $6.50.*

For the sport fisher *First Strike Sportfishing* offers year-round charters guaranteed to get your fish. Call (530) 577–5065 for rate information and reservations.

Soar like a bird over glistening Lake Tahoe below in one of the *Lake Tahoe Balloons.* Float silently over alpine vistas, the snowcapped Sierra Nevadas, and pristine Lake Tahoe. Balloon trips are offered year-round, weather permitting. Reservations are recommended twenty-four to seventy-two hours in advance. FAA-certified pilots will take you on an adventure you will never forget. Call (800) 872–9294 for information and reservations.

A premier event, the *Shakespeare Festival* combines open-air performances at beautiful Lake Tahoe with quality productions of Shakespeare's best-loved works. Dynamic sets, fabulous costumes, and professional theater would make even the Bard envious. The Shakespeare season runs during August and includes afternoon performances for children, such as *Snow White and the Seven Dwarfs* and *Beauty and the Beast.* Dig your feet into the sands and enjoy a picnic while you are entertained. Ticket prices run from $12.00 to $24.00 for midweek performances, $20.00 to $28.00 for weekend performances on Thursday, Friday, Saturday, and $5.00 for the children's performances. For information and tickets call (800) 74–SHOWS.

Other Lake Tahoe annual events include the January Winter Carnival; Paddlewheeler's Race, in May; Wagon Trains, in June; and Star Spangled Fourth, in July. For information write the Tahoe-Douglas Chamber of Commerce, P.O. Box 401, Zephyr Cove 89448, or call (775) 588–4591.

Amy Simpson and Sara Quessenberry have created an intimate dining experience at *Jack Rabbit Moon.* The twenty-six-seat restaurant features murals of fresh vegetables, while the copper-sheeted bar seats twelve. On Fridays a jazz trio creates the perfect mood. The menu rotates with the seasons. With culinary skills honed at the California Culinary Academy in San Francisco, the chefs created rack of spring lamb with ratatouille and grilled polenta and sake salmon on a bed of sushi rice with asparagus spears and cucumber ribbons for the spring menu. Jack Rabbit Moon is located at 907 Tahoe Boulevard, No. 8, in Incline Village. Prices are moderate. Call (775) 832–3007 for reservations.

Start your day out at *Cafe 333,* at 333 Village Boulevard in Incline Village. Owner Mary Young calls her cuisine "Nou-vada Eclectic." Try the Breakfast Strata (a tasty bread pudding) with a supporting cast of espresso and fresh fruit—you'll be pleasantly awakened to a new day. Prices are moderate. For information call (775) 832–7333.

Azzara's Italian Cuisine has been pleasing customers for more than forty years. Start out with the Ravioli di Anitra (duck-stuffed ravioli) for an appetizer and move on to your main course of saltimbocca alla Romana (veal with prosciutto and provolone cheese). Finish up with some coffee and tiramisù. Azzara's is located at 930 Tahoe Boulevard in Incline Village. No reservations are taken, so plan ahead. For information call (775) 831–0346.

The *Mount Rose Wilderness* encompasses 28,000 acres of rugged terrain within minutes of Lake Tahoe and the urban communities of Reno and Sparks. Elevations range from 6,400 feet along canyon bottoms to 10,776 feet at the summit of Mount Rose. Twenty-five miles of trails lead from several trailheads. Wilderness permits are not required for day hikes; however, fire permits and overnight permits are required. Mount Rose Wilderness access maps and permits can be obtained at Carson Pass during regular business hours or from the Carson Ranger District Office, 1536 South Carson Street, Carson City 89701 (775–882–2766).

A Hidden World within Casinos

*C*heck out these amusement centers for kids.

- **Circus Circus.** *Circus performances include flying trapeze, acrobats, jugglers, high-wire walkers, clowns, and more. Carnival games, video arcade, snack bars, restaurants, and gift shop are all housed in the hotel casino. 500 North Sierra Street, Reno; (775) 329–0711 or (800) 648–5010.*

- **Harrah's Tahoe Family Fun Center.** *The 12,000-square-foot center features state-of-the-art arcade and redemption video games. The center features the PlayPal area, a structured soft-play facility for young children. The two-story obstacle course consists of a maze and ball bins. Harrah's Lake Tahoe, Stateline; (775) 588–6611 or (800) eHARRAH.*

- **Nugget Skywalk Arcade.** *The 6,000-square-foot arcade features such popular games as air hockey, the Pogger game, Daytona 500, pinball, and several redemption games for which players redeem tickets for prizes. Staff are on hand to help visitors get acquainted with the facility. John Ascuaga's Nugget, Sparks; (775) 356–3300.*

- **Reno Hilton's Fun Quest.** *The 33,000-square-foot center features 170 state-of-the-art arcade and redemption video games. In addition the center features an interactive laser tag arena, the 5,000-square-foot Q-Zar Laser Tag Center. Also featured is Kid Quest, a soft play area for kids. Reno Hilton, Reno; (775) 789–2000.*

- **Silver Legacy Mother Lode.** *The arcade features a wide variety of games, including the latest arcade games, pinball, and air hockey. Silver Legacy, Reno; (775) 329–4777 or (800) 687–7733.*

The Mount Rose Wilderness is located south of Interstate 80 west of Reno to just north of Lake Tahoe; Route 431 runs along its eastern border. To arrange guided day trips or pack trips into the wilderness, write Tin Cup Adventures, 220 Wayne Road, Carson City 89704, or call (775) 849–0570.

If you lack equipment or wish a guide, Tahoe Trips and Trails offers getaways into spectacular country around Lake Tahoe. For those who like to hike, bike, or kayak, a high-energy option is the Tahoe Sampler in which you choose a different sport each day: kayaking, hiking, rafting, horseback riding, or mountain biking. Prices range from $395 for two-day trips to $1,130 for a five-day sampler. Tahoe Trips and Trails, Box 6952, Tahoe City, CA 96145, or call (800) 581–HIKE or (530) 583–4506.

Located in the back country of Spooner Lake, **Wild Cat Cabin** is a beautiful, hand-hewn, Scandinavian-style log cabin 3 miles from the Spooner trailhead. It sleeps four, has a wood-heating stove and a cooking stove. Continental breakfast included. Located on a rocky bluff looking out at Emerald Bay, a rare treat accessible only by skis or snowshoes. Only 12 miles from Incline Village. Spooner Lake Cross Country, P.O. Box 981, Carson City, NV 89702; (775) 749–5349.

Route 431 brings you to Highway 395 north into Reno, the biggest little city in the world. The slogan on the famous Reno Arch, completed in October 1926, derived from a contest. G. A. Burns came up with the winning slogan and donated the $100 prize to charity. During the Great Depression the city fathers voted in 1932 to turn off the lights on the arch in order to save money. The business community responded with an outcry and raised enough money to turn the lights back on again within three months.

On the University of Nevada at Reno campus, the **Fleischmann Planetarium** provides a series of programs to educate and delight adults and children alike. Special shows rotate throughout the year and include such presentations as "Volcanoes of the Solar System," "Wonders of the Summer Sky, Through the Eyes of Hubble," and "Skywatchers of Ancient Mexico." The SkyDome movie system also presents enticing visuals on earthly topics such as the Grand Canyon and Yellowstone.

Four- and five-day model rocketry classes are available for children ages nine through fourteen. An adjacent museum, Hall of the Solar System, contains many astronomy, earth, and space science exhibits. Be sure to look at all three of the meteorites ever found in Nevada. The planetarium is located at 1650 North Virginia Street. For information write Fleischmann Planetarium, University of Nevada at Reno, Mail Stop 272, Reno 89557, or call (775) 784–4812 for show times. Admission costs $7.00 for those ages thirteen to fifty-nine and $5.00 for others.

Moving from the universe to the planet Earth, stop in at the **Wilbur D. May Arboretum & Botanical Garden,** at 1502 Washington Street. A tour guide/map will lead you through the Songbird Garden, with aromatic flowers and fruits; the Xeriscape Demonstation Garden, featuring native and ornamental plants well adapted to the Great Basin; and the Rose Garden, with a unique collection of miniature, herbitage, and climbing roses.

The May Arboretum and Botanical Garden is open daily from sunrise to sunset and provides a wonderful respite from the city streets. For information call (775) 785–4153.

Trace the history of the automobile at the **National Automobile Museum,** 10 Lake Street, Reno's premier museum attraction and, arguably, the finest automobile collection in the country. See such classics as the 1936 Mercedes-Benz Special Roadster, Duesenbergs, and Cords; celebrity cars such as James Dean's 1949 Mercury, Al Jolson's 1933 V-16 Cadillac, and Lana Turner's 1941 Chrysler Newport (one of only six made); and rarities such as the sleek 1938 Phantom Corsair and the 1907 Thomas Flyer, winner of "The Great Race" from New York to Paris.

> ### Trivia
>
> **Wayne Newton** has performed in the Silver State more than any other entertainer, signing his first contract in 1959 at the age of sixteen.

Admission prices are $7.50 for adults, $6.50 for seniors, $2.50 for children ages six through eighteen, and free for children ages five and under. Hours are from 9:30 A.M. to 5:30 P.M. Monday through Saturday and from 10:00 A.M. to 4:00 P.M. Sunday. For information call (775) 333–9300.

The **Nevada Historical Society,** started in 1904, is Nevada's oldest museum. It serves as the repository of much of Nevada's interesting history. Within its walls you will find priceless baskets made by famous Washo basketmaker Dat-So-La-Lee; the Gridley flour sack, which raised a lot of money for the Civil War Sanitary Commission; and explorer, buckaroo, settler, and casino history. The museum's archives contain more than 350,000 historical photographs and numerous book and manuscript collections. Museum admission runs $2.00 for persons eighteen and older. The facility is located at 1650 North Virginia Street. Hours are from 10:00 A.M. to 5:00 P.M. Monday through Saturday. For information call (775) 688–1190.

Reno hosts the **National Championship Air Races,** the nation's longest consecutive running air race, in mid-September each year. Watch top aviators thrill the audience with death-defying aerobatic feats and maneuvers at the Reno/Stead Airport, north of Reno. Flying formations, solo performers, and fly-bys with antique biplanes will delight all.

A variety of ticket packages are available. For information write National Championship Air Races and Air Show, P.O. Box 1429, Reno 89505, or call (775) 972–6663.

The *National Air Race Museum & Hall of Fame* is located at 1570 Hymer in nearby Sparks. Spend a few hours viewing Jimmy Doolittle's A3C-2 Seaplane; the Italian Macchi M-39, which won the 1926 Schneider Race; and other air-race winners. Entrance fees are $4.95 for adults and $1.95 for children ages six to twelve. The museum is open daily from 9:00 A.M. to 5:00 P.M. For information call (775) 358–0505.

The *Reno Rodeo Parade,* in mid-June, kicks off "The Wildest, Richest Rodeo in the West"; and the *Nugget Rib Cookoff,* in late August, provides plenty of food for thought. For information on these and other Reno activities, write the Development Agency for the City of Reno, 490 South Center Street, P.O. Box 1900, Reno 89505, or call (775) 334–2414 or (800) FOR–RENO.

While we are on the subject of food, *Louis' Basque Corner,* at 301 East Forth Street, serves authentic Basque foods family-style and is a Reno tradition. Prices are moderate. Lunches and dinners are served Tuesday through Sunday. For reservations call (775) 323–7203. Locals also favor *Rapsallion Seafood House & Bar,* at 1555 South Wells Avenue. Its rich wood interior provides a relaxed dining atmosphere. A fine wine selection enhances your dining pleasure. Prices are moderate to expensive. For reservations call (775) 323–1211.

International appetites journey to *Palais de Jade,* at 960 West Moana Lane, No. 107, for high Chinese cuisine such as honey-glazed spareribs, jade sizzling sliced chicken, or Mongolian-style lamb. Prices are moderate. For reservations call (775) 827–5233. Fanciers of raw fish choose the *Sushi Teri,* at 5000 Smithridge Drive. Prices are moderate. Call 827–9191. For northern Italian fare the nod goes to *La Vecchia Varese,* at 130 West Street. Prices are moderate. Call (775) 322–7486.

Sparks grew up as a railroad town and division point of the Southern Pacific Railroad, beginning in 1903. It had one of the world's largest roundhouses during the steam era. Therefore, it is only fitting that the tour of "The Rail City" begins at the *Sparks Heritage Foundation & Museum,* at 820 Victorian Avenue. Pick up a pamphlet entitled *A Railroad Heritage: The Story of Sparks* for an informative walking-tour guide.

Inside the museum you will find a turn-of-the-century barbershop, a display on Prohibition, and, of course, details of railroad history. As you step into the railroad exhibit room, a train whistle blows. For information call

(775) 355–1144. Across the street the visitor center is housed in a replica of the original Sparks Southern Pacific Depot.

The museum is located in Victorian Square, where the Cinco de Mayo Fiesta, September Best in the West Rib Cook-Off, and Sparks Home-towne Christmas festivities are held. For information on these and other annual events, call (775) 353–2284. To arrive at Victorian Square from Reno, take exit 18 off Interstate 80.

Pyramid Lake holds just as much intrigue and mystery as it did when explorer John C. Frémont first set eyes on it. As described in Frémont's 1843 journal,

> It broke upon our eyes like the ocean. The waves were curling in the breeze, and their dark-green color showed it to be a body of deep water, . . . [and it] was set like a gem in the mountains.

> We encamped on the shore, opposite a very remarkable rock in the lake, which had attracted our attention for many miles. It rose, according to our estimate, 600 feet above the water, and from the point we viewed it, presented a pretty exact outline of the great pyramid of Cheops. . . . I called it Pyramid Lake.

To arrive at Pyramid Lake, take Route 445 north out of Sparks for 28 miles. Along the way you'll pass the National Wild Horse and Burro Center in Palomino Valley. Take a left onto Route 445 to drive the last 3 miles to the visitor center in order to obtain a $5.00 day or overnight pass. You are in the heart of the Pyramid Lake Indian Reservation, so pick up a copy of the fishing, hunting, camping, and boating regulations and respect their laws.

Pyramid Lake Legend

*P*yramid Lake Road, north of Reno Highway 445, is the only byway in the nation entirely within a tribal reservation. Stop by the museum for information about the lake and its native Paiute tribe. The formation of this huge lake was once a riddle. Now we know the deep azure waters as the remnants of an ancient inland sea extending south to Walker Lake. Indian legend attributes the lake's appearance to another cause and the famous rock formation at the lake's southeast shore serves as a clue. The rock represents the **Great Stone Mother** waiting for her lost children to return to her. Since the basket at her feet remained empty, her tears over the years filled Pyramid Lake.

Your first view of Pyramid Lake will be as memorable as Frémont's. Plan to spend the better part of a day or more at the lake. There's usually a good breeze here, so bring along your kite for extra fun. The visitor center holds several exhibit rooms, with displays on the wildlife and geology of the area. The marina provides overnight camping facilities and slip rentals. Pyramid Lake's renowned cutthroat trout draw fishers from all over. The lake is the only habitat for the rare cuiui, a fish that first appeared about two million years ago and once served as the main staple of the Paiute people.

Pyramid Lake is a high desert lake with water about one-sixth as salty as seawater. The lake is flanked on the east and west by rugged mountain ranges, and large tufa (calcium carbonate deposits) formations spot the beach areas. Across from the marina is the large pyramid after which the lake derives its name. To get to the pyramid, follow Route 445 southeast until it becomes Route 446. You'll pass what we call Popcorn

Great Stone Mother

Rock on the southwest end of the lake and then swing north on Route 447 at the junction by Nixon.

Continue up Route 447 until you see the sign for the pyramid. It's about 5 miles past Marble Bluff Dam. Turn left and prepare yourself for 8 miles of bone-jarring washboard roads. Stay on the main hard-packed road and be sure to stay out of roads leading into soft sands, unless you want to spend the rest of the day digging yourself out. The main road will swing and circle around to the beach area, where you can get close to Pyramid Rock.

Before you arrive at Pyramid Rock, however, you will pass **Anaho Island,** a national wildlife refuge covered with pelicans. Look up in the sky and see the sun reflecting off circling pelicans as if a giant mobile filled the sky. To the left of Pyramid Rock, with a little sleuthing you will find **Great Stone Mother.** Legend tells us that the woman-shaped rock shed tears for her children, filling the lake with water.

The Pyramid Lake Reservation was set aside in 1859. As noted in the Pony Express Territory chapter, the 1860 Pyramid Lake War led to one of the bloodiest slaughters of Native Americans in Nevada history.

The Donner Party passed south of here, near Wadsworth, on the final stretch of their rendezvous with destiny. Instead of setting up camp near Reno to sit out the winter, they moved on to encounter 22 feet of snow beginning in October and, for some, death and cannibalism on the shores of present Donner Lake in California.

Fifty-six miles north of Nixon on Route 447, you arrive at the gateway to the Black Rock Desert, Gerlach (population 700). For a little town it has much to offer. Dig into some of Gerlach's famous homemade ravioli for lunch or dinner at **Bruno's Country Club.** Prices are moderate; call (775) 557–2220. Spend the afternoon soaking in the hot springs, discovered by Frémont in 1843. Admission is $4.00 for adults and $2.00 for children.

Out-of-the-way Nevada places seem to have an attraction for potters, and Gerlach is no exception. Stop at John Bogard's **Planet X,** a solar-powered pottery studio. Bogard has a reputation for crafting innovative and strikingly beautiful pots, dishes, and vases. To get to Planet X, drive north out of Gerlach, take the left fork (Route 447), and continue for 8 miles.

Trivia
Anaho Island, a rocky island in Pyramid Lake, is one of only eight nesting colonies of American white pelicans in the western United States and Canada. Public access is closed because these birds need solitude for nesting. Frightened adult birds leave unhatched eggs or their young, which, if abandoned, die in the hot summer sun or are attacked and eaten by gulls.

Mountain Biking in the Eastern Sierras

- The **Dog Valley area** is an easy ride over a series of dirt roads that loop around the valley. You can spend a weekend exploring the valley by camping at Lookout Campground. For information, contact the Carson District Office, (775) 831–0494.

- **Spooner Summit to Marlette Lake bike trail** is more challenging, but the trail takes you through pine forests to sparkling Marlette Lake. The Flume Trail continues on the west side of the lake. Contact Lake Tahoe Nevada State Park for information, (775) 831–0494.

- The **Hope Valley ride** takes you to Blue Lakes on the Blue Lake Road through Faith Valley. At Charity Valley the county road turns to dirt and rises in elevation to Blue Lakes. For information, contact Carson Ranger District, (775) 882–2766.

I'll leave you at Black Rock Desert, which has seen its share of history over the aeons. The Black Rock Desert was at the bottom of ancient Lake Lahontan; in places the silt is estimated to be 10,000 feet deep, and in 1992, with the help of excavators, a large mammoth fossil emerged from its depths. One of the main wagon routes west crossed the desert, and at High Rock Canyon pioneers chiseled their names in the canyon rock walls between 1841 and 1849. In the 1940s and 1950s, the desert was used as a bombing range; unexploded shells still appear from time to time—if you see any, leave them where they lie and give them wide berth. In October 1983 a British racing team posted a new world land speed record on the desert playa, reaching an average speed of 633.468 miles per hour.

A word of caution: The playa is unpassable when wet, and there are several bog areas to avoid. Inquire locally about road conditions before you head out. Tell someone where you are going and when you expect to return. There are a number of Black Rock Desert trails, including the High Rock Canyon trail. For tips on enjoying Emigrant Trail Country safely and for Black Rock Desert maps, write the Bureau of Land Management, 5100 East Winnemucca Boulevard, Winnemucca 89445, or call (775) 623–1500.

PLACES TO STAY IN RENO-TAHOE TERRITORY

CARSON CITY/CARSON VALLEY

Best Western–Carson
Station Hotel/Casino,
900 South Carson Street;
(775) 883–0900 or
(800) 501–2929.

Best Western–Trailside Inn,
1300 North Carson Street;
(775) 883–7300 or
(800) 626–1900.

Bliss Mansion
Bed & Breakfast,
710 Robinson Street;
(775) 887–8988 or
(800) 320–0627.

Deer Run Ranch
Bed & Breakfast,
5440 Eastlake Boulevard;
(775) 882–3643.

GARDNERVILLE

Nenzel Mansion,
1431 Ezell Street;
(775) 782–7644.

GENOA

Wild Rose Inn,
2332 Main Street;
(775) 782–5697.

Genoa House Inn,
180 Nixon Street;
(775) 782–7075.

Walley's Hot
Springs Resort,
2001 Foothill Road;
(775) 782–8155 or
(800) 628–7831.

GERLACH

Soldier Meadows
Guest Ranch & Lodge,
Soldier Meadows Road;
(530) 233–4881;
www.soldiermeadows.com.

LAKE TAHOE—NORTH

Lake Tahoe,
Incline Village & Crystal
Bay Visitors Bureau,
969 Tahoe Boulevard,
Incline Village;
(775) 832–1606 or
(800) GO-TAHOE.

North Lake Tahoe
Resort Association,
950 North Lake Boulevard,
Suite #3,
Tahoe City;
(530) 583–3494 or
(888) 434–1262.

Haus Bavaria
Bed & Breakfast,
593 North Dyer Circle,
Incline Village;
(775) 831–6122 or
(800) 731–6222.

The Shore House,
7170 North Lake
Boulevard,
Tahoe Vista,
CA 96148;
(530) 546–7270 or
(800) 207–5160.

Hyatt Regency Resort &
Casino & Lakeside Cottages,
111 Country Club Drive,
Incline Village;
(702) 832–1234 or
(800) 233–1234.

LAKE TAHOE—SOUTH

Lake Tahoe
Visitors Authority,
1156 Ski Run Boulevard,
South Lake Tahoe;
(530) 544–5050 or
(800)-AT-TAHOE.

Camp Richardson Resort,
P.O. Box 9028,
Hwy. 89,
South Lake Tahoe;
(800) 544–1801 or
(530) 541–1801.
Historic hotel,
lakefront cabins, marina,
breakfast on lake at Beacon
Bar and Grill.

Harvey's Resort
Hotel/Casino,
Stateline;
(800) 427–2789 or
(775) 588–2411.

Caesars Tahoe,
55 Highway 50, Stateline;
(888) 829–7630 or
(775) 588–3515.

Sorensen's,
14255 Highway 88,
Hope Valley, CA;
(530) 694–2203 or
(800) 423–9949.

RENO/SPARKS

Bed and Breakfast—
South Reno,
136 Andrew Lane;
(775) 849–0772.

Circus Circus Hotel Casino,
500 North Sierra Street;
(775) 329–0711 or
(800) 648–5010.

Eldorado Hotel/Casino,
345 North Virginia Street;
(775) 786–5700 or
(800) 648–5966.

Harrah's Reno
Casino/Hotel,
219 North Center Street;
(775) 786–3232 or
(800) 427–7247.

Truckee River Lodge
(non-smoking),
501 West First Street;
(775) 786–8888 or
(800) 635–8950.

VIRGINIA CITY
Chollar Mansion B&B,
565 South D Street;
(775) 847–9777.

Crooked House B&B,
8 South F Street;
(775) 847–4447.

Hardwicke House B&B,
P.O. Box 96,
Silver City;
(775) 847–0215.

Gold Hill Hotel,
1540 Main Street,
Gold Hill;
(775) 847–0111.

**PLACES TO EAT IN
RENO-TAHOE TERRITORY**

CARSON CITY
Carlson House Restaurant
(American),
102 North Curry Street;
(702) 888–2030. Casual
dining in Carson City's
second oldest residence,
The Rinckel Mansion,
built in 1876.

Heidi's Dutch Mill
Restaurant (family dining),
1020 North Carson Street;
(775) 882–0486.

Wild Scallion (American),
318 North Carson Street;
(775) 883–8826.

Adele's (Seafood),
1112 North Carson Street;
(775) 882–3353.

Silvana's (American),
1301 North Carson Street;
(775) 883–5100.

GARDNERVILLE
J. T. Basque Bar and Dining
Room (Basque),
1426 Highway 395;
(775) 782–2074.

GENOA
Pink House Restaurant
(American),
Main Street;
(775) 782–3939.

GERLACH
Bruno's Country Club
(American),
Highway 447;
(775) 557–2220.

LAKE TAHOE—NORTH
Old Post Office Coffee Shop
(American),
5245 North Lake Boulevard,
Carnelian Bay;
(530) 546–3205.

Lone Eagle Grille at the
Hyatt (American),
111 Country Club Drive,
Incline Village;
(775) 832–1234.

T's Mesquite Rotisserie
(American Grill),
901 Tahoe Boulevard,
Incline Village;
(775) 831–2832.

Jack Rabbit Moon
(American),
907 Tahoe Boulevard,
Incline Village;
(775) 832–3007.

Cafe 333 (Californian),
333 Village Boulevard,
Incline Village;
(775) 832–7333.

Azzara's Italian Cuisine
(Italian),
930 Tahoe Boulevard,
Incline Village;
(775) 831–0346.

Le Petit Pier (French),
7252 North Lake Boulevard,
Tahoe Vista;
(530) 546–4464.

Crawdaddy's (Cajun),
6873 North Lake Boulevard;
(530) 546–7358.

LAKE TAHOE—SOUTH
Chart House (American),
392 Kingsbury Grade;
(775) 588–6276.

RENO
Louis' Basque Corner,
301 East Fourth Street;
(775) 323–7203.

Rapscallion Seafood
House & Bar,
1555 South Wells Avenue;
(775) 323–1211.

Palais de Jade (Chinese),
960 East Moana Lane;
(775) 827–5233.

Sushi Teri (Japanese),
5000 Smithridge Drive;
(775) 827–9191.

La Vecchia Varese (Italian),
130 West Street;
(775) 322–7486.

Trader Dick's (seafood),
John Ascuaga's Nugget;
(775) 356–3300.

TAHOE'S TOP
WINTER EVENTS

Snowfest,
*North Lake Tahoe,
March; (530) 583–7625.*

**Northern Lights Ski Free
Days** *(with lodging
reservations),
November; (775) 832–1177.*

**Tiny Tim Christmas
Village,**
*Truckee, December;
(916) 582–7720.*

North Lights Festival,
*Incline Village, December;
(800)–GO–TAHOE.*

Torchlight Parade,
*Squaw Valley, December;
(916) 583–5585.*

**Lord of the Boards Season
Championships,**
*Ski Homewood;
(916) 525–2992.*

TAHOE'S TOP
SUMMER EVENTS

**Valhalla Renaissance
Festival;** *jousting, music,
drama, juggling, period
clothing, crafts and food,
Camp Richardson Resort,
Lake Tahoe, early June;
(530) 542–6550.*

**America's Most Beautiful
Bike Ride,** *Lake Tahoe,
early June; (800) 427–7247.*

Mediterraneo Festival,
*North Shore, Lake Tahoe,
mid-June; (530) 546–2875.*

**North Lake Tahoe
Carnival,** *Crystal Bay, late
June; (530) 583–3494.*

**Grunding/Mountain Bik-
ing World Cup Downhill,**
*Squaw Valley, Lake Tahoe,
mid-June; (530) 582–8900.*

For More Information

Carson City Chamber of Commerce
1900 South Carson Street, Suite 100, Carson City 89030
(775) 882–1565

Carson City Convention and Visitors Bureau
1900 South Carson City 89701
(775) 687–7410 or (800) NEVADA–1
www.carson-city.org

Greater Reno-Sparks Chamber of Commerce
405 Marsh Avenue, Reno 89505
(775) 686–3030

Incline Village/Crystal Bay Chamber of Commerce
969 Tahoe Boulevard, Incline Village
(775) 831–4440 or Visitors and Convention Center
(800) GO–TAHOE

Lake Tahoe Visitors Authority
1156 Ski Run Boulevard, South Lake Tahoe, CA 96150
(530) 544–5050 or (800) AT–TAHOE

South Lake Tahoe Chamber of Commerce
*3066 Lake Tahoe Boulevard, South Lake Tahoe, CA
96150; (530) 541–5255*

Virginia City Chamber of Commerce
V&T Railroad Car, C Street, Virginia City 89440
(775) 847–0311

Annual Highway 50 Wagon Train, *as part of its historic ride from Carson City to Folsom, the wagon train is at Lake Tahoe mid-June; (530) 644–3761.*

Lights on the Lake, *one of the largest pyromusicals west of the Mississippi, South Lake Tahoe, July 4; (530) 544–5050.*

Lake Tahoe Summer Music Festival, *summer-long entertainment including Reno Philharmonic, opera dinners, jazz, and musical theater, Lake Tahoe; (530) 583–3101.*

Music at Sand Harbor, *Incline Village, Lake Tahoe, early July; (530) 583–7625.*

North Shore Tahoe Carnival, *Tahoe Biltmore, Crystal Bay, Lake Tahoe, mid-July; (530) 583–3494.*

Lake Tahoe Shakespeare Festival, *North Lake Tahoe's premier cultural event. Enjoy* Romeo & Juliet *and* Twelfth Night *on a white-sand beach overlooking beautiful Lake Tahoe, Sand Harbor, late July to late August; (800) 74–SHOWS.*

Concourse D'Elegance, *North Lake Tahoe's vintage wooden boat show, Carnelian Bay, Lake Tahoe, early August; (530) 581–4700.*

Events at Boathouse Theatre, *Tallac Site, throughout the summer; (530) 541–4975.*

Labor Day Music Festival, *big name entertainment in the natural setting of Sand Harbor State Park, Lake Tahoe, early September; (800) GO-TAHOE.*

Labor Day, *South Shore includes the Great Lake Tahoe Sternwheeler Race and fireworks, Lake Tahoe, early September; (530) 544–5050.*

Native American Snow Dance, *more than one-hundred Native American dancers come together to sing, dance and pray for snow, Incline Village, Lake Tahoe, October; (800) GO-TAHOE.*

Haunted Grand Hall of Valhalla, *Valhalla Grand Hall, Tallac Site, Lake Tahoe, October; (530) 541–4975.*

Autumn Food & Wine Jubilee, *wine seminars, vertical wine tasting, cooking classes, great food, Resort at Squaw Creek, Lake Tahoe, October; (530) 583–3494.*

ALSO WORTH SEEING

National Bowling Stadium, 300 North Center Street, Reno; (775) 334–2695. The world's largest and most technically advanced bowling center. This massive, six-story building in downtown Reno sports eighty championship lanes and a giant silver dome, which contains a theater showing films of special events in Reno/Lake Tahoe.

The Castle, 70 South B Street, Virginia City; (775) 847–0275. Once referred to as "the house of silver doorknobs," this house was built in 1868 by Robert Graves. The magnificent white home features richly appointed rooms, crystal chandeliers, steel engravings, and yes, silver doorknobs.

Las Vegas Territory

Clark County

Enter Nevada via Arizona Route 68 or 95 at Laughlin, on the banks of the Colorado River. Laughlin lies in the heart of desert country and regularly records summer temperatures well in excess of 100 degrees Fahrenheit. It owns the dubious honor of having Nevada's highest recorded temperature: 125 degrees Fahrenheit, hit in 1994. To escape the sweltering heat, enjoy one of the many activities centered on the Colorado River.

The **Fiesta Queen** provides a fully narrated *Colorado River Cruise* for a unique look at Davis Dam from the water. You will be transported back to the era when steamboats plied the river. The cruise provides a history of the town and surrounding area, as well as live entertainment. Five cruises depart daily, leaving every two hours between noon and 6:00 P.M. For information and reservations call (702) 298–1047 or (800) 228–9825.

If you want to furnish your own power, consider a *canoe or kayak Colorado River experience.* Back Bay Canoes & Kayaks provides rentals for half-day, one-day, and custom trips and for multi-day trips to match your schedule. Write Back Bay at 1450 Newberry Drive, Bullhead City, AZ 86430, or call (520) 758–6242.

Combine your room accommodations with a water vacation via a houseboat rental. *Houseboats* can be reserved at Lake Mohave Resort, just north of Davis Dam near Laughlin. For information call Seven Crown Resorts at (800) 752–9669.

The earth and rockfill *Davis Dam and Powerplant* was created in Pyramid Canyon in 1953 by the Bureau of Reclamation to control flash floods and generate hydroelectric power. The dam stands 200 feet high and creates Lake Mohave,

---

White-Knuckle Rides

*On the 180-foot **Skycoaster** at the MGM Grand at 3799 Las Vegas Boulevard South (877–880–0880), three riders are hoisted to the top of the tower where they pull their own ripcord and drop. The world's highest thrill rides are at the Stratosphere Tower Hotel & Casino at 2000 Las Vegas Boulevard South (800-99-TOWER).*

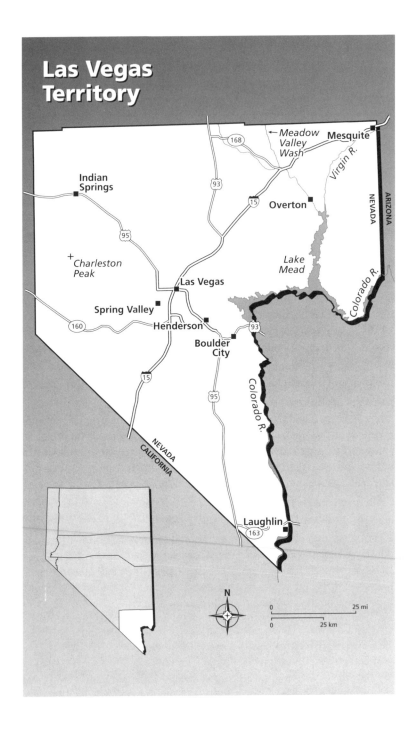

Las Vegas Territory

Indian Springs

Charleston Peak

Las Vegas

Spring Valley

Henderson

Boulder City

Laughlin

Overton

Mesquite

Meadow Valley Wash

Virgin R.

Lake Mead

Colorado R.

Colorado R.

NEVADA

ARIZONA

NEVADA

CALIFORNIA

168

93

15

95

160

15

95

93

163

N

0   25 mi

0   25 km

AUTHOR'S TOP PICKS

Las Vegas Strip

Natural History Museum, Las Vegas

Stratosphere Tower observation deck, Las Vegas

Hoover Dam, Boulder City

Lake Mead Houseboating, Callville Bay Marina

Valley of Fire, 55 miles northeast of Las Vegas

Red Rock Canyon, outside Las Vegas

Secret Garden, Mirage, Las Vegas

Cirque du Soleil, Bellagio, Las Vegas

Lost City Museum, Overton

with 200 miles of shoreline. Rainbow trout and bass abound in the clear water. Free self-guided tours of the facility are available weekdays from 7:30 A.M. to 3:30 P.M. The tour begins at the dam's main office and gives you an inside view of the workings of the five-turbine power plant. To reach Davis Dam, take the Davis Dam Road off Route 163 west of Laughlin north and follow the road to the Davis Dam and Powerplant. For information call the Laughlin Visitors Bureau at (702) 298–3321 or (800) 452–8445.

Railroad buffs will want to climb aboard **Old No. 7** for a nostalgic ride. The train is a narrow-gauge replica of Genoa, the steam engine that hauled freight and passengers on Nevada's famed Virginia & Truckee Railroad more than a hundred years ago. All of the railroad equipment is authentic. The train circles the twenty-seven-acre property of Ramada Express and departs every twelve minutes from morning to night. The cost of a ride is one smile. The train is located at 2121 South Casino Drive in Laughlin.

Many people describe **Laughlin** as "What Las Vegas used to be." The sunny little gambling mecca on the Colorado River has great showrooms, including one at the Gold River Hotel and Casino at 2700 South Casino Drive at (702) 298–2242 or (800) 835–7904.

Collector car fans can check out the rotating exhibit at the **Classic Auto Exhibition Hall,** in Don Laughlin's Riverside Resort & Casino. Your eyes will feast on more than seventy of the world's most distinctive automobiles, with an estimated value in excess of $10 million. The collection includes such rarities as a 1931 Rolls-Royce Imperial Cabriolet valued at more than $400,000 and a 1965 Mustang prototype specially built for the James Bond epic *Goldfinger.* The auto collection is located at 1650 Casino Drive. For more information call (800) 227–3849.

Prepare yourself for a stampede to **Laughlin Rodeo Days,** in spring. A full schedule of bareback riding, saddle bronco riding, bull riding, calf roping, steer wrestling, team roping, barrel racing, and clown acts will keep you entertained during the day, while an evening concert caps off the festivities. Rodeo tickets run $10.00 to $12.00 for adults and $5.00 for children under age twelve. For information on rodeo tickets or concert packages, call the Laughlin Chamber of Commerce at (702) 298–2214 or (800) 227–5245.

For a taste of Italy and fine dining, check out the **Alta Villa,** at the Flamingo Hilton. Specialties include several varieties of veal (marsala, piccata, Française, and saltimbocca), as well as tournedos bardolino (tenderloins of beef with mushrooms in a red wine sauce) and fettuccine al'aragosta (fettuccine tossed with shrimp and lobster in a cream sauce). Prices are moderate to expensive. Alta Villa is located at South Casino Drive. It is open Friday through Tuesday from 5:00 to 10:00 P.M. and Saturday from 5:00 to 11:00 P.M. For reservations call (702) 298–5111.

As you head out of Laughlin, be sure to swing by **Grapevine Canyon & Christmas Tree Pass.** Ancestors of the Mojave Indians (Pipa Aha Macave, or "the people by the river") journeyed up to Grapevine Canyon during the summer to escape the heat. According to legend, the spiritmentor, Mutavilya, created the Colorado River and its plants and animals and instructed the Pipa Aha Macave in the arts of civilization. The Native Americans were successful farmers and traders, with networks extending as far away as the Pacific Ocean. They have left behind intriguing petroglyphs as testimony to their lifestyle and beliefs.

The Grapevine Canyon area is an excellent spot for camping, hiking, taking pictures, and just plain exploring. A short walking trail off the parking area leads you to the ancient petroglyphs among wild grapes in the narrow canyon. To reach Grapevine Canyon, take Highway 163 west out of Laughlin for about 6³/₁₀ miles, where you will see a sign; turn right and travel 2²/₁₀ miles on a gravel road, then turn left into the parking area. For information call (702) 298–3321.

When you are finished, continue on the gravel road over Christmas Tree Pass. Use your imagination and look for Rabbit Rock, about 2¹/₂ miles down the road on the left. Farther on look for gaping rock jaws to the right. Search out your own unusual rock formations and pinnacles the rest of the way, as well as gliding hawks. Alongside the road pine trees decorated with tinsel and ribbons announce Christmas Tree Pass. The bumpy, winding gravel road eventually straightens and smooths before dropping you onto Highway 95, just south of Cal Nev Ari.

Continue north on Highway 95 about 10 miles to **Searchlight.** The historical marker alongside the road tells you that G. F. Colton discovered gold here in 1897. The town boasted 1,500 residents in the early 1900s but by 1910 the decline had set in. Total district production is estimated at more than $5 million. A quick drive around town rewards you with dilapidated

TOP ANNUAL EVENTS

*Best of the West Grand
Prix Motorcycle Race,*
Mesquite, January;
(702) 457–5775.

*Race Track/Sand
drag races,* April through
October, Amargosa;
(702) 372–5658.

*Las Vegas International
Marathon,* February;
(702) 876–3870.

*Desert Inn PGA Interna-
tional Golf Tournament,*
Las Vegas, March;
(702) 733–GOLF.

Snow Mountain Pow Wow,
Las Vegas, May;
(702) 386–3926.

Las Vegas Indian Days,
October; (702) 386–3926.

Nevada Day Parade,
Las Vegas, October;
(702) 882–1565.

National Finals Rodeo,
Las Vegas, December;
(702) 731–2115.

miners' shacks and weathered wooden head-frames worthy of a photo. Local lore claims that Colton found gold while lighting his pipe with Searchlight brand matches, thus giving birth to the mining camp name.

The local museum—situated in the Searchlight Community Center, at 200 Michael Wendoll Way, 89046 is open Monday through Friday from 9:00 A.M. to 5:00 P.M. and Saturday from 9:00 A.M. to 1:00 P.M. For information call (702) 297–1642.

The federal government created **Boulder City** (population 15,567), beginning in 1931, in con-junction with construction of Boulder (Hoover) Dam, due to the remote location of the large con-struction project. Boulder City housed 4,000 engineers and dam construction workers. The government hired pioneer and noted city planner Saco Reink DeBoer from Denver. DeBoer created a lovely city with government buildings situated at the crest of a hill and a large park serving as the city's focal point. The National Register of Historic Places lists the original townsite as the Boulder City Historic District.

Pick up a copy of the **Boulder City Historic District Walking Tour** brochure at the Chamber of Commerce office in the **Boulder Dam Hotel,** at 1305 Arizona Street. The hotel is listed on the National Register of Historic Places. For information call (702) 293–2034.

Start your tour at the 1933 hotel, built to accommodate dignitaries and guests visiting famous Hoover Dam. It is currently under restoration, with plans to reopen hotel rooms to the public in a few years. A $1 million restoration has, however, revitalized the building that houses the **Boulder City Art Guild Gallery** and **Tiffany's Ristorante.** Browse through the art gallery and then enjoy a delicious dinner at Tiffany's. Eating fare ranges from chicken marsala to duck a l'orange. Prices are moderate to expensive. The restaurant is open daily from 4:00 to 10:00 P.M. For restaurant information call (702) 294–1666.

Before you head to Hoover Dam, stop in at the **Boulder City/Hoover Dam Museum,** at 444 Hotel Plaza in Boulder City. Photo exhibits, town and dam memorabilia, and an interesting diorama bring the historic project to life. Of particular note is the 8-by-8-foot mural canvas of Ragtown by famed Las Vegas artist Roy Purcell. The museum is open from 10:00 A.M. to 5:00 P.M. Monday through Saturday and from noon to 5:00 P.M. on Sunday. For information call (702) 294–1988.

In his Dedicatory Address on September 30, 1935, President Franklin D. Roosevelt said:

> Ten years ago the place where we are gathered was an unpeopled, forbidding desert. In the bottom of a gloomy canyon, whose precipitous walls rose to a height of more than 1,000 feet, flowed a turbulent, dangerous river. The mountains on either side of the canyon were difficult of access, with neither road nor trail, and their rocks were protected by neither trees nor grass from the blazing heat of the sun. The site of Boulder City was a cactus-covered waste. The transformation wrought here is a twentieth-century marvel.

To reach Hoover Dam from Boulder City, take Highway 93 northeast about 8 miles. Beat the heat and the crowds and go early in the morning or late in the day. Park in the relatively new parking ramp exhibiting Art Deco styling, tying it artistically to the 1930s-era architecture of Hoover Dam buildings. To be sure, the engineering marvel of the dam will attract your attention. The dam is not only a National Historic Landmark but also a National Historic Civil Engineering Landmark.

Hoover Dam rises to a height of 770 feet at its crest, with a top width of 45 feet spanning the Black Canyon. Work crews placed 4.25 million cubic yards of concrete in its construction. Seventeen generating units create in excess of 2,000 megawatts of power. Behind the dam Lake Mead encompasses 550 miles of shoreline and has a maximum depth of 500 feet. It is the largest man-made lake in the Western world.

Hoover Dam and subsequent downstream dams enable use of Colorado River water to irrigate more than one million acres of land in the United States and an additional half-million acres in Mexico; provide domestic water needs for more than eighteen million people in Las Vegas, Los Angeles, San Diego, Phoenix, Tucson, and other southwestern towns and Native American communities in Arizona, Nevada, and California; and generate low-cost hydroelectric power to those same states.

The visitor center's movie theater presents a twenty-five minute film showing the construction of the dam. The cost of the dam exceeded $165 million, which has been recovered through power sales. In addition, take

Trivia

The Rat Pack were the five biggest names in show business in the 1960s: Frank Sinatra, Sammy Davis Jr., Dean Martin, Joey Bishop, and Peter Lawford. They performed together at the Sands while in Vegas to film Ocean's Eleven.

a look at the photo and other display exhibits in the visitor center. Bureau of Reclamation guides conduct thirty-five-minute walking tours through Hoover Dam daily, except Christmas and Thanksgiving Day. Tours are from 8:30 A.M. to 5:30 P.M., start in the visitor center, and leave every ten minutes. Tours cost $10 per person. You can still ride the old elevator inside the dam if you take the seventy-five-minute hard hat tour. Hard-hat tour costs $25. Visit them at www.hooverdam.usbr.gov or call (702) 294–3517.

Two of our favorite Hoover Dam sites you will not find in the brochures are the gravesite of the construction crew's mascot and the dedication platform. Just before the down escalator, look on the wall to the left for a plaque. It tells you about the puppy found by work crews and adopted as the **construction mascot.** He was accidentally run over by a truck in 1941 and was buried on-site. Go around the escalator and proceed to the September 30, 1935, **Dedication Area.** The stone mosaic at your feet was set in place by putting the stones on blocks of ice; as the ice melted, the stones slipped into their appropriate locations. The mosaic contains exact settings for star positioning at the exact moment of dedication, 8:56:2.25 A.M. The flagpole was also positioned to point to the center of the equinox at that time. Flanking the flagpole on either side are two 1930s statues with hands and wings raised to the sky in triumph.

You can take a quick drive across the top of the dam into Arizona and then reenter Nevada for the second time over the top of a dam, the first being north of Jarbidge. Note the artwork at the center columns above the brass doors.

Heading back toward Boulder City on Highway 93, stop at the visitor center at the junction of Highway 93 and Route 166. Inside you will find information on recreational activities around the Lake Mead area. From the visitor center you can see the beginning of the **Historic Railroad Hiking Trail.** Start your hike by reading the *Desert Hiking* brochure for safety and comfort tips. The railroad trail is open to both hikers and bicyclists, so be on the alert for either. It leads you along the railroad grade and takes you through several railroad tunnels. Lookout for ravens' and owls' nests and on the watch for rattle-snakes and scorpions. Be careful where you stop to sit down. It is a $2^{6}/_{10}$-mile walk from the gate to the entrance to Tunnel No. 5, which is closed to traffic. A number of other Lake Mead walking trails are yours for the choosing. Get a copy of the flyer describing the hiking trails and their locations.

Howard Hughes

*Billionaire recluse **Howard Hughes** once lived for four years in the Desert Inn Hotel behind heavily draped windows. At the time of his death, Howard Hughes owned casinos, an airline, stretches of undeveloped and commercial properties, mining claims, Hughes Aircraft, and the Howard Hughes Medical Institute. Hughes died in 1976, mad from drug abuse, weighing ninety-two pounds. He also died without a will. Who would control or inherit his $6.2 billion fortune? Con artists by the thousands presented wills. Even the states of California and Texas claimed Hughes as a resident to get inheritance tax money. The big winners were finally the heirs, the tax man, Howard Hughes Medical Institute, and Nevadans. Spring Mountain Ranch State Park, west of Las Vegas, once owned by Howard Hughes, is now a 520-acre shady retreat for picnics and outdoor concerts.*

Lake Mead campgrounds are available on a first-come, first-served basis. Campground fees are $19 per night. The Lake Mead Visitors Center holds interpretive programs on such topics as bird watching, wildflowers, and fishing. For information and schedules call (702) 293–8990.

Turn onto Route 166 and take a right at the ***Lake Mead Lodge*** sign, a few miles down the road. Relax by the swimming pool, launch your own boat or rent one for a day of fishing or other water sports, or take a scenic drive along Lake Mead, using the lodge bungalows as your home base. Against the background of desert mountains, the lodge rests only a stone's throw from Lake Mead. Area wildlife of bighorn sheep, roadrunners, and cottontail rabbits abound, and even a distant coyote can be heard. Your days can be filled with activity and the night can come alive as the rising moon and stars shimmer across the lake surface.

Rooms run from $50 per night for a queen-size bed to $65 per night for rooms with two queen-size beds to $125 per night for a three-room suite with fireplace and two baths. The lodge is located on the lakeside and 1 mile from the marina. For information and reservations contact Seven Crown Resorts at (800) 752–9669.

Forever Resorts rents houseboats at the marinas in Callville Bay on Lake Mead and Cottonwood Cove on Lake Mohave. Seven Crown Resorts has houseboats docked at Echo Bay, Lake Mead, and Temple Bar marinas on Lake Mead and at Lake Mohave Resort on Lake Mohave. Houseboats rates range from $800 for three days up to $2,950 for seven days. Prices are higher in summer. For information contact Forever Resorts at Callville Bay Marina, HCR-30, Box 100; (702) 565–8958 or (800) 255–5561; Forever Resorts at Cottonwood Cove Marina, P.O. Box 1000; (702) 297–1464 or (800) 255–5561; Seven Crown Resorts, (800) 752–9669.

Lake Mead Cruises' 300-passenger paddlewheeler travels to and from Hoover Dam. Sightseeing trips start at $14.50; costs are $28.50 for a breakfast buffet, $39.50 for an early dinner, and $51.00 for a dinner dance excursion. Write Lake Mead Cruises, Box 62465, Boulder City 89006, or call (702) 293–6180 for departure information and reservations.

Experience the awesome sights of the Black Canyon by floating along the Colorado River on a three-hour guided *Black Canyon raft tour.* Float from Hoover Dam to Willow Beach on large comfortable rafts. The $64.95 fee includes transfer to and from Expedition Depot, as well as lunch (for $5.00 off clip out the coupon in the tourist magazines). For information and reservations write Black River Canyon Raft Tours, Expedition Depot, Boulder City 89005, or call (702) 293–3776 or (800) 696–RAFT; www.rafts.com.

Return to Boulder City and then head northwest to Henderson (population 117,890), 9 miles away via Highway 95. World War II gave birth to Henderson in order to produce magnesium used in the manufacture of instruments, lightweight equipment, and incendiary bombs for the war effort.

A large deposit of magnesite near Gabbs furnished the ore, and electrical power from Hoover Dam provided the power to process the ore. The magnesium processing plant stretched $1^1/_2$ miles long and $^3/_4$ mile wide. Several thousand men and women worked in the facility. The War Production Board shut down the plant in late 1944, resulting in a virtual overnight ghost town. Fortunately, conversion to private industry allowed prosperity to return. Today Henderson ranks as Nevada's third largest city.

Turning from magnesium, Henderson is home to *Ethel M Chocolates* and *Ron Lee's World of Clowns,* both of which offer factory tours.

Ethel M Chocolates combines a chocolate factory tour with an informative cactus garden tour. Learn about the art of hand-crafted chocolates and then study more than 350 species of cacti, succulents, and other desert plants. Tours are available daily from 8:30 A.M. to 7:00 P.M. For information call (702) 458–8864. Ethel M is located near the corner of Sunset Way and Mountain Vista.

Finish up with Ron Lee's World of Clowns, featuring a Fun Factory Tour with a clown museum, a 30-foot carousel, and Jitters Gourmet Coffee Cafe. Ron Lee's is located at 330 Carousel Parkway. For information call (702) 434–1700 or (800) 829–3928. Both tours are free and are within a 3-mile radius.

Visit a pueblo of the Ancient Ones, climb aboard a 1944 caboose, explore the prehistoric Gypsum Cave, and tour pioneer homes—you can do all of these and more at the *Clark County Heritage Museum* in Henderson.

Mormon settlers arrived at Las Vegas in 1855, sent by Brigham Young to establish a way station on the Mormon Road from Utah to a settlement in San Bernardino, California.

Exhibits cover Clark County history, including mining, railroading, pioneering, Henderson's World War II contribution, Hoover Dam, and a resurrected ghost town. The museum is open daily from 9:00 A.M. to 4:30 P.M. and is located at 1830 South Boulder Highway, 89015. Admission runs $1.50 for adults and $1.00 for children and seniors. For information call (702) 455–7955.

Return to Highway 95 and drop down into Las Vegas. As far back as the sixteenth century, the Las Vegas area's natural springs and meadows served as a popular stop for travelers. In 1829 missionaries and traders established the oldest trail in Nevada, the Spanish Trail, crossing the southeast corner of the state near Las Vegas. Later a portion of that trail was incorporated in the San Bernardino–Salt Lake Wagon Road used by emigrants. In 1844 Frémont also used this route in his explorations, stopping at the Las Vegas springs. The name Las Vegas derives from Spanish and means "the meadows."

Early Spanish traders dubbed the 55 dry miles separating Las Vegas from the Muddy River the Journada de Muerto (Journey of Death). John C. Frémont crossed the Journey of Death in 1844 and recorded the following:

> We ate the barrel cactus and moistened our mouths with the acid of the sour dock. Hourly expecting to find water, we continued to press on to midnight, when after a hard and uninterrupted march of 16 hours, our wild mules began running ahead; and in a mile or two we came to a bold running stream [the Muddy River].

In 1855 Brigham Young dispatched a group of Mormon colonists to establish a fortified mission in the Las Vegas area as a link between California and Utah. The settlement was abandoned in 1858. The adobe remnant of the original mission, known as **Old Mormon Fort,** is the oldest building in Nevada and listed on the National Register of Historic Places. The fort is located at 908 North Las Vegas Boulevard, 89101. It is open daily; hours vary. Admission is free. For information call (702) 486–3511.

Located next door, at 900 North Las Vegas Boulevard, 89101, is the **Las Vegas Natural History Museum.** Kids of all ages will be thrilled with huge animated dinosaurs, international wildlife displays, a shark exhibit, and an extensive wildlife art collection. Many hands-on exhibits keep kids interested for hours. Museum tours cost $5.50 for adults, $4.50 for seniors and members of the military, and $3.00 for children ages four and above; children under four are admitted free. Hours are from 9:00 A.M. to 4:00 P.M. daily. For information call (702) 384–DINO.

Down the block and across the street, the **Lied Discovery Children's Museum** piques the interest of children with more than one hundred hands-on exhibits that allow them to pilot a space shuttle, play disc jockey at KKID Radio, and achieve star status on the Performing Arts Stage. Hours are from 10:00 A.M. to 5:00 P.M. Tuesday through Saturday, with Wednesday's closing extending to 7:00 P.M., and from noon to 5:00 P.M. Sunday (closed Monday). Admission runs $6.00 for adults; $5.00 for seniors, military, and children ages twelve and older; and $3.00 for children ages eleven and under. Lied Discovery Children's Museum is located at 833 North Las Vegas Boulevard, 89101. For information call (702) 382–KIDS.

Travel south on Las Vegas Boulevard to another kids' favorite, the **Guinness World of Records Museum.** Three-dimensional displays bring the world of amazing facts and figures to life. Stand next to the world's tallest man (Robert Wadlow, at 8 feet, 11.1 inches tall), step on the family-size scale to see how your family weighs in against the world's heaviest man (Robert Hughes, at 1,069 pounds), or view historic footage of man's space highlights. The Guinness jukebox, filled with record-breaking tunes, always gathers a big crowd. The museum is open daily. Entrance fees run $6.00 for adults; $5.00 for students, seniors, and military; and $4.00 for

Cougie

*C*ougie the mountain lion is a star in Las Vegas, admired by the hundreds of people who visit the **Southern Nevada Zoological-Botanical Park** each week. But when visitors watch the cat romp around his enclosure or nap in his favorite grassy spot, few realize that Cougie arrived ten years ago as a five-week-old cub close to death. It was winter in Nevada, and a miner near Battle Mountain had stumbled upon the nearly frozen mountain lion cub curled up in the rut of a logging road, apparently abandoned by his mother.

The miner scooped up the cub and took him to the Nevada Division of Wildlife office in Elko. They contacted Pat Dingle at the Southern Nevada Zoological-Botanical Park, the only place in Nevada that could care for the cat. But how could he get the animal from Elko to Las Vegas, nearly 500 miles away, quickly enough to save its life? Dingle called on the Nevada Highway Patrol. From Elko to Vegas, the 5-pound cub was relayed from patrol car to patrol car. He arrived near death, but was nursed back to health.

children ages twelve and under. The museum is located at 2780 South Las Vegas Boulevard, 89019. For hours call (702) 792–3766.

In America's glittering city in the desert, casinos and resorts grow more lavish and imaginative every year. The **Vegas Strip** is the only place in the world you can promenade past a giant Egyptian pyramid, a medieval castle, the streets of Manhattan, a Roman temple, a fiery volcano, and a Caribbean lagoon, and 1,001 Arabian Nights at Aladdin Resort Hotel's Desert Passage. Bellagio welcomes you with a choreographed ballet of water, music, and lights on a nine-acre lake. Masquerade Village brings Mardi Gras to Las Vegas: The Venetian brings Venice: Mandalay Bay brings a tropical paradise: and Paris Casino Resort brings the Eiffel Tower and other landmarks of the French capital (opens in 2000). Check out the big names on the marquees—Liza Minnelli, the Temptations, Wynonna, Penn and Teller, Kenny Rodgers, and Howie Mandel the theatrical spectaculars—from Siegfried and Roy's magic show to the aerial gymnastics of Cirque de Soleil.

Las Vegas debuts "O," the show of the century, at Bellagio Resort. Through **Cirque du Soleil**'s cunning mix of diving, synchronized swimming, aerial acrobatics, character actors, and musicians, "O" rises to the apogee of live entertainment. The stage is the first of many surprises. Performing in, on, and above a 1.5-million-gallon pool, the cast appears otherworldly: stunningly masked, costumed, and painted. To the creators of Cirque du Soleil, imagination is without limits as long as reality is well masked. A team of fifteen divers changes sets underwater. Props are continuously raised, lowered, and docked. Bubbles from a perforated hose along the bottom of the pool mask this flurry of

What Would You Do for Fame?

You'll find the world's most bizarre answers to this question at the **Guinness World of Records Museum.**

Check out the museum's Crazy Eating display, which definitely stretches the boundaries of "good taste." Here you'll see videotapes of people setting records by stuffing their mouths with the most eels, pickled onions, raw eggs, and other unappetizing items.

Other creative record-holders whose stories are featured at the museum include Krystyne Kolorful, the Most Tattooed Lady, and Louise J. Greenfarb, aka the Magnet Lady, who collected her way to stardom by amassing more than 21,000 magnets (no duplicates).

Guinness World of Records Museum and Gift Shop, 2780 Las Vegas Boulevard South, 89109; (702) 792–3766.

underwater activity. Performances begin at 7:30 P.M. and 11:00 P.M., Friday through Tuesday. Tickets are available seven days in advance to the public, ninety days in advance to guests of Mirage Resort hotels. For information call (888) 488–7111 or (702) 693–7722.

Four Seasons is the first deluxe non-gaming hotel on the strip, also the first hotel within a hotel—424 guest rooms atop the Mandalay Bay Resort tower. Aside from the stunning views, the hotel has a private pool and gardens, as well as Mandalay Bay's 11-acre tropical water park with a sand-and-surf beach, lazy river ride, and swimming pools—one with a swim-up shark tank. Shark Reef is more than a typical aquarium: It is a total sensory undersea adventure. You view nearly seventy-five species of sharks, reptiles, marine invertebrates, and rays. Ask for the thirty-ninth floor for views of Red Rock Canyon. Four Seasons Hotel, 3960 Las Vegas Boulevard South; (702) 632–5000.

The next day on Las Vegas Boulevard head to 3535 South for a look at one of the largest privately owned auto collections in the world and the world's largest Model J Duesenberg collection, at the *Imperial Palace Auto Collection.* Among the 200-plus automobiles on display daily are such classics as a 1907 Franklin Type D Landaulet, a 1928 Cadillac Dual Cowl Phaeton, a 1939 Mercedes-Benz (used by Hitler in the 1940 Berlin victory parade), and a 1947 Tucker. A gift shop holds a wide selection of automobile memorabilia and books for the auto enthusiast. The collection is open daily 9:30 A.M. to 9:00 P.M. Admission runs $6.95 for adults and $3.00 for seniors and children (scour the tourist magazines for a free entry coupon). For information call (702) 794–3174.

Moving from classic cars to stars, drop in at the *Liberace Museum,* at 1775 East Tropicana Avenu, 89119. Mr. Showmanship continues to amaze audiences with exhibits of his dazzling jewelry, priceless antiques, million-dollar wardrobe, and collection of antique pianos. Pay particular attention to the rare Moser crystal from Czechoslovakia. For those who did not get enough cars at the Imperial Palace Auto Collection, feast your eyes on the one-of-a-kind Rolls-Royces adorned with thousands of mirror tiles or rhinestones. The Liberace Museum is open daily; hours are 10:00 A.M. to 5:00 P.M. Monday through Saturday and 1:00 to 5:00 P.M. Sunday. Admission is $6.95 per adult, $4.95 per senior, and $2.00 per child under six. For information call (702) 798–5595.

Taking another historical theme, *King Tut's Tomb and Museum* transports you back to 1922, when Howard Carter discovered the tomb. The full-scale reproduction includes all aspects of the tomb, including vestibule, passageway, antechamber, annex, burial chamber, and treasury. The tours lasts approximately thirty minutes and costs $5.00. King Tut's Tomb and Museum is located at the Luxor, at 3900 South Las Vegas Boulevard, 89119. It is open daily from 9:00 A.M. to 11:00 P.M.; Friday and Saturday until 1:00 A.M. For information call (702) 262–4000.

Enter the space frame at the **Fremont Street Experience** for an out-of-this-world light and sound show, featuring 2.1 million lights capable of producing more than 65,000 color combinations. It takes thirty-one computers to choreograph the extravaganza, and it takes forty-five hours to load the graphic display computers to produce a six-minute show. Light shows are free and run nightly after dark on the hour until midnight. Recently erected are the Hacienda Horse and Rides, Aladdin's Lamp, Anderson Dairy Milkman, and the Fifth Street Liquor sign. For more information call (702) 678–5777 or (800) 249–3559.

In Las Vegas you'll be fascinated by the animals at the hotels. At the Mirage take a mini-safari through the jungles of the **Secret Garden,** home to six rare animal breeds, including the White Lions of Timbavati and Siegfried and Roy's Royal White Tigers. I saw the white tigers and a new family of white lions. The white cubs are a target for poachers and trophy hunters, so Siegfried and Roy not only have begun a white tiger and lion breeding program, but also provide the animals with a lavish "jungle" at their sprawling Las Vegas home. There are also tawny-colored tigers, which carry the recessive genes that produce pure-white offspring. The number of white tigers in the illusionists' show has grown from two to forty, and Siegfried and Roy have dubbed them the Royal White Tigers of Nevada. For more information contact the Secret Garden of Siegfried and Roy, The Mirage, 3400 Las Vegas Boulevard South; (702) 791–7111. Admission of $10 includes the dolphin habitat.

For a more earthly experience, journey over to 3701 West Alta for the **Desert Demonstration Gardens.** Eleven theme gardens and more than 180 varieties of plants give you a new perspective for the abundance of life in our nation's deserts. Learn about teddy bear cholla, Mohave yucca, organ pipe, and the giant saguaro. Admission is free. Hours are from 8:00 A.M. to 5:00 P.M. Monday through Friday and from 8:00 A.M. to 4:30 P.M. weekends. Call (702) 258–3205 for information.

World champion bronco riders, calf ropers, steer wrestlers, and bull riders converge on Las Vegas for the **National Finals Rodeo** every December for a more than a week of competition to determine bragging rights for the year. Up-and-coming contenders are pitted against world-class cowboys and cowgirls the likes of Ty Murray, six-time all-around champion, and Kristie Peterson, world-champion barrel racer. In addition to bragging rights and saving face, more than $3 million in purse money is at stake. For the current year's dates and for ticket information, call (702) 731–2115.

A rodeo, a carnival (at the largest midway in Nevada), and concerts headline *Helldorado,* a Las Vegas tradition held during mid-May. Events kick off with a trail ride, followed by a barbecue/entertainment-filled evening. Other attractions include the Helldorado Parade and Native American art and exhibits. For dates and ticket information, call (702) 895–3900 or (702) 870–1221.

Also in May, the *Snow Mountain Pow Wow* attracts Native Americans from across the country to perform traditional dances and carry on the heritage of their rich culture. Native American crafts such as handmade jewelry, beadwork, and clothing are on display and for sale. Artisans demonstrate their skills. You will be welcomed in many languages: Uchum (Southern Paiute), Yah-ah-teeh (Navaho), and Kamathu (Mojave).

Men's traditional dance represents storytelling in dance form. The story typically relates feats of bravery as the men move in a counterclockwise circle. The whirling movements of the fast-paced fancy dancers are accented by the men's brightly colored feather bustles or women's fringed shawls.

The Mafia

*S*iegel, Lansky, and Spilotro are some members of the **Mafia** who transformed a sandy desert into a multimillion-dollar business called Las Vegas. Explore the Mafia connection in these five books:

- Beyond the Mafia: Italian Americans and the Development of Las Vegas, *by Alan Richard Balboni.*

- The Black Book and the Mob : The Untold Story of the Control of Nevada's Casinos, *by Ronald A. Farrell and Carole Case.*

- Bugsy, *by James Toback.*

- The Enforcer: Spilotro—The Chicago Mob's Man over Las Vegas, *by William F. Roemer.*

- War of the Godfathers: The Bloody Confrontation Between the Chicago and New York Families for Control of Las Vegas, *by William R. Roemer.*

Admission is free, but there is a nominal parking fee. The powwow runs from 7:00 P.M. to midnight on Friday, from noon to midnight on Saturday, and from noon to 6:00 P.M. on Sunday. To reach the Snow Mountain Pow Wow, take Highway 95 north to the Snow Mountain exit. Turn left to the powwow grounds. For dates and other information, call the Pow Wow Hotline at (702) 386–0758.

Las Vegas' heritage is celebrated with an annual festival at Freedom Park, located at Lamb Boulevard and Mojave Road. *Cinco de Mayo* activities include marching bands and entertainers from Mexico and throughout Nevada and the West. Dance to the mariachi and chow down on some Tex-Mex food for a grand time. Cinco de Mayo commemorates a battle between the French and Mexican armies that took place in Puebla, Mexico, on May 5, 1862. Led by Generals Ignacio Zaragoza and Profiria Diaz, the Mexican Army defeated the highly regarded French forces.

Join the *Las Vegas High Rollers and Strollers* for any one of a series of 5-kilometer and 10-kilometer walks. Those in better shape could go the distance in the 10-kilometer to 20-kilometer Volksmarches. To get in step, write the group at P.O. Box 30153, North Las Vegas 89036.

Having worked up a good appetite on your Volksmarch, you can reward yourself with a stop at *Albina's Italian and American Bakery,* at 3035 East Tropicana Avenue, Suite A2. The family bakery specializes in such Italian delicacies as cannoli (vanilla and chocolate shells filled with cannoli cream) and sfogliatelle (flaky shells stuffed with Italian cheese and citrus fruit). For information call (702) 433–5400.

For more substantial fare Las Vegas offers a variety of eating options to satisfy any palate. Dive into USDA prime aged steaks or Nova Scotia lobsters at the *Palm Restaurant.* The Palm flies with its famous creamy cheesecake from S&S Cheesecake Company in the Bronx. Customers say that this family-owned bakery is simply the best. Prices are moderate to expensive. The Palm is located at 3500 South Las Vegas Boulevard. It is open for lunch and dinner; reservations are recommended. Call (702) 732–PALM.

The *Rosewood Grille* offers an exquisite wine list and wonderfully prepared seafood and steaks. Opt for the Maryland crab cakes accompanied by a creamy Dijon hollandaise sauce to start your meal; you won't be disappointed. The Rosewood Grille is located at 3339 South Las Vegas Boulevard. Prices are expensive. Call (702) 792–5965 for reservations.

Two Italian restaurants garnered our attention. *Sergio's Italian Gardens,* at 1955 East Tropicana Avenue, serves up a wide selection of pasta, veal, and other dishes. Chef Sante Norlatti taught at a culinary academy near Rome. Prices are moderate to expensive. The restaurant is open daily for dinner from 5:30 to 11:00 P.M.; call (702) 739-1544. **Battista's Hole in the Wall,** at 4041 Audrie, delivers casual dining in an Old World setting. Entrees range from veal piccante to pizza. The unlimited house wine is a bonus. Prices are moderate to expensive. The eatery is open daily at 4:30 P.M.; call (702) 732-1424.

Try **Yolie's Brazilian Steakhouse** for a welcome twist on steak preparation. Top off your meal with a serving of bananas smothered in caramel sauce. Lunch is served from 11:00 A.M. to 3:00 P.M., while dinner takes place between 5:00 and 11:00 P.M. Yolie's is located at 3900 Paradise Road, Suite Z. Prices are moderate to expensive. For reservations call (702) 794-0700.

Authentic Japanese fare can be had at **Ginza,** a delightful restaurant serving sushi, sukiyaki, tempura, and beef teriyaki, as well as specialties such as yosenabe (Japanese bouillabaisse). Ginza is located at 1000 East Sahara. It is open from 5:00 P.M. to 1:00 A.M. Tuesday through Sunday, and prices are moderate to expensive. For reservations call (702) 732-3080.

Relax in the French country atmosphere of **Pamplemousse,** at 400 East Sahara. Fresh seafood, duck, veal, and steaks are enhanced by the restaurant's own special recipes. Prices are moderate to expensive. Seatings at 6:00, 6:30, 9:00, and 9:30 P.M. For reservations call (702) 733-2066.

Take a drive out to **Floyd Lamb State Park,** located 10 miles off Highway 95. The green oasis is a great haven for bird watching, fishing, or just having a picnic under the groves of trees. Native Americans used this spot as a watering hole for generations. Later it became a privately owned working ranch, as well as a guest/dude ranch. The park encompasses sixteen acres of land and a seven-acre lake. It's open daily from 8:00 A.M. to 8:00 P.M. For information call (702) 486-5413.

Load your camera with film for a day of spectacular scenery. Located less than 20 miles from the Las Vegas strip, red sandstone ledges and magnificent rock formations rise from the earth. Throw in beautiful desert flowers and you have the makings of a great excursion. To reach **Red Rock Canyon,** drive west on Charleston Boulevard (it becomes Route 159, the Blue Diamond cutoff) to the Red Rock Canyon loop. Stop at the visitor center for maps and information on climbing, hiking, bicycling, and other activities. Inquire about special programs sponsored by the Bureau of Land Management. The visitor center is open daily from 8:00 A.M. to 5:00 P.M. For information call (702) 363–1921.

The loop drive is a one-way, 13-mile paved road through the Red Rock Canyon National Conservation Area "Calico Hills," a scenic outcrop of Aztec sandstone domes seamed by narrow, red rock canyons. Be alert for plenty of wildlife, such as lizards, bighorn sheep, mule deer, and roaming burros. A word of caution: The burros are wild animals and can be dangerous. Every year people are kicked or bitten by these burros. There is a $1,000 fine for feeding wild burros.

The Keystone Thrust Fault represents the most significant geologic feature of the Red Rock Canyon. More than sixty-five million years ago, two of the earth's crustal plates collided with impact enough to force part of one plate up and over younger sandstone. The thrust is clearly identified by the sharp contrast between the gray limestone and the red sandstone. A 2-mile round-trip hike into Pine Creek Canyon leads to the ruins of a historic homestead surrounded by large ponderosa pines; other hiking trails can be found out at the visitor center. If the heat gets to you, stop at Ice Box Canyon for a breather. Plan your trip to end about sundown and you will be rewarded with class 1 stargazing.

Red Rock National Conservation Area is also a prime vacation destination for rock climbers, and **Sky's the Limit** can give you a leg up on the sport. The company is lead by rock-climbing guru Randal Grandstaff, who with other guides teaches classes ranging from half-day instruction for beginners ($150) to multiday excursions on the rocks for serious climbers ($200 to $250). Grandstaff conducts day hikes in Red Rock and winter ice-climbing and cross-country treks at Mount Charleston. Call Sky's the Limit, (800) 733–7597 or (702) 363–4533, or write HCR 33, Box 1, Calico Basin NV 89124–9204.

Las Vegas is a popular destination for adventure excursions. You can tour Red Rock Canyon with **Red Rock Downhill Bike & Hike Tours.** Wayne Combs and Ron Miller lead half-day and full-day tours through the most exciting terrain; call (702) 617–8965. Or you can travel the canyon on horseback. Red Rock Canyon and Mt. Charleston riding stable offer guided horseback riding, mustang viewing, campfire music, and cowboy poetry; call (702) 838-8001; www.cowboytrailrides.com. Motorists can cruise the one-way scenic drive of the Red Rock Canyon National Conservation Area for a fee of $5.00 per vehicle. Along the drive are self-guided trails, picnic areas, and scenic overlooks.

Spring Mountain Ranch lies at the base of the grand Wilson Cliffs in Red Rock Canyon. The 520-acre state park sponsors cultural and theatrical events at the amphitheater during the summer, and docents provide guided tours through the historic ranch buildings on weekends. The main ranch house serves as the visitor center. Among remaining buildings are the stone blacksmith shop (1864), stone cabin (1864), foreman's residence (1929), milking barn, poultry house, and farm implement shed. Previous owners of the ranch included Jim Wilson, Sr., and sons; Willard George, a prominent Hollywood furrier; and Vera Krupp, wife of a German industrialist. The shaded picnic area is open daily from 8:00 A.M. to dusk. An entrance fee is charged per vehicle. For information call the Spring Mountain Ranch at (702) 875–4141 or the Bureau of Land Management Las Vegas District Office at (702) 647–5000.

Saddle up with *Silver State "Old West" Tours,* a division of Golden West Land & Cattle Corporation, and hightail it to a scenic trail ride through Red Rock Canyon and Spring Mountain Ranch. Prices range from $25.00 to $97.50, depending on the tour package chosen. Overnight and multiday tours are also available. For information and reservations call (702) 798–7788. If you prefer to travel by covered wagon, call *Wagons West* for a variety of excursions along the Old Spanish Trail and into Red Rock Canyon. Dinner rides and overnight pack trips are available. Rates vary, depending on the length of the trip. For information call (702) 875–1978.

Leave the heat and dust of the desert behind as you escape to *Mount Charleston Resort,* deep within the Toiyabe National Forest. Begin to immediately cool off as you face the sheer cliffs of Mount Charleston and start your climb up Kyle Canyon to your mountain getaway with green trees and cool breezes. The peak, at an elevation of 11,918 feet, was named in 1869 by a U.S. Army survey party mapmaker after his hometown of Charleston, South Carolina. In 1906 the Charleston Lumber Company cut 80,000 board feet of lumber per day. The lumber company burned down in 1910.

Your destination—your own private log cabin—sits perched on the cliff at 7,800 feet elevation. Inside you'll be pampered with a double-width whirlpool, gas fireplace, and king-size bed. The cabin is decorated with log furniture. A private deck with a swing overlooks the canyon for a fantastic view. Before you turn in for the evening, the cookie fairy leaves several fresh-baked chocolate morsels by your door. In the morning a breakfast basket awakens you to the new day. Sit on the deck and enjoy your breakfast with hummingbirds fluttering about.

For your pleasure Mount Charleston Resort provides horse-drawn winter sleigh rides, summer hayrides, group barbecue parties, riding stables for trail rides, and information on area hiking trails. Go explore this pristine mountaintop and be alert for bobcat, deer, elk, gray fox, mountain lion, and turkey. To soothe your body, Swedish and American massage treatment can be arranged through the Nevada Corporate Wellness Center.

The adjacent Mount Charleston Restaurant & Lounge serves lunch and dinner. Famed for its Mount Charleston Coffee and wild game specialties, the restaurant has been a popular local gathering spot for decades. Choose from elk Oscar, buffalo steak peppercorn, paired stuffed roasted quail, rabbit Florentine, pheasant pignolia, or venison Charleston. Guests at Mount Charleston Resort receive a complimentary bottle of wine with their meal. Meal prices are moderate to expensive. The restaurant's floor-to-ceiling windows bring the outdoors in with grand views of the mountains. Live entertainment compliments your flavorful meal. In 1973 Barbara and Collie Orcutt first purchased the Mount Charleton Restaurant, and in 1995 Barbara earned the Nevada Restaurateur of the Year Award.

Trivia

*In 1994, the **Hoover Dam**, which harnesses the lower Colorado River, was named one of America's seven Modern Civil Engineering Wonders.*

The twenty-four log cabins fill up fast, so make your reservations early for an unforgettable retreat. Rates range from $120 to $180 per night. For information and reservations call (702) 872–5408 or (800) 955– 1314. To reach Mount Charleton Resort from the Interstate 15/Highway 95 interchange in Las Vegas, take Highway 95 northwest 17 miles, then turn left on Route 157 (Kyle Canyon Road) and proceed 21 miles farther to the resort.

Nevada's ever-changing landscape of mountain and desert scenery provides one final surprise: skiing and snowboarding just an hour's drive northwest of Las Vegas. *The Las Vegas Ski and Snowboard Resort* has an 8,500-foot base elevation and a 9,500-foot peak. It is located in the Spring Mountains' Lee Canyon, a beautiful area of Humboldt-Toiyabe National Forest. To get there, you follow a designated Nevada Scenic Byway along Lee Canyon Road (State Route 156), a portion of Charleston Park Road (State Road 157) and Deer Creek Road. For information call (702) 645–2754 or visit www.skilasvegas.com.

Northeast of Las Vegas you will discover an archaeological and geological wonder. The *Valley of Fire* encompasses 36,800 acres of unusual

Valley of Fire

sandstone formations, ancient petroglyphs, and camping facilities. Between 1930 and 1950, this was a popular site to film Westerns. Within Nevada's oldest state park, breathtaking views abound as you travel through rugged rust-colored rock outcroppings.

One look and you'll fall in love with the Nevada desert. The Valley of Fire was formed millions of years ago from the great shifting of sand dunes. Oxidized iron gives the park its name and eerie appearance. Basins, canyons, uplifts and overthrust belts, and mountain ranges represent a geologist's dream. Several loop roads within the park lead you to intriguing sites, hiking trails, and picnicking and camping areas. To reach the Valley of Fire, take Interstate 15 northeast out of Las Vegas for 34 miles and turn right on Highway 169, which leads to the western park entrance. Fees run $4.00 per car. The next 20 miles leads you down into the Valley of Fire, with an exit at the eastern park entrance.

The visitor center is located in the center of the park, just off the main road. It has excellent displays on geology and the Valley of Fire area. The visitor center sponsors a variety of interesting and informative programs, including desert survival, desert wildflowers, moonlight hikes, snakes, and archaeology and geology.

You can get a copy of the *Valley of Fire* brochure with road map and list and locations of park features at the visitor center, but try to pick one up at a Nevada visitor center before you arrive at the park so you won't have to double back to see some sights. You can also, in advance of your trip, write the Nevada Division of Parks, Capital Complex, Carson City 89710; contact Valley of Fire State Park, P.O. Box 515, Overton 89040 (702–397–2088); or call the Nevada Commission on Tourism at (800) NEVADA–8.

Take the scenic loop road that goes off to your left to Atlatl Rock. This is the site of many petroglyphs carved high on the rocks. More than eighty steps and two landings later, you will be high above the desert floor and face to face with ancient rock carvings. One depicts the atlatl, a notched stick used to add speed and distance to a thrown spear. It was a predecessor of the bow and arrow.

Stop at the Beehives, unusual sandstone formations weathered by eroding wind and water into the shape of beehives. Proceed to the Petrified Logs, washed into the area from ancient forests more than 225 million years ago. Next it's time to take out your camera for a shot of Rainbow Vista and the towering red giants. A ½-mile hiking trail takes you through a sandy canyon to Mouse's Tank; along the way interpretive trail signs point out petroglyphs. For fantastic shaded picnic areas with outdoor grills, choose between the one at the Seven Sisters rock formations and the one at the 1930s Civilian Conservation Corps stone cabins.

Before you depart the east entrance, take the short marked hiking trail from the entrance station to view Elephant Rock. All of the above sites and more are indicated on the park brochure.

If you are driving a four-wheel-drive vehicle, you can opt for a journey along the 28-mile **Bitter Springs Trail,** which is off the beaten path through remote basins and canyons. The alert and adventuresome can view coyote, kit fox, wild horses, burros, roadrunners, and desert tortoises.

Lost City Museum

*I*n Overton is the site of the finest Native American exhibit in Nevada. The southern Paiute lived around the springs of Las Vegas Valley and the tributaries of the Colorado River. Their predecessors were known as the Anasazi. More than 1,000 years ago, the ancient ones constructed large adobe colonies along the Muddy River in the Moapa Valley south of Las Vegas. Artifacts from the area, as well as a full-size model of the pueblo homes of the Anasazi, are on display at the **Lost City Museum** in Overton. The first weekend in November, the Lost City Museum hosts the Festival Americana, (702) 397–2193.

Picturesque geologic formations include buttes, natural arches, and windows. There are ample opportunities for backpacking, hiking, and camping. A bonus is the remnants of a historic borax mining operation.

The trail is accessible from the Valley of Fire State Park Road. For a detailed map of the Bitter Springs Trail, a Nevada Back Country Byway, write the Bureau of Land Management Las Vegas District Office, 4765 West Vegas Drive, P.O. Box 26569, Las Vegas 89126, or call (702) 647–5000.

Exiting from the Valley of Fire State Park at the east entrance, turn north on Route 169 and travel 8 miles to Overton. On the edge of town, stop at the *Lost City Museum.* The excellent museum houses one of the nation's most complete collections of early Pueblo Indian artifacts, including a full-scale *reconstruction of a Pueblo structure.* Learn the history of the Anasazi (the Ancient Ones) and the Pueblo Grande de Nevada ruins, situated along the Muddy and Virgin River Valleys until the people mysteriously disappeared 1,200 years ago. The Lost City ruins were discovered by explorer Jedidiah Smith around 1826. In 1924 Nevada governor James Scrugham arranged for a New York archaeologist, M. R. Harrington, to investigate the sites.

The Anasazi had established a highly developed culture and were engaged in agriculture, mining, and trade. They cultivated corn, beans, squash, and cotton and developed permanent dwellings along the entire

Reconstructed Anasazi Pueblos

length of the Moapa Valley before they disappeared. The museum, built in 1935, captures the Lost City's culture with displays of baskets, pottery, jewelry, and interpretive exhibits. Paintings on bowls reflect pottery designs unique to the western periphery of the Virgin River Branch Anasazi. Most of the original Lost City has lain beneath the waters of Lake Mead since the 1930s, with the construction of Hoover Dam. Overall, 21 sites with more than 600 buildings were excavated and investigated.

The museum is located at 721 South Moapa Valley Boulevard. Hours are from 8:30 a.m. to 4:30 p.m. daily. Admission is $2.00 for adults; children get in free. For information call (702) 397–2193 or write P.O. Box807, Overton 89040.

In Overton, the *Moapa Valley Art Guild Art Gallery,* at 401 Moapa Valley Boulevard, offers a selection of fine arts, hand-crafted gifts, and pottery. The gallery is open from 11:00 A.M. to 5:00 P.M. Tuesday through Saturday in the winter and from 11:00 A.M. to 5:00 P.M. Thursday through Saturday during the summer. For information call (702) 397–8323.

Now that you have scratched the surface of the "real" Nevada, keep coming back to discover more and more.

**PLACES TO STAY IN
LAS VEGAS TERRITORY**

LAUGHLIN
River Palms Resort
and Casino,
2700 South Casino Drive;
(702) 298–2242 or
(800) 835–7904.

Riverside Resort Hotel
& Casino,
1650 Casino Drive;
(702) 298–2535 or
(800) 227–3849.

MESQUITE
Oasis
Resort, Hotel, and Casino,
(Green Valley Spa),
1137 Mesquite Boulevard;
(702) 346–5232 or
(800) 216–2747.

MOUNT CHARLESTON
Mount Charleston
Golf Resort,
Kyle Canyon Road;
(702) 872–4653.

Almost Heaven B&B,
123 Rainbow Canyon
Boulevard;
(702) 872–0711.

Mount Charleston Hotel,
2 Kyle Canyon Road;
(702) 872–5500 or
(800) 794–3456.

SEARCHLIGHT
El Rey Lodge,
430 South Hobson at
Highway 95;
(702) 297–1144.

PRIMM/JEAN
Buffalo Bill's,
I–15 South at Stateline;
(702) 382–1111 or
(800) 386–7867.

LAS VEGAS STRIP
Caesar's Palace,
3570 Las Vegas
Boulevard South;
(702) 731–7110 or
(800) 634–6661;
www.caesars.com.

Circus Circus Hotel
& Casino,
2880 Las Vegas
Boulevard South;
(702) 734–0410 or
(800) 634–3450;
www.circuscircus–lasve-
gas. com.

Desert Inn/Monte Carlo
Restaurant,
3145 Las Vegas
Boulevard South;
(702) 733–4444 or
(800) 634–6906.

Excalibur Hotel/Casino,
3850 Las Vegas
Boulevard South;
(702) 597–7777 or
(800) 937–7777.

Four Seasons Las Vegas,
3960 Las Vegas Boulevard
South; (702) 632–5000.

Imperial Palace,
3535 Las Vegas
Boulevard South;
(702) 731–3311 or
(800) 634–6661;
www.imperial-palace.com.

Luxor Hotel Casino,
3900 Las Vegas
Boulevard South;
(702) 262–4000 or
(800) 288–1000;
www.luxor.com.

MGM Grand Hotel/Casino,
3799 Las Vegas
Boulevard South;
(702) 891–1111 or
(800) 929–1111.

The Mirage,
3400 Las Vegas
Boulevard South;
(702) 791–7111 or
(800) 627–6667;
www.themirage.com.

Monte Carlo Hotel Casino,
3770 Las Vegas
Boulevard South;
(702) 730–7777 or
(800) 311–8999;
www.monte-carlo.com.

New York,
New York Hotel Casino,
3790 Las Vegas
Boulevard South;
(702) 740–6969 or
(800) 693–6763.

Treasure Island
at the Mirage,
3300 Las Vegas
Boulevard South;
(702) 894–7111 or
(800) 944–7711;
www.treasureisland
lasvegas.com.

For More Information

Las Vegas Chamber of Commerce
3720 Howard Hughes Parkway, Las Vegas 89109
(702) 735–1616

Las Vegas Convention & Visitors Authority
3150 Paradise Rd., Las Vegas 89109
(702) 892–0711 or (800) 332–5333
www.lasvegas24hours.com

North Las Vegas Chamber of Commerce
1023 East Lake Mead Boulevard
North Las Vegas 89030; (702) 642–9595

Las Vegas Indian Center
2300 West Bonanza Road, Las Vegas 89109
(702) 647–5842

Boulder City Visitors Center
100 Nevada Highway, Boulder City 89005
(702) 294–1252

Laughlin Visitors Bureau
1555 South Casino Drive, Laughlin 89029
(702) 298–3321 or (800) 452–8445.

Hoover Dam Visitors Services
Box 60400, Boulder City 89006
(702) 294–3523; www.hooverdam.com

Moapa Valley Chamber of Commerce
Highway 169, Box 361, Overton 89040
(702) 397–2160

Stratosphere Tower Hotel
& Casino,
2000 Las Vegas
Boulevard South;
(702) 380–7777 or
(800) 99–TOWER.

PLACES TO EAT IN LAS VEGAS TERRITORY

BOULDER CITY
Boulder Dam Hotel
(lunch weekdays),
1305 Arizona Street;
(702) 293–7731.

LAS VEGAS
Monte Carlo Restaurant,
Desert Inn Resort,
four diamond rating
(French),
3145 Las Vegas
Boulevard South;
(800) 634–6906.

El Sombrero (Mexican),
807 South Main Street;
(702) 382–9234.

Shanghai Lilly (Chinese),
Mandalay Bay,
3950 Las Vegas Boulevard
South; (702) 632–7409.

La Chandele
(Mediterranean),
Lake Las Vegas Resort,
1600 Lake Las Vegas
Parkway;
(702) 564–1600.

ALSO WORTH SEEING

*Fashion Outlet
of Las Vegas* has 400,000
square feet of high fashion
from world-renowned
retailers, the largest outlet
mall under one roof in
the United States. In fact
to explore each of the
mall's 140 stores you'll
need your jogging shoes.
A few miles south of the
Strip on Las Vegas Boule-
vard, the mall now
includes Calvin Klein,
Neiman Marcus, J. Crew,
and casino logo
merchandise.
(702) 874–1400.

Index

INDEX

INDEX

About the Author

Donna Peck is a prolific travel writer and editor whose travel guide to San Francisco, *Romantic Days and Nights in San Francisco* (The Globe Pequot Press), is now in its third edition. She is the author of *Access San Francisco* (HarperCollins) and *Access California Wine Country* (HarperCollins).